Book 2

Ideas of Authority

Edited by Lynda Prescott and Fiona Richards

This publication forms part of the Open University module A105 *Voices, texts and material culture*. Details of this and other Open University modules can be obtained from the Student Registration and Enquiry Service, The Open University, PO Box 197, Milton Keynes MK7 6BJ, United Kingdom (tel. +44 (0)845 300 60 90; email general-enquiries@open.ac.uk).

Alternatively, you may visit the Open University website at www.open.ac.uk where you can learn more about the wide range of modules and packs offered at all levels by The Open University.

To purchase a selection of Open University materials visit www.ouw.co.uk, or contact Open University Worldwide, Walton Hall, Milton Keynes MK7 6AA, United Kingdom for a catalogue (tel. +44 (0)1908 858779; fax +44 (0)1908 858787; email ouw-customer-services@open.ac.uk).

The Open University, Walton Hall, Milton Keynes MK7 6AA

First published 2014.

Edited and designed by The Open University.

Typeset by The Open University.

Printed in the United Kingdom by Bell & Bain Ltd, Glasgow.

ISBN 978 1 7800 7821 2

1.1

Contents

Introduction

The second book of A105 *Voices, texts and material culture* is underpinned by the idea of authority. The book divides into two halves, and you will encounter six different disciplines within it: Religious Studies, Music and Art History in the first half, and History, Classical Studies and Literature in the second half. From the first book, you will already be conscious of the importance of cultural factors in shaping objects, texts, processes and performances. In this second book, awareness of social and cultural context is angled towards some specific questions, as we explore the structures that confer authority.

It is no accident that the term 'authority' contains the word 'author'. This is because the two words have a common root, the Latin verb *augere*, meaning 'to increase, promote, originate'. Although our contemporary use of 'author' is usually restricted to someone who produces written works, the word also has a more general meaning of 'maker', as in the expression that we are 'authors of our own lives'. The author, then, is an individual agent, and authorship implies potential for creativity. The term 'authority', although originally springing from the same root, has over time become associated with social forces and is linked to ideas of power, often via expert knowledge. So there is a tension between the two words: 'author' is about the individual, but 'authority' is about a collective dimension of our lives.

One of the themes of Book 2 is the interplay of power and authority. Across a vast spectrum of subjects, from politics to the physical sciences, 'power' can suggest forces at work, either causing change or preventing things from changing. To take one example, the authority of religion has continued to shape western culture even outside the formal structures of religious practice, as you will discover in your study of Art History in Chapter 3. The idea of going back to an originary source is often the starting point for structures of power – hence Graeco-Roman antiquity has been one of the major sources of authority in western culture, at least since its textual and artistic legacy was rediscovered in the period known as the Renaissance (the term means 'rebirth', and it refers to the period from roughly the end of the fourteenth century to the end of the sixteenth). In the second half of this book in particular, and especially in Chapter 4, we see power as a dynamic concept, while authority, in its various guises, is often an attempt to dress power in permanent-seeming clothes: the power to command respect not just today, but in the long run. Sometimes permanence, or at least long-lastingness, is embodied in traditions, rules and conventions and in the respect people have for them.

The first three chapters of Book 2 focus on the kind of authority that is granted to certain works after they have been in circulation for a time. Here you will encounter the concept of canons in relation to Religious Studies, Music and Art History. The term 'canon' originated in ancient Greek as a word for a measuring stick and came to signify a rule or standard. This original meaning finds an echo in modern usage when critics describe a work as a 'yardstick' against which other works may be judged. Later, the term came to mean a catalogue of religious texts that were recognised as genuine and authoritative. Today, however, it is frequently used about works in a number of fields that are recognised as worthy of special attention and respect. Thus a canon is a catalogue or list of works whose importance is backed by some kind of collective authority: 'canonical works' have been given a seal of approval by relevant authorities.

The concept of the canon is generally governed by judgements about quality and status, the central question being: which musical works, artistic products or literary texts are considered important enough to merit continuing attention? However, as we shall see, the idea of a canon of religious texts, music or paintings is not absolutely rigid. Closely related to the canon is the idea of the 'classic'. Originally, this term referred to the works of authors considered to be of the highest importance and value. For centuries, the only texts that were accorded the status of classic were works by ancient Greek and Latin authors. This usage is still preserved in the name of the academic discipline Classical Studies. In Art History, too, classicism is still primarily associated with the legacy of Graeco-Roman antiquity. However, in other disciplines these terms can be applied much more broadly to include a wide range of canonical works. In Literature, for example, a classic may be any highly admired work, extending almost to the present; a highly admired work of recent literature, for instance, may be published in a series of 'modern classics'. Similarly, it is standard to speak of 'classical music' – a term which means more than just 'music of the Classical period'. You will therefore need to be alert to different usages when the same term crops up in different contexts.

Another term that you will find used in slightly different ways is 'genre'. In Book 2 you will encounter the concept of genre attached to some discipline-specific meanings, though for now we shall consider it in its most general sense, replacing the French term with its closest English parallel, 'type'. In considering canons, we'll be asking which types of musical works, paintings and so on are regarded as the most important. Does a folk song have the same claim to musical importance as an opera? Can a caricature sit in the Art History canon alongside an oil painting? In trying to answer this kind of question, we shall probably recognise that genre-distinctions change over time, and so does the status of individual genres. Sometimes genre and context raise other questions, and in Chapters 2 and 3 you will study works that, while 'religious' in subject matter, are not religious in function. You might like to think of these and other similar works as part of the continuing cultural authority of Christian culture, even when the context is art or music.

In the second half of Book 2 we examine some of the ways in which cultural authority can be challenged or 'remade'. The idea of challenges to authority is very much the focus of Chapter 4, where we consider attitudes towards religious objects during the European Reformation of the sixteenth century. Chapter 5 explores the way in which the work of Homer has been presented and re-presented to modern English-speaking audiences. A different classical text, Sophocles' play *Antigone*, features indirectly in Chapter 6, as we study a short South African drama, *The Island*, created during the era of apartheid. The political prisoners who performed *Antigone* in the notorious Robben Island prison were not only appropriating a classic ancient Greek text but also mounting a challenge to contemporary authority.

Activity

I'd like to end this introduction with an activity intended to tease out some of the connotations of the word 'authority'. Here are a few sentences in which the word 'authority' is used with slightly different meanings:

You should allow about 15 minutes for this activity.

(a) 'By the authority invested in me as Vice-Chancellor of The Open University, I confer on you the degree of BA (Honours) in Humanities.'

(b) 'Our local authority seems uninterested in community-building.'

(c) 'Someone in authority needs to sort this out.'

(d) 'I have it on good authority that the 16.55 from Euston arrived on time.'

(e) 'We'd like our next team-captain to be someone with authority.'

(f) 'She's an authority on International Relations in the 1920s.'

Now find the *Oxford English Dictionary* online by following the link on the Study Planner of the module website. (You can also find the *OED* by following the link in the 'Databases' section of the OU Library website.)

Look up the list of possible meanings for 'authority'. You'll see that they are grouped into two main branches: 'I. Power to enforce obedience' and 'II. Power to influence action, opinion, belief'. Without worrying too much about the finer distinctions under each of these headings, try grouping the sentences above under the two main definitions offered by the *OED*.

Discussion

While the various senses of 'authority' tend to shade into each other, the first three sentences would fit under the first definition, with its ideas of 'power over others', and the last three under the second, involving 'power to influence'. The distinctions are made more complicated, though, by the fact that sometimes when we use the term 'authority' we are referring not to power itself, but to a person or group of people who exercise that power (sentence (b) is an especially good example). In some cases, such as in sentence (f), assumptions about knowledge and/or judgement are rolled up into the idea of authority, too.

If you found it difficult to disentangle the two sets of meanings, don't worry too much: dictionary definitions can take us only so far towards an understanding of a complex concept such as authority. We can probably get to grips with it only by looking at it in detail, from a number of different angles, as we shall do in the course of this book.

Consensus, collective opinion and accepted forms or conventions are an important aspect of study in the Arts and Humanities, and as you work through this book you will begin to analyse the means by which texts are either granted authority or draw on conventions of authority. We hope that by the time you have worked through these varied study materials, you will have a full and rich understanding of how authority comes to be associated with particular works, and how traditions are invoked and challenged.

Chapter 1
Voices of authority and truth: the *Metta Sutta*

Helen Waterhouse with Fiona Richards

Contents

Aims

This chapter will:

- develop your knowledge and understanding of the ways in which religious texts acquire authoritative voices within specific communities through the establishment of a canon

- explore how the authority of canonical texts is invoked and demonstrated in religious practice

- introduce you to the musical aspects of chant as used in religious practice

- look at some of the problems associated with the voices of religious texts in translation.

Materials you will need

In this chapter, you will need to listen to the following audio recordings, which can be found on the module website:

- Recitation of the *Metta Sutta*
- Discussion of the *Metta Sutta*.

You will also need to watch the following films, which can be found on the module website:

- Pali *sutta*s recited by young Sri Lankan monks
- Pali *sutta*s recited by a Sri Lankan community.

Introduction

We are going to begin this chapter on the voices of authority by looking at a traditional canonical text. As you have seen in the introduction to this book, the term 'canon' originated in ancient Greek and signified a rule or standard. It was used later to describe a body of religious texts that were accepted as authentic within a tradition over a long period of time. As often happens, a word that was first used to describe a religious concept is now used much more widely, and you will explore the development of the idea of the canon as this book unfolds. Here, though, we shall concentrate on a text that is part of a religious canon. Rather than base this discussion on the Bible or the Qur'an, the religious texts with which people in western cultures are perhaps most familiar, we shall be focusing on a Buddhist text; an encounter with something belonging to a less familiar culture can often help us to take a fresh look at what we might otherwise take for granted or simply dismiss. We shall be looking in some detail at the story of a short Buddhist text, at the ways in which this text is used today and at some of the challenges associated with the translation of the text into new languages. To complement your study of the way in which a sacred text may be used today, the chapter includes a brief section introducing you to the musical aspects of chant as used in religious practice. To begin with, however, I shall introduce, very briefly, some of the general problems associated with canonical religious texts in the modern world. You may notice as you read that the chapter does not engage with the questions of whether religious texts are true or if they merit their authoritative status. These questions, though important and legitimate, are not our focus here.

1.1 Religious texts and the modern world

Most of the religious texts (often called 'scriptures', from the Latin verb meaning 'to write') that provide a basis for religions practised today became fixed in canons many centuries ago. These texts, such as the Christian and Jewish Bibles or the Islamic Qur'an, provide a range of content, including an explanation of history, stories about the activities and sayings of founders and other important individuals, and ethical injunctions. Such texts deal with mundane matters and so can be applied to everyday life, but they are also concerned with ultimate questions such as those about the meaning of life and death. The texts offer answers to these big questions; indeed, the Christian, Jewish and Islamic traditions hold that their canonical texts are authoritative in a definitive way because they were revealed by God rather than constructed entirely by human minds.

We might expect that, down the centuries, there has been agreement about the content of the scriptural canons. However, if we take the Christian biblical canon as an example, we find that it has not been uncontested and that even now there are disagreements between, for example, Roman Catholics and Protestants about some of the biblical books. Roman Catholics include within the canon some texts, such as the Books of Tobit and Judith, and the first and second Books of the Maccabees, that are not accepted by Protestants. Despite this, though, there is a comparatively high degree of agreement about the content of the Christian canon.

It is common outside Christianity to find that religious traditions recognise different categories of sacred writings within their canons. Some of these texts are more authoritative than others. For example, Judaism has its Bible, but a vast collection of ethical and legal guidance for living also forms an integral part of the Jewish canon. This material has developed partly because revelations or the pronouncements of a religious teacher, no matter how authoritative they may be within a tradition, often need interpretation or explanation for a new time and place or in new circumstances. Some of the ethical dilemmas we face today simply did not apply when these texts were compiled. Even so, members of the communities that recognise their authority expect them to speak to people in different places and cultures and in different eras:

the texts are regarded as universally applicable. Such interpretations can become authoritative in their own right.

In the following activity, you are asked to think about how communities who accept religious texts as authoritative might use them to address contemporary issues.

Activity

Think about a modern scientific development, such as the human capacity to construct and use nuclear arms. How can religious texts written before the development of modern science help religious communities develop a view on such contemporary issues?

Discussion

It is clear that today's religious leaders cannot turn to sections in their canonical texts that discuss weapons of mass destruction. But they can apply the broad principles found in the texts to develop views on modern problems. Many religious texts include prohibitions against killing, for instance, but they may also recognise occasions when action is better than inaction. There are plenty of other examples of modern-day issues that were simply unknown and undreamed of when these texts were originally put together. This is why religious traditions have to interpret their canonical texts. It is useful to bear this in mind when you hear representatives from religious traditions speaking authoritatively in the media on modern matters.

People often think of religious traditions as discrete entities, and in popular parlance and in the media it is often implied that there is *a* Christian or *a* Hindu or *an* Islamic view of, for example, abortion or God or the afterlife. In reality, divisions within traditions may be deep-rooted and significant. There is seldom one agreed view on any issue, and internal conflict can be just as strong as common understanding. These disagreements, many of which are centuries old, often have their basis in different interpretations of canonical texts. The texts were written in particular times and places but they are expected, by the traditions that revere them, to be relevant at all times and in all places. Christians or Muslims arguing among themselves, for instance about the roles that women ought or ought not to play, all cite canonical texts, but co-religionists may come to different conclusions.

Texts such as the Christian Bible remain authoritative for some people in our own time because they identify with the religious traditions such texts represent. However, the Bible is not just authoritative for people who practise or 'believe in' Christianity. The ideas and stories contained within it have been influential throughout western culture: its legal systems have been based on a combination of Roman law and biblical principles of morality and justice, and allusions to biblical narratives are found in canonical works of literature throughout the western world. In these ways the Bible has been authoritative for the development and underpinning of western cultural identity regardless of choices that individuals might now make. Similar arguments can be made about the role of canonical religious texts in other cultures.

1.2 A Buddhist canonical text: the *Metta Sutta*

We now turn to look at a short example of a canonical religious text from a tradition that has its roots outside Europe. This text, called the *Metta Sutta*, comes from the Buddhist tradition. Buddhist teaching, including this text, is based on the sermons of the Buddha (the word 'Buddha' means 'the awakened one'). There is some disagreement about the Buddha's precise dates (Cousins, 1996; Bechert, 1992), but it is generally accepted that he lived in northern India in the fifth and fourth centuries BCE. Buddhists believe that the Buddha (Figure 1.1) 'woke up' from ignorance and delusion when he came to an understanding (usually called enlightenment) about 'the way things really are'. His followers believe that his awakening gave him wisdom and knowledge and that the sermons he preached and the instructions for living he gave during his long life preserve that wisdom.

The Buddha was brought up with assumptions about how the world works and about the place of humanity and gods within it that were very different from the Judaeo-Christian tradition that underpins much of western cultural life. After the Buddha's death, his teachings travelled across Asia over the course of many centuries. The countries to which they spread include China, Japan and Korea in east Asia, and Afghanistan and Uzbekistan in central Asia. Buddhism is now also increasingly evident in western countries, for instance in North America and Europe (Waterhouse, 2001).

In contrast with the Christian Bible, which can be contained in one handheld volume, the Buddhist canon is vast, containing many thousands of texts, some of which are very short, just a few lines, and some of which are thousands of pages long. There is much more disagreement about which texts are canonical in Buddhism than there is in Christianity. Indeed, we could say that three distinct Buddhist canons survive today (Gethin, 1998, p. 40). These three canons belong to different geographical areas: the southern tradition of Sri Lanka and southeast Asia; the eastern tradition of China, Japan and Korea; and the northern tradition of Tibet. There is much common material in the three canons, but Buddhists from different areas of Asia and from contrasting schools of the tradition have their own ideas about which canonical text or texts are most important. Some texts that are highly influential in parts of Asia are rejected outright in other areas of the

Figure 1.1 Seated Buddha, first century CE, red sandstone. National Museum of New Delhi, inv. 55.25. Photographed by Angelo Hornak. Photo: © Angelo Hornak/Alamy

Buddhist world. For example, the most important text for many east Asian Buddhists, the *Lotus Sutra*, does not feature at all in the canon recognised by the southern Buddhists of Sri Lanka, Thailand and Burma.

The *Metta Sutta* is recognised as canonical by Buddhist scholars across Asia and it features in all canonical collections, but it is of particular significance for the Buddhist practitioners who live in south and southeast Asia. For these Buddhists, the *Metta Sutta* is not simply part of a canon of texts; it is in regular use. In what follows I shall trace the way in which the text became part of the canon and discuss how it is used. You will discover that religious texts are not simply read or studied by adherents, but are also put to work in other ways.

Translated from the **Pali** language in which it is written, the word ***sutta*** means 'thread'. It refers to a discourse or teaching said to have been given by the Buddha, which extends threadlike, connecting the Buddha to those who hear it. *Metta* is usually translated into English (as here) as 'loving-kindness', but alternative translations are 'goodwill' or 'universal love'. The *Metta Sutta* is therefore a discourse on loving-kindness that is believed to have been taught by the historical Buddha. It is difficult both to date this text and to ascribe it in a historically reliable way to an author; however, that does not prevent it from occupying a place in the Buddhist canon.

Activity

The *Metta Sutta* is reproduced below. Read the text through a couple of times in order to familiarise yourself with it.

The citation at the end of the text refers to Saddhatissa. Why do you think this passage is ascribed to Saddhatissa if, as I've just said, Buddhists believe that the text represents the voice of the Buddha?

You should allow about 20 minutes for this activity.

Metta Sutta (Loving-kindness): In praise of love and goodwill towards all beings.

1 He who is skilled in welfare, who wishes to attain that calm state [**nibbana**], should act thus: he should be able, upright, perfectly upright, of noble speech, gentle and humble.

2 Contented, easily supported, with few duties, of light livelihood, with senses calmed, discreet, not impudent, not greedily attached to families.

3 He should not pursue the slightest thing for which otherwise men might censure him. May all beings be happy and secure, may their hearts be wholesome!

4–5 Whatever living beings there be: feeble or strong, tall, stout or medium, short, small or large, without exception; seen or unseen, those dwelling far or near, those who are born or those who are to be born, may all beings be happy!

6   Let none deceive another, nor despise any person whatsoever in any place. Let him not wish any harm to another out of anger or ill-will.

7   Just as a mother would protect her only child at the risk of her own life, even so, let him cultivate a boundless heart towards all beings.

8   Let his thoughts of boundless love pervade the whole world: above, below and across without any obstruction, without any hatred, without any enmity.

9   Whether he stands, walks, sits or lies down, as long as he is awake, he should develop this mindfulness. This they say is the noblest living here.

10 Not falling into wrong views, being virtuous and endowed with insight, by discarding attachment to sense desires, never again is he reborn.

(Saddhatissa, 1994, pp. 15–16)

Discussion

I hope you enjoyed reading the *Metta Sutta*. This text has been in circulation for hundreds of years. Nevertheless, regardless of your attitude to religion in general or to one religion in particular, you may think there is content within it that can speak to modern people. The academic study of religion is less concerned with personal reactions to religious texts and practices, important as these reactions are, than with understanding the reactions of others.

The reason why the passage is ascribed to Saddhatissa has nothing to do with whether or not the Buddha spoke the words of the text. Rather, it makes reference to modern scholarly conventions. As you know, when you quote someone else's words, as I have done here, you must tell your reader where you took them from. The citation above in brackets refers you to the full reference at the end of this chapter. The book from which this translation of the *Metta Sutta* was taken was compiled and edited by the Venerable Dr Hammalawa Saddhatissa (1914–1990). Saddhatissa also made the translation of the text from Pali into English. The citation therefore refers you to where you can find this text, rather than to the person who first created it. In this chapter I have referred you to English-language sources and, where appropriate, to the Pali name of a text or group of texts. I have not used the specialist scholarly system of referencing the Pali canon, which would be much less useful to you. The point of references is that academic arguments are stronger – more authoritative – if they are supported by evidence from other people's research. References also provide useful information about sources that can be checked and followed up by others.

The Buddha taught mainly within the northwest of India. He lived in a culture in which texts were transmitted orally from generation to generation. [Access to these texts was controlled by elite families who would pass them on to their sons.] This oral method of preserving texts may seem unreliable to people in modern western societies who are used to having easy access to books and not so used to memorising large sections of poetry and prose, but it was an established system in India at that time and was probably no less reliable than copying written texts by hand. Scholars have argued, in fact, that the system allowed for a high degree of accuracy in transmission (Witzel, 2005).

The Buddha changed this tradition in some ways. The texts that developed from his teaching were not as tightly controlled as earlier Indian religious texts had been and they were not controlled within families, but the oral tradition persisted. Indeed, there is no evidence of writing of any kind in India in the Buddha's time (Gombrich, 1988, p. 53). According to Buddhist tradition, the disciples who heard the Buddha's teachings, including the *Metta Sutta*, remembered them and passed them on to others by word of mouth. In this way, large numbers of teachings were remembered and preserved. It was the task of monks to remember the teachings and, then as now, monks spent much of their time in study, which in Buddhist tradition entails learning texts by heart. Later in this chapter, you will watch two films that illustrate this tradition. One film shows young trainee monks reciting texts together; the other shows laypeople reciting together, led by a monk.

Buddhist tradition records that, when the Buddha died, all the monks gathered together to recite the teachings they remembered. The gathering is known as the First Council. Tradition has it that each text unanimously agreed on by all 500 monks was accepted as part of the canon. Modern scholarship calls into question this traditional account (Prebish, 2005, p. 2035). Though we are told in other canonical texts that all the monks who had followed the Buddha were present at this meeting (Harvey, 1990, p. 73), not all monks thought the communal recitation was useful (Gethin, 1998, p. 46). It also seems likely that in fourth- or fifth-century India there were monks who did not manage to get to the venue in time to participate.

In the next activity you will read a passage from another Pali *sutta*, the *Mahaparinibbana Sutta*. The passage is taken from a conversation between the Buddha and Ananda, one of the Buddha's closest disciples, which took place when the Buddha was close to death. The term **dhamma** is the Pali-language version of the perhaps better-known **Sanskrit** word *dharma*. In Buddhism, *dhamma* is taken to mean 'the truth of how things are', and the practices that lead to knowledge and understanding of that truth. 'Discipline' refers to the way of life the Buddha recommended for his followers.

Activity

You should allow about 10 minutes for this activity.

Now read the following extract. What does the Buddha say here about what would happen to his authority after his death?

> And the Lord said to Ananda: 'Ananda, it may be that you will think: "The Teacher's instruction has ceased, now we have no teacher!" It should not be seen like this, Ananda, for what I have taught and explained to you as Dhamma and discipline will, at my passing, be your teacher'.
>
> (Walshe, 1995, pp. 269–70)

Discussion

In this passage the Buddha explains to Ananda that after his death, when 'instruction has ceased', explanation and, indeed, authority will reside in the teachings that he has given. The Buddha did not appoint a successor, instead telling his disciples that he was leaving behind what he had taught them as the *dhamma* and the discipline.

The texts record that the Buddha gave his disciples guidance about how to decide whether a text was genuine. All teachings were required to have been given by the Buddha himself or by one of his most senior disciples, and any new teaching that sought admission to the canon had to conform to the already accepted teachings and rulings (Gethin, 1998, p. 47) The texts had authority because everything they contained, regardless of their 'author', appeared to be the thought and the voice of one mind (Harvey, 1990, p. 3).

Small disagreements about the authentic canon of texts arose quite soon after the Buddha's death and led to the formation of schools of Buddhism that took slightly different attitudes and developed their own canons. These disagreements usually began in relation to small points of monastic discipline rather than about significant doctrinal matters. The Pali canon is the only one of these early collections to survive. Within the tradition that preserves it, called Theravada Buddhism (meaning 'the Buddhism of the Elders'), the canon is assumed to have been settled at this very early time. Modern scholarship challenges this claim (for example, Collins, 1990), but, within the Theravada tradition, the canon acquires part of its authoritative standing from its early date.

Remembering such a large amount of text would be a significant and very unusual feat for any individual, so, before the canon was committed to writing, monks were each assigned a manageable portion to memorise. A large part of a monk's job continues to be committing the texts to memory (Gombrich, 1988, p. 152), and there are regular occasions on which to recite them.

Activity

Why was it so important for the texts to be passed on to subsequent generations?

You should allow about 10 minutes for this activity.

Discussion

As you have seen, before he died the Buddha told his disciples that what he had taught them represented the truth, as he had understood it. He did not appoint a successor because he said that the *dhamma* would be the teacher. According to the tradition, the reason that it was important to pass on the texts, and indeed to maintain their accuracy, was that they were an authoritative source of the truth as the Buddha had understood and taught it.

The oral texts were first written down in Sri Lanka, in the middle or towards the end of the first century BCE (Lopez, 2008, p. 9; Gombrich, 1984, p. 77). The texts were written on dried palm leaves, which were collected together in baskets according to their content (Figure 1.2). Buddhist practitioners and scholars still refer to the Pali-language canon as the 'three baskets' (***tipitaka***).

Figure 1.2 A Cambodian example of the Pali canon written on bamboo.
Photo: © World Religions Photo Library/C. Stout

The method by which the texts were collected together is clearly of scholarly interest, but for Buddhists in Sri Lanka the voice of the texts is of far more importance than the ways in which they were gathered and preserved. We could say that it is a matter of trustful confidence for Buddhists that the texts collected in the three baskets of palm leaves represent the voice of the Buddha. Of these early writings, the *Metta Sutta* is probably the most widely used and popular short text (Gombrich, 1984, p. 88).

1.3 The voice of the Buddha?

Whose voice does the *Metta Sutta* represent? As with many religious canonical texts, this question has no straightforward answer. According to Buddhist tradition, the words of the texts were spoken by the Buddha. All the texts said to have been recited at the First Council were prefaced by the words 'Thus have I heard'. In this way the monks affirmed that they had heard the Buddha (or others approved by him) speak the texts. In this sense, then, the *Metta Sutta* represents the voice of the Buddha. However, the Buddha taught that he was not revealing a new truth. The translation of the *Metta Sutta* that you have read contains cultural references to India in the fourth or fifth century BCE, but the Buddha certainly thought that what he was teaching was simply 'the way things are' and that others had the potential to understand that. [In this sense the tradition recognises the *Metta Sutta* as the voice of truth or wisdom and this text, like the rest of the Buddhist canon, derives its authority from that status.]

Activity

Do you think the *Metta Sutta* has authority? If you do, where do you think that authority comes from?

You should allow about 10 minutes for this activity.

Discussion

You may not recognise the authority of this text at all, perhaps because you don't agree with what it says or because you can't accept that religious texts have any authority. If you do agree with some of the ideas it contains, you may think that its authority comes from the fact that it is observably true: that it is good, for example, not to despise or deceive people or to wish them harm. In that case, the fact that the text is ascribed to the Buddha might seem less important to you than the fact that what it teaches is true in your experience. This view accords with Buddhist tradition, in which testing the Buddha's teaching for oneself is an important principle.

One thing that Buddhists and non-Buddhists can agree on is that the *Metta Sutta* acts as a legitimate, authoritative voice of the Buddhist tradition. Whatever we may think individually about the text, we must accept that it is an authoritative representation of the ways in which Buddhists are taught to see the world. Because that is the case, this discussion of the *Metta Sutta* as a text would be incomplete if we did not consider the ways in which Buddhists use this text. We shall look at this in the next section.

1.4 Putting theory into practice

The discipline of Religious Studies has a complex history. It arose in the 1960s, at a time when undergraduates studying religion spent most of their time working with early religious texts. Little attention was paid to the more contentious issue of the contemporary practice of religion (Cunningham, 1990, p. 21). Ancient texts are to some extent self-contained and manageable, whereas religious practice can be difficult to understand, confusing and even sometimes alarming. The early scholars of religions other than Christianity laid a good foundation for what followed, but their understanding of religion was incomplete because they avoided taking seriously the practice of religious adherents and the ways in which generations of practitioners had related to their texts. It does not help us to understand a religious or cultural tradition if we look only at the theory; we also need to see how the theory is put into practice.

The voice of Buddhist practice

The next three activities give you an opportunity to watch and listen to Pali chanting. When you have done that, we shall look in more detail at the ways in which the *Metta Sutta* is used.

Activity

First, you should find the audio recording 'Recitation of the *Metta Sutta*' on the module website. This is a recitation of the *Metta Sutta* in Pali by the Sri Lankan monk Mahinda Deegalle.

Listen to Mahinda's recitation. What do you notice about the way he recites the *sutta*?

You should allow about 20 minutes for this activity.

Discussion

The recitation is very regular. You can probably get a sense from the rhythm of the whole that each verse is recited separately but with similar intonation. There is no sense that Mahinda is trying to articulate the meaning of the text as he chants it. There is a degree of modulation in his voice as he recites each verse and we might discern a very basic tune, but the chanting doesn't quite make it into the category of what we commonly understand as music. The modulation would help monks to remember the text, but because the degree of intonation is not great, it does not offend against the rule that monks may not listen to music.

Activity

You should allow about 20 minutes for this activity.

You should now find the audio recording 'Discussion of the *Metta Sutta*' on the module website. In this recording, Mahinda Deegalle talks about how the *Metta Sutta* is used in Sri Lanka, where he was born and brought up.

Listen to the discussion now. Can you pick out from Mahinda's description some of the ways in which the *sutta* is used?

Discussion

Mahinda's description gives an indication of how often the *Metta Sutta* is recited. He tells us that it is recited at home and in the temples. He also suggests that, because the *sutta* is about loving-kindness, it is a good focus for thoughts last thing at night, and he tells us that he was encouraged to chant it before he went to sleep when he was a small boy. [This shows the status of the text; it is taught to children when they are very young and because there are many opportunities to recite it, the text stays in the memory throughout life.]

Activity

You should allow about 20 minutes for this activity.

Finally, you should find the films 'Pali *sutta*s recited by young Sri Lankan monks' and 'Pali *sutta*s recited by a Sri Lankan community' on the module website. In these films, you will see Sri Lankan monks and laypeople reciting texts in a temple near Colombo. The laypeople are reciting popular devotional verses, some of which are based on Pali *sutta*s.

Watch the films now. What strikes you about these examples of *sutta* recitation?

Discussion

In 'Pali *sutta*s recited by young Sri Lankan monks', the chanting is not as rhythmic as it might be. As you can see, these monks are mostly young and therefore comparatively inexperienced. No senior monks are present on this occasion, and the monks are reciting as much to learn the texts as for any other reason. In 'Pali *sutta*s recited by a Sri Lankan community', the verses are recited by laypeople, the majority of whom will have known these texts all their lives. They are clearly very comfortable with the chanting.

Some musical aspects of Buddhist chant

Fiona Richards

Chant is common to many different south Asian cultures, which feature a wide range of chanted poetry as well as examples of chant in a variety of religious contexts. In most examples of chant the text is of primary importance.

In the film 'Pali *sutta*s recited by young Sri Lankan monks', there are only three clearly discernible different pitches (by **pitch** we mean the way in which notes sound high or low in relation to one another). In the opening section one pitch assumes a much greater importance than the others. This is the first note you hear, sung clearly by the young monk, and much of the chant is based on this pitch. A second and third higher pitches, each only one step apart, are the other most commonly used musical notes in the film, and the voices oscillate between these three sounds for much of the chant. The meditative characteristic of the chant is largely due to the drone-like qualities induced by this very limited use of melodic pitches and the mellifluous rocking between them.

If we were to notate the opening section of the chant it might look something like Figure 1.3. This is a basic outline of the first 30 seconds or so of the film. The lowest 'blob' is the lowest and most important pitch; the others are the higher pitches. The different sizes are a rough representation of the importance of each pitch, and are intended to show you that some words are held for slightly longer, while others are chanted more quickly.

Figure 1.3 A graphic representation of Pali chant

Use of the *Metta Sutta*

The uses to which the *Metta Sutta* may be put can be divided into three categories. Like many categories, these three overlap – but for the sake of convenience they are discussed separately. The three are **meditation**, teaching and protection.

Meditation

In his discussion of the *Metta Sutta*, Mahinda has more to say about meditation than about teaching and protection. He refers to the calming effect of the *Metta Sutta*; as a boy, he used it to help him sleep. Calming and quietening the mind is basic to all meditation because it is not until the mind is calm that Buddhist meditators can begin meditation techniques to acquire insight and wisdom. It is not possible to think about anything in a careful way if the mind is flitting from one topic to another. The *Metta Sutta* is used to calm the mind ready for developing insight, but the text can also be a focus for insight meditation in its own right. Meditating on loving-kindness is a way to counteract hatred and to acquire a calm attitude to life in general. Indeed, reciting the *Metta Sutta* with the mind fully concentrated on its meaning is one of the most common meditation practices among Buddhists in southeast Asia (Gombrich, 1984, p. 88). Meditation, though difficult to do well because of the concentration it involves, can be a simple practice.

Activity

You should allow about 20 minutes for this activity.

One of the aims of meditation is the development of good qualities. What are the qualities that the *Metta Sutta* commends?

Discussion

The *Metta Sutta* affirms many qualities, including uprightness, noble speech, gentleness, humility, contentment, calm senses, discretion, happiness, security and boundless love. The text uses the example of a mother's love for her children to suggest the kind of unconditional love that beings ought to have for each other. You may also have noticed that the text emphasises the need for loving-kindness to reach out across the world.

Teaching

As we have seen, the canon to which the *Metta Sutta* belongs represents for Buddhists the voice and the word of the Buddha. They therefore listen to that voice and try to learn from it. Until comparatively modern times the word 'Pali' meant only 'Buddhist canonical text'; it did not refer to a language. The Theravada school of Buddhism, which preserved the Pali canon of which the *Metta Sutta* is a part, used Pali in a similar way to that in which ancient Indian religions used the Sanskrit language, or the Roman Catholic Church used Latin (Gombrich, 1984, p. 78). Pali is a textual language, not a language for everyday speech, but such is the popularity of this text that Buddhists who do not know Pali understand the content of the text. Anyone who can listen to monks or laypeople chanting the *Metta Sutta* and understand its content will hear a sort of sermon or exhortation (Gombrich, 1991, p. 242). They may not understand the text word for word, but they will know what it expresses.

Many religious canons narrate stories about beginnings and endings, or the cycle of time, or the activities of the founders. Alongside these stories are found complex doctrinal treaties and inspirational devotional verses. The Buddhist canon is no different. Many of the texts in the Pali canon are detailed, methodical expositions of doctrine or enumerations of the rules by which monks should live. The *Metta Sutta* is more accessible than many texts and it probably gained its popularity because of that. It is also inspirational in nature and so has an ability to arouse interest in Buddhism. Although the content of the *sutta* is accessible to non-Buddhists, like all religious texts it stands within a sophisticated doctrinal system. To get the maximum meaning out of the *Metta Sutta* it is necessary to understand the references within it. Although when you first read the text you may not have understood references to, for example, *nibbana*, people who live in Buddhist cultures are able to make these connections, so that each time the *Metta Sutta* is chanted it reaffirms Buddhist teaching for those who chant it or listen to it. Texts in other religious traditions have a similar teaching function – for instance, the Lord's Prayer (beginning 'Our Father, who art in heaven') for Christians, or the Shahada ('There is no God but God and Mohammad is his messenger'), which is the most important declaration of faith for Muslims. Each time these words are repeated, they reinforce the ideas they contain and act as teaching texts.

Protection

The third way in which the *Metta Sutta* is used is as a protective chant to ward off all kinds of ills and to bring about well-being. Because of its authoritative status, it may – along with other favoured texts – be recited when someone dies, at the opening of Parliament, to consecrate a new building, to get a good harvest, to do well in an exam, or at a sickbed. Like adherents of other Indian religions, including Hindus and Sikhs, many Buddhists believe that sound has intrinsic power. Certain sounds, whether or not they convey meaning, are powerful because they represent truth in sound form. This is why **mantra**s, which are believed to be made up of sacred syllables, are used extensively within Buddhism and other Indian religions. Buddhists in Sri Lanka believe that the recitation by monks of this and other *sutta*s in chorus is highly efficacious because the practice combines the words of the Buddha with recitation by religious specialists. As they recite the texts, a thread (called a *pirit*, or 'protection' thread) may be held by the monks and by the person for whom the blessing is intended. In Figure 1.4 Buddhist monks are shown holding a *pirit* thread as they chant.

Figure 1.4 Buddhist monks chanting. Photo: © KLJ Photographic/Alamy

The Buddhist scholar Peter Harvey (1990, pp. 180–1) puts forward five reasons for why chanting the *Metta Sutta* has a protective function.

First, chanting the *Metta Sutta*, or listening to a monk chant it, is soothing and so leads to calm because of the quality of the sound and because of the meaning of the text. Being calm is thought to be generally beneficial. It helped Mahinda sleep at night and it is good in any crisis. Sick people are more likely to recover if they stay calm, whether the root of the illness is bad **karma** or a flu bug.

Second, if hostile people hear the *Metta Sutta* being chanted they may become better disposed towards the chanter and others listening; their mood will be improved and so they will feel less aggressive and be less likely to act in a hostile way. A canonical story is told about the Buddha in which an enemy, his cousin Devadatta, released a rogue elephant with the intention of killing him. The Buddha was able to subdue the elephant simply by the forceful power of his loving-kindness (Gethin, 1998, p. 26).

Third, chanting the *Metta Sutta* is simply thought to be a good thing to do. In Buddhist thought, all good actions lead in time to good results; therefore it is always worth carrying out good actions.

Fourth, the gods who are the protectors of Buddhism like to hear the *Metta Sutta* being chanted, so they may offer their protection and help when they hear it.

The final reason Harvey suggests that reciting the *Metta Sutta* has a protective function relates to what was said above about teaching. Reaffirming virtues or good qualities in oneself is thought also to affirm and encourage those qualities.

According to the Buddhist law of karma, it is inevitable that good actions lead to good results and that bad actions lead to bad results. Buddhism does not support the idea that a student will pass an exam just by chanting the *Metta Sutta*. Instead it teaches that misfortune (in the form of an illness, say) can come about as a result of bad karma accrued in a past life and/or from a simple infection or injury. Buddhism does not teach that chanting the *Metta Sutta* at the bedside or in other situations will bring about an immediate cure or other change of fortune. However, as you have just seen, there are reasons why Buddhists think chanting the *Metta Sutta* might help anyway.

1.5 The voice of the translator

In some ways, the translation of the *Metta Sutta* you read earlier in this chapter represents the voice of Saddhatissa, who translated it from Pali into English, as well as the voice of the Buddha and of Buddhist tradition. Saddhatissa was a Sri Lankan monk and scholar. He became a novice monk in Sri Lanka when he was 12 years old, a traditional age for boys to begin their training. As well as receiving a traditional monk's education, he also received a higher education in the west, including at London and Edinburgh universities. He spent many years at the School of Oriental and African Studies in London and continued to live as a monk while he worked there (Walshe, 1970, p. 7). As a result of this, he [was able to use his knowledge and experience of Buddhism and his understanding of western culture to produce translations of Buddhist texts that he believed were both true to their original intention and accessible to native English speakers.] His book was first published in 1985 and he tells us in the preface that he had taught the text to undergraduates in India and in Canada before he finalised the translation.

Saddhatissa writes: 'It should be understood that it is not a strict translation but rather a [rendering of the spirit of the *suttas*'] (1994, p. vii). You can see from this comment that, rather than translate the *Metta Sutta* and other *sutta*s word for word, he has prioritised maintaining the sense, or the 'spirit', of the text. To facilitate this, he has prepared a prose version rather than a poetic version. [In prose the text loses some of the rhythmic impetus] that made it easy for countless generations of Pali chanters to memorise, but it probably gains in clarity because it is not constricted by metrical form. The British Pali scholar Richard Gombrich says of the Pali version of the text that [content was far more important than literary grace'] (1984, p. 88). He is referring to the fact that the meaning of the text is more important than its form. Of course, the fact that content is more important than form does not mean that form is unimportant.

There are many alternative translations of the *Metta Sutta*, some of which are in verse form. We shall consider one of these shortly. But first consider the questions in the following activity. (You will return to the topic of different approaches to translation in Chapter 5, when you study some extracts from an ancient Greek poem, Homer's *Iliad*.)

Activity

Does the identity of the translator affect the authority of a text? If so, how does it do this and why? In thinking about this question you should draw not only on what you have just read, but also on your life experience.

You should allow about 20 minutes for this activity.

Discussion

I think the answer to this question is that it does. As a reader you will want to be sure that the translator has great facility with both the original language and the language you are reading. It is easy to spot a translation into your own language that has been made by someone who doesn't speak the language well. This kind of translation can lead, for example, to amusing signs or explanations for tourists. But it is much more difficult to spot that a translator doesn't fully understand the language and culture he or she is translating from. You would certainly want to be sure that you really are reading the text you set out to read rather than a misunderstanding of that text. Within religions there is another factor to add in. As you have seen, religious canonical texts have authority as the voice of a founder and of a tradition and even as the voice of truth. In the case of Christianity, Judaism and Islam, followers believe that their canonical texts in some sense represent the voice of God. It is obviously important for adherents of a religion that the translator hasn't made a mistake. Saddhatissa has said that he has tried to retain the 'spirit of the *suttas*'. It is therefore legitimate to ask by what authority he can decide what the spirit of a *sutta* is. That is why in the preface to the volume in which Saddhatissa's translation is published we are given his credentials both as a scholar and as a monk.

Here is a different translation of the *Metta Sutta*. I'll call it the 'Amaravati version', after the name of the Buddhist community in Buckinghamshire, England that published this version. This community attracts Thai followers but caters mainly for westerners, many of whom, though they have no intention of becoming monks or nuns, take their practice of Buddhism very seriously.

> This is what should be done
>   By one who is skilled in goodness,
> And who knows the path of peace:
>   Let them be able and upright,
> Straightforward and gentle in speech,
>   Humble and not conceited,

Contented and easily satisfied,
      Unburdened with duties and frugal in their ways.
Peaceful and calm and wise and skillful,
      Not proud or demanding in nature.
Let them not do the slightest thing
      That the wise would later reprove.
Wishing: In gladness and in safety,
      May all beings be at ease.
Whatever living beings there may be;
      Whether they are weak or strong, omitting none,
The great or the mighty, medium, short or small,
      The seen and the unseen,
Those living near and far away,
      Those born and to-be-born –
May all beings be at ease!

Let none deceive another,
      Or despise any being in any state.
Let none through anger or ill-will
      Wish harm upon another.
Even as a mother protects with her life
      Her child, her only child,
So with a boundless heart
      Should one cherish all living beings;
Radiating kindness over the entire world:
      Spreading upwards to the skies,
And downwards to the depths;
      Outwards and unbounded,
Freed from hatred and ill-will.
      Whether standing or walking, seated or lying down
Free from drowsiness,
      One should sustain this recollection.
This is said to be the sublime abiding.
      By not holding to fixed views,
The pure-hearted one, having clarity of vision,
      Being freed from all sense desires,
Is not born again into this world.

(Amaravati Sangha, 2013)

Activity

What strikes you about this translation?

You should allow about 15 minutes for this activity.

Discussion

The most obvious difference between the Amaravati translation and Saddhatissa's translation is that the Amaravati version is in poetic form. My colleague Bill Greenwell, whom you will encounter in Book 3, says that what struck him when he read the Amaravati translation for the first time was that the language is slightly artificial, as if mimicking sacred texts first translated into English in previous centuries.

Certainly, the language is formal and uses idioms that we would be unlikely to use in everyday speech, such as: 'Wishing: In gladness and in safety,/May all beings be at ease.' The verse form also requires some repetition in order to maintain the rhythm, as in 'Even as a mother protects with her life/Her child, her only child,' which flows differently from Saddhatissa's 'Just as a mother would protect her only child at the risk of her own life'.

The two translations were made for different purposes. The Amaravati translators probably had in mind the fact that their version would be recited within an English-speaking community in a similar way to that of the Sri Lankan monks and laypeople chanting Pali verses in the films you watched earlier in the chapter. Saddhatissa's translation was made largely for students and to explain the content of the text.

As with all translations, Saddhatissa and the translators of the Amaravati version have made decisions about how to express unfamiliar ideas in English. The good qualities that the *Metta Sutta* commends are relatively easy to pick out, but there are other ideas in this text that are less familiar. Here is a discussion of two of these.

The first comes at the end of verse 2 of Saddhatissa's translation, where the text exhorts the reciter and listener not to be 'greedily attached to families'. You'll notice that there is no mention of families in the Amaravati translation. According to the preface to the *sutta*, the *Metta Sutta* was taught by the Buddha to a group of monks who had settled in a forest for the Indian rainy season. This context is important. Monks are full-time religious practitioners who are not permitted to earn a living. They therefore rely on others for support and were and are used to receiving alms from their families. Saddhatissa saw fit to keep the reference to families, while the Amaravati translators simply

context

refer to not being 'demanding in nature'. It may be that the Amaravati translators were more conscious than was Saddhatissa that they were addressing many more laypeople than monks, and so selected words for the translation that reflected the different audience.

The second phrase is 'This they say is the noblest living here' in verse 9. The Amaravati version translates this as 'This is said to be the sublime abiding'. Gombrich prefers 'This they say is the Sublime State in this life' (1984, p. 88). This is another reference to *nibbana*, the state in which someone lives their life without greed, hatred and delusion.

unfamiliar cocepts

It is a matter for debate which of these three phrases expresses *nibbana* more clearly, but obviously all three translators have set out to convey its meaning as best they can. It is difficult to express in a succinct way, in English, a concept that is not native to western cultures. Indeed, it is difficult to understand the meaning of a religious text at all without knowing something of the context in which it was written. That does not mean that when we start to study religion we cannot learn from these texts. When you first read an unfamiliar text it might seem impossible to understand – and some religious texts are much more difficult to get to grips with than the *Metta Sutta* is. But the more you know about the context in which a text was written and about how that text is used and interpreted, the better you can understand it. At the same time, the texts themselves are part of the context for understanding a religious tradition. A text is hard to understand without the context and a context is hard to understand without the text. By studying both text and context, and using each to shed light on the other, you will make progress.

As Buddhism spread from India into other parts of Asia, including China, Japan and Tibet, the texts were translated into vernacular languages, the languages that people spoke in those areas. They were inevitably changed in the process, as concepts in the texts were expressed in terms that already carried meaning in the languages into which they were translated. In the same way, when Buddhist texts are translated into English, for example, words that are familiar from Christianity, such as 'faith' or 'god', may be used to express Buddhist concepts that do not quite match up in meaning with their Christian counterparts. Like Saddhatissa, translators have always been aware of the need to preserve the authority of sacred texts when they are expressed in new languages. The same process continues, as Buddhist converts and students who think about the world in twenty-first-century idioms try to understand the meaning of ancient texts. This is perhaps why religious people sometimes talk about the 'true' meaning of texts, as though there are other meanings that are 'untrue', or perhaps 'less true'.

Religious canonical texts carry a particular kind of authority. It is therefore also important to some translators that the results of their work can be understood by people who are not used to books or to sophisticated religious language. They will be especially keen to balance accuracy in translation with language that a reader can understand. You can draw your own conclusions about the accessibility of the two translations of the *Metta Sutta* that you have read in this chapter.

Conclusion

In this account of the *Metta Sutta* you have considered how the text came to be part of the Buddhist canon. You have also looked at the ways in which the text is used in Sri Lanka and at issues concerning its translation out of Pali and into other languages. Texts are important sources of authority for religious traditions. They are not the only sources of authority: tradition itself is authoritative, and so are charismatic individuals and personal experience, but texts represent continuity in religions and are cited both by traditions and by teachers.

Religious texts are also sources of cohesion and division. The *Metta Sutta* is not a source of authority for Christians, just as the Christian Bible carries no authority for Buddhists. Buddhists and Christians may appreciate each other's texts but they do not rely on them. Even within a tradition, certain texts are authoritative for some but not for others. The *Metta Sutta* is as close as it can be to a Buddhist text accepted by all Buddhists, but other Buddhist texts are not accepted by Buddhists in the same way. The same can be true of texts preserved in other religious traditions, and certainly the ways in which texts are interpreted can be a source of division.

You will have seen from this account of the *Metta Sutta* that scholarly understanding of canonical religious texts is not a simple matter of reading the texts and working out whether or not you agree with them, or what they might mean to you. Canonical texts are important to communities and they provide a focus or a context for religious teaching and for religious practice. For Buddhists it is not enough to know the content of the *Metta Sutta*; it is also important that the text is recited and put to use in approved ways. The same is true for the religious texts of other traditions. When we study religion it is important to recognise that texts have complex voices. In this case, the voices are those of the Buddha and of the tradition and practices that follow him.

References

Amaravati Sangha (2013) 'Karaniya Metta Sutta: the Buddha's words on loving-kindness', Sn 1.8 (trans. from the Pali), *Access to Insight (Legacy Edition)*, 2 November [Online]. Available at http://www.accesstoinsight.org/tipitaka/kn/snp/snp.1.08.amar.html (Accessed 22 April 2014).

Bechert, H. (1992) 'The date of the Buddha reconsidered', *Indologica Taurinensia*, no. 10, pp. 29–36.

Collins, S. (1990) 'On the very idea of the Pali canon', *Journal of the Pali Text Society*, no. 15, pp. 89–116.

Cousins, L. (1996) 'The dating of the historical Buddha: a review article', *Journal of the Royal Asiatic Society*, third series, vol. 6, no. 1, pp. 57–63.

Cunningham, A. (1990) 'Religious studies in the universities' in King, U. (ed.) *Turning Points in Religious Studies*, Edinburgh, T&T Clark, pp. 21–31.

Gethin, R. (1998) *The Foundations of Buddhism*, Oxford, Oxford University Press.

Gombrich, R. (1984) 'The evolution of the Sangha' in Bechert, H. and Gombrich, R. (eds) *The World of Buddhism*, London, Thames and Hudson, pp. 77–89.

Gombrich, R. (1988) *Theravada Buddhism*, London, Routledge & Kegan Paul.

Gombrich, R. (1991) *Buddhist Precept and Practice*, Delhi, Motilal Banarsidass.

Harvey, P. (1990) *An Introduction to Buddhism*, Cambridge, Cambridge University Press.

Lopez, D.S. (2008) *Buddhism and Science: A Guide for the Perplexed*, Chicago and London, University of Chicago Press.

Prebish, C. (2005) 'Councils: Buddhist councils', in Jones, L. (ed.) *Encyclopedia of Religion*, 2nd edn, vol. 3, Detroit, Macmillan, pp. 2034–9.

Saddhatissa, H. (1994) *The Sutta-Nipāta*, Richmond, Curzon.

Walshe, M. (1970) 'Foreword', in Saddhatissa, H., *Buddhist Ethics*, London, George Allen & Unwin, pp. 7–8.

Walshe, M. (1995) *The Long Discourses of the Buddha*, Boston, Wisdom.

Waterhouse, H. (2001) 'Representing western Buddhism: a United Kingdom focus', in Beckerlegge, G. (ed.) *From Sacred Text to Internet*, Aldershot, Ashgate, pp. 117–60.

Witzel, M. (2005) 'Vedas and Upaniṣads', in Flood, G. (ed.) *The Blackwell Companion to Hinduism* [Online], Oxford, Blackwell Reference. Available at http://www.blackwellreference.com/subscriber/book.html?id=g9780631215356_9780631215356 (Accessed 12 May 2014).

Further reading

If you would like to find out more about Buddhist traditions, you could start with the BBC website and with Damien Keown's introductory volume (2013):

BBC (2014) 'Buddhism' [Online]. Available at http://www.bbc.co.uk/religion/religions/buddhism/(Accessed 28 February 2014).

Keown, D. (2013) *Buddhism: A Very Short Introduction*, Oxford, Oxford University Press.

Chapter 2
The musical canon

Fiona Richards

Contents

Aims

This chapter will:

- examine the concept of the canon as it is used in Music
- introduce case studies of some canonical vocal and instrumental genres
- develop your understanding of notions of authority and musical texts
- develop your ability to write about music.

Materials you will need

In this chapter, you will need to listen to the following audio recordings, which can be found on the module website:

- Handel, 'Hallelujah' chorus (version 1)
- Handel, 'Hallelujah' chorus (version 2)
- Musical examples 1–4
- O'Connor, 'Anything goes'
- Stone, 'Anything goes'
- Vaughan Williams, 'The Vagabond'
- Beethoven, Eighth Symphony, first movement
- Beethoven, Eighth Symphony, second movement
- Beethoven, Eighth Symphony, third movement
- Beethoven, Eighth Symphony, fourth movement
- Beethoven, First Symphony, first movement
- Beethoven, Ninth Symphony, first movement
- Beethoven, Sixth Symphony, second movement, 'By the brook'
- Dvořák, Violin Concerto, last movement
- Raga Jaunpuri: II. Intermezzo in Shikartaal
- Adams, El Niño, 'For with God no thing shall be impossible'
- Adams, extract from *The Dharma at Big Sur*
- John Donne, 'Batter my heart'.

You will also need to watch the following films, which can be found on the module website:

- Opera in Classical Vienna
- 'Batter my heart', from Adams, *Doctor Atomic*.

Introduction

This chapter focuses on the idea of canon and authority. You met the term 'canon' in your work on Buddhism in the previous chapter. Although the meaning of the term in Music is related to the way it is used in Religious Studies, there are important differences, too. Following some broad-ranging examples drawn from different musical repertories, the focus here narrows to two case studies. The first of these returns to the work begun in Book 1, and explores in more detail questions of canon and authority and the Stradivarius violin. The second looks at the work of the American composer John Adams alongside study of the words of the English seventeenth-century preacher and poet John Donne. Although these two artists may seem worlds away from each other, there is, as you will discover, a link that enables us to engage in an interdisciplinary study of a single text.

The idea of a musical canon

In classical music the word 'canon' is used to describe a body of works in particular genres, such as symphonies, concertos and operas, that have become recognised as 'masterpieces' by a range of critics, performers and audiences. However, this musical canon is not a strict and defined list of pieces, but rather an assumed understanding that certain types of music – the works of particular composers – have what might be called a benchmark status. *Messiah*, by George Frideric Handel (1685–1759), the operas of Wolfgang Amadeus Mozart (1756–1791) and the symphonies of Ludwig van Beethoven (1770–1827) might fit into this category. As with works of art (as you will discover in the next chapter), central to the canon is the idea of the masterpiece, which, in the context of music, signifies a work by a key figure in one of the major musical genres, such as opera or the symphony.

Linked to this canon of musical works are people, institutions and performing organisations. For example, names such as the Berlin Philharmonic Orchestra, BBC Radio 3 and Luciano Pavarotti are associated with exceptional standards and approaches to performance. Equally, important venues such as the Royal Albert Hall in London (Figure 2.1) and the Musikverein in Vienna (Figure 2.2) have a high status and carry a sense of authority in the musical world.

However, there is not just one musical canon, but several. It might be argued that in addition to a wider canon of classical music, there are

Figure 2.1 Royal Albert Hall, London. Photo: © Enigma/Alamy

Figure 2.2 Wiener Musikverein, Vienna, Austria, 2009. Photographed by
B. O'Kane. Photo: © B. O'Kane/Alamy

also smaller canons of nineteenth-century piano music, of string quartets, of Viennese waltzes, and so on – subsets, as it were. Equally, there are canons in other types of music. Names such as Louis Armstrong and Charlie Parker would undoubtedly figure in thoughts of a jazz canon. If we were to think of a canon of pop groups it would be impossible to ignore the Beatles, but it is also possible to think of a body of music from smaller and more defined periods such as the 1970s or the 1980s that has become canonical. My own candidates for canonical songs from the 1980s might include music by the Police, Human League, Pet Shop Boys, Adam Ant and the Smiths. But another person's 1980s' canon could look quite different, maybe more like this: the Jam, Madness, U2, Eurythmics, a-ha. It has to be said, however, that this type of 'canon' of recent songs is more a reflection of personal taste or assumed knowledge than of works that have stood the test of time. In the case of, say, an opera by Richard Wagner (1813–1883), its canonical status has been shaped and established by musicians, critics, audiences and institutions.

So how do we know when a work is canonical? There is no formal list of canonical music, and views evolve and change. Handel's music was very successful and popular during his lifetime, but performed much less frequently after his death until it was revived by the Victorians. In the above example of music from the 1980s, there are songs that have become known as canonical, 'classic' songs of the decade for a range of reasons – maybe because of their continued sales or their association with the era (such as the use of music by the Jam in the film *Billy Elliot* (2000), or Duran Duran's association with the James Bond film *A View to a Kill* (1985)).

This process of change is often reflected in images and design details, for example on covers of sheet music produced in the late nineteenth and early twentieth centuries.

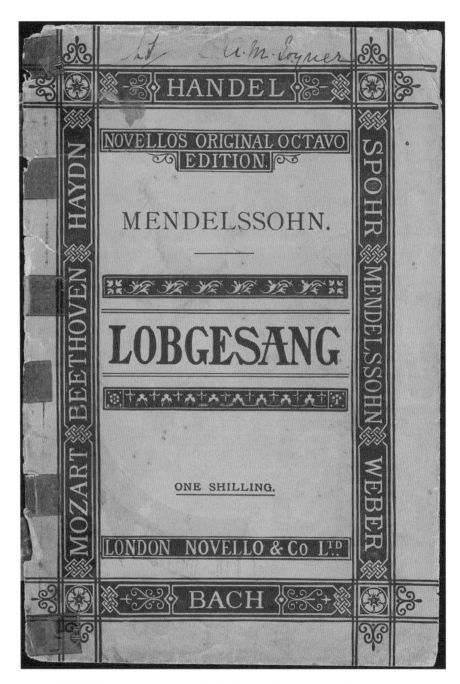

Figure 2.3 *Lobgesang*, cover for Felix Mendelssohn's musical score.
Produced by Novello and Co., London

Activity

Figure 2.3 shows the cover of *Lobgesang* ('Hymn of Praise', 1840), a choral work composed by Felix Mendelssohn (1809–1847). It was produced by Novello and Co., a leading publisher of classical music. Look closely at the names of composers used in the borders on the cover and make a list of them. Then put the names in order, from the most canonical to the least known.

You should allow about 10 minutes for this activity.

Discussion

These are the names in my order:

- Beethoven
- Mozart
- Bach
- Handel
- Haydn
- Mendelssohn
- Weber
- Spohr.

Your order might differ slightly. For example, you might place Mozart at the top. The Victorians prized the **Baroque** composers, and you can see evidence of the considered musical canon of this time on this cover: Handel and Bach are in pride of place at the top and bottom, and around them appear the names Spohr, Mendelssohn, Weber, Mozart, Beethoven and Haydn. However, while you may have heard of the last three composers, you may not have come across Louis Spohr (1784–1859), whose music is now neglected by comparison with the others.

2.1 Canonical vocal works

Next, I'll introduce you to some short examples of what might be considered pieces belonging to a musical canon, all of which involve voices.

Activity

You should allow about 20 minutes for this activity.

You should now find the audio recording 'Handel, "Hallelujah" chorus (version 1)' on the module website. The words are shown in Reading 2.1.

Listen to the recording now. As you listen, concentrate on the words and on the voices and orchestra performing them, and try to note in very simple terms what you are hearing.

Discussion

This is possibly the best-known example of a piece of choral music. It is written for a traditional chorus, which usually consists of four different voice types, which range from the highest female voices (sopranos) to the lowest male voices (basses). In between there are other female (alto) voices and male (tenor) voices, too. This is the standard make-up of a conventional mixed-voice choir, often abbreviated as SATB (soprano, alto, tenor, bass). The piece that you hear uses a mixture of **unison** and contrapuntal writing. In some places the voices sing together in **harmony**, or in **chord**s. In other places one voice follows another in imitation or two different melodic lines are woven against one another: this type of writing is called **counterpoint**.

The 'Hallelujah' chorus comes from a larger work, *Messiah*, written by Handel in 1741, while he was living in Brook Street, London, and first performed in Dublin in 1742. *Messiah* is an oratorio: a canonical musical genre used by composers for the last 400 years. In music, a genre is a type of musical work – for example symphony, opera, oratorio. I shall return to this subject when we move on to look at Beethoven.

Oratorio

An oratorio is a large musical composition for voices and orchestra, including a choir and soloists. Structurally it has some similarities with opera, but is an unstaged concert piece performed in a church or concert hall by singers who are not costumed as actors. The work usually concerns a story on a sacred topic – in the case of Handel's *Messiah*, the life of Jesus – and is structured in acts divided into a number of small movements, some of which are for soloists, some for chorus. *Messiah*, for example, has three parts (or acts) following events described in the Christian Bible. Part 1 deals with the Advent and Christmas stories, Part 2 centres on the Easter story and Part 3 is based on events in the Book of Revelation.

Messiah has become part of the musical canon for a variety of reasons: its superb music, its popularity as a work that can be performed by both professionals and amateurs, and its importance over many generations. It is from the Baroque period, which in terms of music lasted from around 1600 to 1750. Mozart made his own arrangement of *Messiah* with a larger orchestra, and nineteenth- and early twentieth-century British performances of the work favoured huge orchestras (which sometimes additionally included brass bands) and choruses as a way of praising God through music (Figure 2.4).

However, in a study that considers 'authority', you might regard it as interesting that there is no definitive musical text for *Messiah* because of the many changes Handel himself made during the seasons it was performed in the 1740s and 1750s. Some numbers were recomposed or altered to suit a particular soloist. And later changes by editors have meant that there is no authoritative printed edition of the work.

Activity

Before you start this activity, you might like to remind yourself of the musical terms introduced in Book 1, Chapter 2, Section 2.1.

You should then find the audio recording 'Handel, "Hallelujah" chorus (version 2)' on the module website. Before you listen to it, listen again to the recording from the last activity: 'Handel, "Hallelujah" chorus (version 1)'. In the table below note, very generally, the differences between them. The duration of each piece is noted on the module website.

You should allow about 20 minutes for this activity.

	Version 1	**Version 2**
Duration		
Speed		
Voices		
Orchestra		

Figure 2.4 *Messiah,* George Frideric Handel. Conducted by F. Cowen at the annual festival, Crystal Palace, 1905. Photo: © Lebrecht Music and Arts Photo Library/Alamy

Discussion

Close listening is one of the core skills in the study of Music as a discipline, and one of the features of the approach used in this chapter is to offer different versions of the same pieces, to help you develop your listening skills. I hope you managed to hear some of the principal differences between these two recordings. My comments are shown below.

	Version 1	**Version 2**
Duration	4 minutes 44 seconds	3 minutes 47 seconds
Speed	Quite ponderous	Much more lively, with a bouncy feel
Voices	Mixed voices, both male and female – very 'operatic' in sound	Only male voices
Orchestra	Full symphony orchestra, heavy and weighty	Smaller orchestra with a lighter sound

Version 1 was recorded some time ago now, in 1960, and features Leonard Bernstein conducting the New York Philharmonic Orchestra with the Mormon Tabernacle Choir. I hope you logged that it was almost a whole minute longer than the second one. A performance of this type – quite ponderous – might now be viewed as not in keeping with the spirit of the music. Version 2 was recorded in 1980 and has now entered the canon of highly regarded recordings of *Messiah*. This is because it sets out to be an 'authentic' performance, one that adheres to the performance conventions and values that applied when Handel wrote this work. In practice, what this means is that the choir consists of only male voices: boys taking the soprano line, with male altos, tenors and basses. In addition, the orchestral instruments used are as close as possible to the instruments played in the 1740s, while other issues such as **tempi** (speeds) and balance are carefully considered within their Baroque context. For example, it is much quicker than Bernstein's version. The conductor Christopher Hogwood founded the orchestra playing this version, the Academy of Ancient Music, in 1973, with the express purpose of trying to re-create, as far as is feasible, the intentions of the composer, both in notation and in performance.

Activity

Now it's up to you to comment on some musical examples. Find the audio recordings entitled 'Musical examples 1–4' on the module website. Listen to each of the four pieces. For each example, describe what you hear. You might ask yourself: is this one voice with an orchestra, or a vocal group? Is it accompanied or unaccompanied? The words of each piece are shown in Readings 2.2, 2.3, 2.4, and 2.6.

You should allow about 20 minutes for this activity.

Discussion

Example 1 is sung by male voices – boys and men with organ. Example 2 is a solo male voice (**baritone**) and orchestra. Example 3 is a recording of a solo female voice and small jazz band. Example 4 features a solo male voice with piano.

You'll now build on your initial work with these examples, adding more information and considering why each example might be considered to be canonical. Before you read on, though, listen to 'Musical examples 1–4' again as many times as you wish, to familiarise yourself with the pieces.

The first example, 'I vow to thee, my country', might be considered to be canonical for a number of reasons. It is a well-known and popular hymn, but it has also become associated with important events. The words of the first verse refer to the sacrifice of those who died during the First World War, and were set to music by the British composer Gustav Holst (1874–1934). Holst took the tune from an existing piece of his own orchestral music, *The Planets* (1914–16). The hymn is now a regular feature of Armistice memorial ceremonies. It was sung at both the wedding and the funeral of Diana, Princess of Wales (in 1981 and 1997, respectively). Through its poignant lyrics, familiar tune and range of nationalistic and political associations, it has come to carry a sense of authority.

Hymn

A hymn is a type of song, usually religious, written for the purpose of praise, adoration or prayer. Ancient examples include an important collection of Hindu hymns called the Vedas. The western tradition of hymnody – that is, the singing or composition of hymns – begins with the Greek Homeric hymns, dating from the eighth century BCE. Christian hymns are often written for particular events such as Christmas or Easter. Most of today's well-known hymns are written in four parts using the same standard layout, SATB. In many church services only the top line is sung, with the other parts played on the organ. Hymn accompaniments vary enormously, depending on the particular form of worship involved, and range from synthesised instruments or small bands to unaccompanied voices.

The second example is an extract from one of Mozart's operas, which are an undisputed part of the canon of important **Classical** music. Mozart wrote operas in German and in Italian, and had a hugely significant impact on operatic writing in the nineteenth century. *The Marriage of Figaro* is an example of comic opera, known as **opera buffa**, and was first performed in Vienna in 1786. Vienna at this time was a remarkable creative centre of music, with four of the most significant composers of Classical music based there – Joseph Haydn (1732–1809), Mozart, Beethoven and Franz Schubert (1797–1828). Mozart spent the last ten years of his life in the city, and most of his major operas were composed for performance there. This opera was considered quite risqué at the time it was written, as the opera's librettist, Lorenzo da Ponte, adapted the story from a banned play by Pierre-Augustin Beaumarchais. It is an excellent example of the portrayal of character in opera, where particular types of music tend to be allotted to male and female characters. The **aria** you've heard is a typical example of the way in which music might be viewed as gendered. It is sung by the opera's protagonist, Figaro, and is correspondingly predominantly *forte* (loud) throughout; is a march in a bright, major key; uses an orchestra with prominent brass and timpani; and has a full **texture**. The **melody** sung by Figaro is based on chords and has many bold, assertive, rising **phrase**s.

Opera

An opera is a dramatic musical work in which singing takes the place of speech. Like a play, an opera is often structured in acts and scenes. Opera has its origins in late sixteenth-century Florence. Many operas contain standard features: an overture (an orchestral opening), choruses, duets and other ensembles. Operas often use recitative, which is a declamatory, speech-like style of singing used to carry the plot forwards. An aria in an opera is a song sung by a particular character, which allows them to have a moment of reflection.

In the next activity you will watch a short film giving you some contextual background to the performance of Mozart's operas in the eighteenth century. The film shows you some images of the Burgtheater in Vienna, where many works were performed, and then moves on to a theatre in Český Krumlov in the Czech Republic, close to the Austrian border. This theatre holds a marvellous archive of opera sets from the late eighteenth century and in the film you will see these sets in operation, along with some extracts from *The Marriage of Figaro*.

Activity

Find the film 'Opera in Classical Vienna' on the module website. Watch it through now. What does this tell you about the impact of Viennese nobility on cultural life?

You should allow about 30 minutes for this activity.

Discussion

In this film you see a surviving – and stunning – eighteenth-century theatre. Many Viennese noblemen at this time owned vast country estates outside the city, with extensive gardens, theatres and lavishly decorated rooms. This estate belonged to the house of Schwarzenberg and the theatre was built in the 1760s. It has fabulous sets requiring a team of operators. Composers saw their works performed in theatres such as this, and Italian singers were brought in to perform them, though not during Lent, when no operas were performed.

The third musical example you listened to was 'Anything goes', a song that is regarded as belonging to the 'Great American Songbook', sometimes known as GAS. The Great American Songbook is a term used to refer to a body of songs from the 1920s to the 1960s, drawn from a range of backgrounds such as musical theatre and films, which have become a core part of the repertoire of singers and jazz musicians. There is no definitive list of songs, but such names as Irving Berlin (1888–1989; 'Cheek to Cheek', 'White Christmas'), George Gershwin (1898–1937; 'Summertime', 'I Got Rhythm'), Jerome Kern (1885–1945; 'Smoke Gets in Your Eyes') and Cole Porter (1891–1964; 'Anything goes') are all considered to belong to a group of iconic composers of great American songs.

Many of the songs in the Great American Songbook share a common musical structure featuring a verse and a chorus. The chorus is usually a 32-bar AABA or ABAC form, where there is a repeating A section with contrasting music for the B and C sections. Many singers and musicians have recorded or performed these songs, and you will find numerous versions of them, in very contrasting styles. One interesting performance of the song by Caroline O'Connor is included on the module website (though in a slightly different version in terms of the text, with two additional verses, as shown in Reading 2.5). A third version of 'Anything goes', by Lew Stone and His Band, is also included on the module website.

The fourth example is a German song, or *Lied*, one of the principal genres of the Classical period and the nineteenth century. Schubert's song 'Erlkönig' is a setting of words by someone who is viewed as part of the literary canon of great German writers, Johann Wolfgang von Goethe (1749–1832). Its narrative tells of a child who dies in his father's arms, killed by a supernatural being, the Erl-king (the elf-king, or alder-king, a type of malevolent spirit). In the poem a young boy is being carried home at night by his father on horseback. As the poem unfolds, the son begins to see and hear spirits that his father does not: both the Erl-king and other ghostly presences. The father initially talks these away as nothing more than fog or leaves. But the child's increasing terror gradually convinces the father that something is wrong. The climax of the son's fright comes as he shrieks that the Erl-king has attacked him. The father rides faster, but his son lies dead in his arms.

Lied

The German word for song is *Lied* and its plural is *Lieder*. Both words are commonly used to refer to examples of German song, especially from the nineteenth century. The origins of the Romantic *Lieder* repertory lie in the late eighteenth century, but the best-known works in the genre were composed after 1800 by Beethoven, Schubert, Robert Schumann (1810–1856), Johannes Brahms (1833–1897) and Hugo Wolf (1860–1903).

What makes Schubert's song so special is the way in which one voice sings four characters – narrator, father, son and the Erl-king – while the piano plays the part of the horse, with constant pounding movement. Schubert places each role in a slightly different vocal range, and in this particular performance the singer also gives each role a slightly different vocal nuance. Thus the narrator is in the middle range of the voice, the father in the low range and the boy in a higher range. The Erl-king's vocal line snakes up and down and is sung more quietly to mirror the fact that only the boy can see him. In addition, each time the boy sings his phrase is slightly higher and louder, to create the sense of mounting terror. One interesting feature of Schubert's approach to words is that he made a practice of returning to poems he had already set to music and viewing them from a new angle, often setting the words in a radically different manner. While he did not do this with 'Erlkönig', it is a feature of his fascination with word-setting. This particular song has been much discussed as an example of the exceptional bringing together of voices and texts, as this passage demonstrates:

The extent to which Schubert, in his eighteenth year, had developed this control of an aspect of song-writing in which art and craft meet shows itself nowhere more dazzlingly than in 'Erlkönig'. 'Erlkönig' is, of course, a dramatic ballad, this time by the greatest of Schubert's poets, Goethe. […] A poem exuding such mystery, suspense and excitement, and driving relentlessly forward on waves of juvenile fear and paternal anxiety – both approaching panic – was bound to encourage Schubert to draw upon the more dramatic elements of his musical vocabulary. 'Erlkönig' is a highly charged, graphic portrayal of a nightmarish tale, missing no opportunity to point up its passing details yet maintaining a galloping momentum from start to finish.

(Newbould, 1997, p. 57)

The song cycle

Each of the pieces you've heard so far has been discussed as a separate entity, though in two cases the item is part of a bigger whole – the Handel chorus is from an oratorio and the Mozart aria from an opera. The Schubert piece is an individual song, but there is also a larger-scale canonical song genre called a song cycle.

A song cycle is a group of songs and poems, either for voice and piano or for voice and ensemble orchestra, that relate to one another in some way. Sometimes the songs may be only loosely connected, but in the nineteenth century this type of musical genre more commonly came to comprise sets of songs that either had a narrative thread or expressed a common theme. Some cycles set the words of only one poet, whereas in others poems by different poets are brought together as a set. Sometimes musical cross-quotations between songs create strong links across the song cycle as a whole. Two important examples include Schubert's *Winterreise* ('Winter Journey', 1827; words by Wilhelm Müller) and Schumann's *Dichterliebe* ('Poet's Love', 1840; words by Heinrich Heine).

We are now going to look at a song cycle from the twentieth century. In a hierarchy of twentieth-century English music, Ralph Vaughan Williams (1872–1958) would feature quite highly. He had an interest in the revival of Tudor music, he was an important collector of folk songs and he was equally important as one of the first composers to establish

English song in the first part of the twentieth century. His choice of lyrics spanned nineteenth-century poets such as Algernon Charles Swinburne and Alfred, Lord Tennyson, his contemporaries A(lfred) E (dward) Housman and Fredegond Shove, and earlier writers including William Blake and Geoffrey Chaucer. One of the most successful and popular of his early works was a song cycle, *Songs of Travel* (1901–04). This is a collection of settings of verse by the Scottish poet Robert Louis Stevenson (1850–1894). One of the attractions of Stevenson's words is that they were conceived with melody in mind and all have simple, stanzaic structures that lend themselves to song-setting.

Activity

You can find an audio recording of the first song from *Songs of Travel*, 'The Vagabond', on the module website. The words are shown in Reading 2.7. Listen to the recording now and answer the following questions:

You should allow about 20 minutes for this activity.

1   If you take verse 1 to be the 'A' material, what is the overall structure of the song? Listen to see if this 'A' material repeats, and if there are places where it is altered.

2   What is the most obvious way in which Vaughan Williams captures the spirit of the poem in the music?

Discussion

1   There are two main passages of music, giving the overall pattern AABA. Thus verses 1, 2 and 4 use the same music, while verse 3 has a change of mood and new music.

2   I would say that the most obvious way in which Vaughan Williams captures the spirit of the poem is in the characteristic tramping figure that opens the song. The performance indications in the score of 'The Vagabond' enhance the sense of tramping movement; for example, the performers are instructed to play *pesante* (heavily) and *robustamente* (robustly). The AABA structure of the song could also be interpreted as encapsulating the mood of the words: the only point at which the protagonist dreams of the 'fireside haven' is in the third stanza, where the music changes. By the fourth stanza the inexorable onward tramping has returned.

The overall theme of the songs in this cycle is that expressed in the title of the song cycle: travel. The image of a journey, especially a rural adventure, was something that pervaded much of the literature of the latter part of the nineteenth and early part of the twentieth centuries, and Stevenson's poems are part of a wider literary and artistic culture. Vaughan Williams made significant contributions to the development of English song as a genre in the first decade of the twentieth century, and he produced a number of song cycles.

2.2 Beethoven and the symphony

So far we've focused on vocal music, but we're now going to move to a different area of study. Of all instrumental genres, the symphony is the most likely to feature in the canon of western Classical music, and Beethoven is probably the name that would appear on any list of composers of great symphonies. Although he was born in Bonn, Beethoven spent his adult career in Vienna and all his mature music was composed in that city. He wrote nine symphonies in total, covering the period from 1800 to 1824.

Other names renowned for their contributions to the symphony include:

* Haydn

* Mozart

* Schubert

* Schumann

* Tchaikovsky

* Dvořák

* Brahms

* Bruckner

* Mahler.

You might notice that most of these names are German or Austrian. Although there are examples from other countries, including England, France, Italy and Russia, the symphony developed mainly in these two countries. One of the reasons for this was that the Austro-Hungarian empire was centred on the city of Vienna, which became one of the major political, cultural and artistic centres of Europe – as you saw in your study of a Mozart opera. This is one of the contributing factors in the establishment of the symphony as an important instrumental genre. Another reason that some genres and composers achieve a particular status is through publications and their dissemination. In the case of Beethoven, his music was widely available in contemporary catalogues and newspapers, and also attracted many reviews. This commentary on the first appearance in print of the Eighth Symphony, for example, gives you some indication of the reception of the work:

> The true music lover will welcome with open arms this brilliant and magnificent work by the inexhaustible Beethoven, who stands

not only as equal with his older brothers in the art, but perhaps even surpasses many of his predecessors in his variety, the ingenious working out of themes, the novelty of his ideas, and in the most original use of instrumental combinations.

(Anonymous, 1818)

I'm now going to move on to explore the characteristic features of the symphony in more detail. This section will include extracts taken from several of Beethoven's works, in order to give you a broad sense of his output.

Symphony

The word 'symphony' quite literally means 'sounding together'. As the word came to be used during the Classical period, it referred to a large-scale composition for orchestra, usually in four movements. A standard pattern was established of:

1   an opening fast movement, sometimes with a short, slow introduction

2   a slow movement

3   a **minuet** or **scherzo**

4   a fast closing movement.

Activity

You should allow about 10 minutes for this activity.

You can find short audio recordings of the openings of the four movements of Beethoven's Eighth Symphony (the one you read about above) on the module website. Each of the four movements conforms to the descriptions above, although in this instance the first movement doesn't have a slow introduction. Listen to the four passages now, considering them according to these descriptions.

If you have ever watched a modern symphony orchestra in performance, you will notice that the performers are usually arranged on the platform according to the 'families' to which their instruments belong, a concept you have already come across in Book 1 in your study of classification. Although the exact layout varies slightly according to conductor preference and the repertoire performed, as a general rule strings sit together, as do woodwinds, brass and percussion. The table below is a summary of the most common instruments used in a symphony orchestra. Since many musical scores use Italian, I have included the most commonly used Italian names and abbreviations here.

Family	English name	Italian name (plural)	Italian abbreviation
Woodwind	Flute	Flauto (Flauti)	Fl
	Oboe	Oboe (Oboi)	Ob
	Clarinet	Clarinetto (Clarinetti)	Cl
	Bassoon	Fagotto (Fagotti)	Fg
Brass	Horn	Corno (Corni)	Cor
	Trumpet	Tromba (Trombe)	Tr
	Trombone	Trombone (Tromboni)	Tbni
Percussion	Kettledrums (usually just called Timpani nowadays)	Timpani	Timp
Strings	Violin	Violino (Violini)	Vl
	Viola	Viola	Vla
	Cello	Violoncello (Violoncelli)	Vc
	Double bass	Basso (Bassi)	Cb

You should allow about
an hour for this activity
and the next two.

Activity

This next short series of exercises uses musical scores. You do not need to be able to read music, as the purpose is for you to use the scores as a means of understanding instrumental groupings.

Turn to Reading 2.8 and have a look over it. This is an extract from the beginning of the third movement of Beethoven's Third Symphony, known as the 'Eroica'. Identify the instruments used in it from the list above and comment on their grouping on the score.

Discussion

The instruments in the score are arranged in 'families', bracketed together, within which they appear in order of pitch, with the highest at the top each time. There is one exception to this: the horns are usually placed between woodwind and brass because of their particular role in the orchestra. In this example you see flutes, oboes, clarinets, bassoons, three horns, two trumpets (but no trombones), timpani and strings, with the violins divided into violins 1 and violins 2, which is usual for symphonic writing.

As an aside, in 1805, when it was first performed, the 'Eroica' was the longest symphony yet written. It also betrays a fascination with the number three: its key signature has three flats, it uses three horns, and the first movement is in three-time.

Activity

Now turn to Readings 2.9 and 2.10, each of which is taken from the opening of a Beethoven symphony. Reading 2.9 is from the First Symphony, first performed in 1800. Reading 2.10 is from the Ninth Symphony, from 1824. What differences do you notice? Focus your attention on the horns and double bass and ignore all the markings 'in C', etc. Also note that in this particular 'edition', the trumpets are labelled 'clarino' rather than 'tromba'.

Discussion

There are actually very few significant differences, although the two woodwind parts are written out on separate staves. In the Ninth Symphony the part marked 'Corni' has two more horns (the Corni in B basso), and the double bass is independent, whereas in the First Symphony it shares a part with the cellos. Both examples are representative of the 'average' eighteenth-century orchestra, which included double woodwinds and horns.

Activity

Find the audio recordings of the extracts from the first movements of Beethoven's First and Ninth Symphonies on the module website. These are the extracts shown in Reading 2.9 and 2.10. Listen to them now in order to hear the differences between them. In particular, you might notice that a larger orchestra is used for the later work.

The constitution of the orchestra changed surprisingly little from the works of Haydn and Mozart to the Eighth Symphony by Beethoven. However, in the fourth movement of the Ninth Symphony there are some striking developments, as you can see in the score extract included as Reading 2.11. Here there are added trombones, piccolo, a double bassoon, more percussion instruments, four vocal soloists and a chorus. During the intervening years the orchestra was gradually growing in size and shape, and by the time of the symphonies of Gustav Mahler (1860–1911) had reached epic proportions.

The examples so far have been included to show you some of the typical features of this canonical genre. Beethoven consolidated it, using the prototype established by Haydn and Mozart, and also made innovations, some of which can be seen in his Sixth Symphony. This is an example of programme music (music of a narrative or descriptive kind). The work was published as *Sinfonia pastorale* ('Pastoral Symphony') and assigns an inscription to each of its five movements:

1 'Awakening of Happy Feelings on Arriving in the Country'

2 'By the brook'

3 'Merrymaking of the Country Folk'

4 'Storm'

5 'Shepherds' Song: Joy and Gratitude after the Storm'.

From as early as 1829 there were stage productions of this symphony and numerous subsequent images of Beethoven writing the work while sitting in the countryside.

You should allow about 10 minutes for this activity.

Activity

You should now listen to a short section taken from 'By the brook', the second movement of Beethoven's Sixth Symphony. You can find this audio recording on the module website.

How does Beethoven imitate the sounds of nature in this passage?

Discussion

This is a highly imaginative passage, a type of pastoral tableau in which Beethoven creates birdsong, represents flowing water and introduces drone basses. The passage you've just heard is intended to represent three birds, hence the use of three woodwind instruments and decorative melodic writing. Beethoven even wrote into his score the words for nightingale, quail and cuckoo to identify precisely the birds he was trying to imitate.

Beethoven became a canonical figure not only for his music, but also on account of aspects of his life and reputation. His deafness in later life, his position as the 'Romantic' artist, his own Heiligenstadt testament (a letter in which he expressed his despair over his increasing deafness and his desire to find a way of overcoming his affliction), his turbulent relationships and the images of him as brooding or wild – these have all contributed to Beethoven's status. His funeral on 29 March 1827 was a huge affair, with a procession witnessed by 20,000 people, constituting a tenth of the population of Vienna (see Figure 2.5). Schools and theatres were closed in mourning; at the graveyard, speeches were forbidden by the authorities. Many of Beethoven's contemporaries, including Schubert, participated in the funeral procession as pall-bearers or torch-bearers. After his death, Beethoven's reputation remained undimmed and arguably grew.

Two case studies close this chapter. In each of these you look at a canonical work and its transportation to a different context. This idea of canons and their transformations will be developed further in Chapters 3 and 5 of this book.

Figure 2.5 Franz Stober, *Funeral of Ludwig van Beethoven* (detail), 1827, watercolour on paper. Beethoven Haus, Bonn. Photo: © Beethoven Haus/Giraudon/The Bridgeman Art Library

2.3 Case study: voices of authority – instruments, makers and performers

By far the most important orchestral genres in the latter part of the eighteenth century and early years of the nineteenth century were the symphony and concerto, and this short case study is intended to bring together a canonical genre, instrument and performer.

> **Concerto**
>
> A concerto is a piece for one or more soloists and orchestra, featuring contrast between the orchestral ensemble and the solo instrument(s). Concertos are usually in three movements, but there are also many exceptions. During the nineteenth century the solo concerto became a vehicle for virtuoso display.

In Book 1 you considered the lives of objects, and looked briefly at the significance of the Stradivarius violin. Remind yourself of this by revisiting Book 1, Chapter 1 and re-reading 'Lives of violins' (in Section 1.4). Then note this assessment of the lasting importance of the Stradivarius:

> More than 250 years after his death, Stradivari's violins and cellos remain the best in the world. On song and in the right hands they are magnificent, projecting a glorious tone to the back of the largest concert hall. A violinist who is attuned to his [*sic*] Strad, and knows that it will do everything required of it, can relax into playing, confident that he will not have to force to be heard. Of five soloists in a recent season at London's Royal Festival Hall, four played Strads. They are the ultimate rebuke to the arrogance of the modern age: science does not have all the answers; Renaissance technology still cannot be bettered.
>
> (Faber, 2005, pp. xvii–xviii)

In addition to the Stradivari family, other renowned violin-making dynasties include the Amati, Guadagnini, Guarneri and Tononi families. Often the musicians who play these instruments develop a very close bond with them: the violinist Maxim Vengerov describes his relationship with his instrument as a marriage, and in Vikram Seth's novel *An Equal Music* the main character, Michael, expresses his almost physical passion for his instrument: 'I love it and it loves me. We have grown to know each other [...] We have been together for twelve years. Its sound is my sound. I can't bear to part with it' (Seth, 1999, p. 69).

A musician who developed a similarly close bond with his instrument was Nathan Milstein (1903–1992), one of the great violinists of the twentieth century. For most of his performing life Milstein used a 1716 Stradivarius violin. Born in Odessa, he emigrated from Russia in 1925, living first in Paris and London and later in the United States, becoming an American citizen in 1942. Milstein made his debut with the New York Philharmonic Orchestra in 1929 and went on to perform with them many times: between 1943 and 1965 he appeared as soloist in a concerto 40 times, playing works by, among others, Brahms, Dvŏrák, Mendelssohn and Tchaikovsky.

Activity

Read the two passages below. The first is from a dictionary entry on Milstein, the second from his obituary. In a couple of sentences, summarise the points made about Milstein's playing style.

You should allow about 10 minutes for this activity.

Passage 1

He began his career as a virtuoso and matured into a most individual interpreter. His fiery temperament was firmly disciplined, his line classically pure. His tone, though not large, had great carrying power: he changed his bowing frequently to produce power through sweep rather than by pressure. His intonation was incomparably true because his vibrato never became too wide or cloying. His interpretations of the great concertos were full of nobility and revealed a stimulating mind.

(Schwarz, 2007–14)

Passage 2

From the beginning, his playing was constantly described as 'flawless,' 'aristocratic' and 'elegant.' A supreme technician, he nevertheless refrained from flaunting his extraordinary bow and finger dexterity. Instead he concentrated on the substance of the music, interpreting it in a warm, unaffected, personal manner.

His playing, virtuosic as it could be when the music demanded, always gave the feeling of intimacy. It was characteristic that he elected to use a Stradivarius. The Stradivarius is a more subtle instrument with a smaller sound than the Guarnerius del Jesu instruments favored by more exhibitionistic players.

As with all Romantics, it was with the expressive side of music that Mr. Milstein was primarily concerned. But he never paraded any spurious emotions onstage. His interpretations were marked by a sweet, pure tone produced by an infallible bow arm, by vaulting melodic phrases and a keen sense of the music's structure.

(Schonberg, 1992)

Discussion

From the two pieces above, I would pick out the emphasis on Milstein's 'sweet, pure tone', his perfect intonation (tuning) and fluency, all of which are linked to the instrument on which he played.

Activity

You should allow about 15 minutes for this activity.

Now find the audio recording of an extract from the last movement of Dvořák's Violin Concerto on the module website. This features Milstein playing his 1716 Stradivarius. Listen to the recording and see if you can hear some of the characteristics described in the obituary. I think the pure, sweet tone is evident from the outset.

Milstein's violin was purchased by wealthy businessman Jerry Kohl in 2006, and has since then appeared in a variety of different contexts. We're going to conclude this section with a very different recording of this same violin, played by Robert Gupta, a musician in the Los Angeles Philharmonic. In 2011, in the iconic Walt Disney Concert Hall, he made an album embracing different styles and continents.

Activity

You should now find the audio recording of 'Raga Jaunpuri: II. Intermezzo in Shikartaal' on the module website. This features Robert Gupta playing the violin, along with tabla, which are Indian hand-played drums. Write some notes to describe what you hear.

You should allow about 20 minutes for this activity.

Discussion

Drums open the extract, playing a soft **rhythm** over a very quiet drone. The violin enters, extemporising over the drums, using only a few pitches. You then hear the voice saying rhythmic syllables. This new, more playful mood continues to the end, with the violin repeating fragments until all instruments come together to conclude.

Raga and tala

The melodic aspect of this piece is founded on a raga. In Indian music a raga is a series of pitches that form the basis of a vocal or instrumental piece. Each raga has its own unique aesthetic quality. In north India a raga is associated with a time of day or season. In this particular example the Jaunpuri raga is linked to late morning, and Jaunpur is a city northwest of Varanasi. The rhythmic element of the piece, specifically a cyclical pattern that develops, is known as 'tala'.

Gupta wrote of the background to this piece, 'Raga Jaunpuri: II. Intermezzo in Shikartaal':

> Although I have never formally studied the vast musical genre of Indian classical music, this is the first music I heard. I grew up in a traditional Bengali household, one in which my mother always sang while cooking, the strains of a sitar or a voice accompanying most daily activities. I discovered this particular raga when I heard *New Dawn Mind*, an album which includes two morning ragas, *Jaunpuri* and *Bhairavi*, by the famous Bengali sitarist Purbayan Chatterjee. [...] The composed *Jaunpuri* you hear on this album is an amalgam of various instrumental and vocal elements from the

great masters. I use the violin – maverick emulator that it is – to express a wide range, from the sultry lyricism of the voice to the percussive twang of the sitar.

(Gupta and Roy, n.d.)

Thus Gupta gives a fresh take on a canonical style, using an eighteenth-century violin in a modern context.

2.4 Case study: John Adams and John Donne

This final short case study looks at the important American composer John Adams. Born in 1947, he has produced a number of vocal works, using a wide range of often controversial material and texts in different languages, and embracing several of the genres that you've studied above, for example song cycle and opera. Notable operas have included *Nixon in China* (1987) and *The Death of Klinghoffer* (1991). In 2000 he created a version of the Nativity story, *El Niño*, using texts from English, Spanish and Latin sources. He has also written many large-scale orchestral works, such as *The Dharma at Big Sur* (2003), a concerto for electric violin and orchestra which draws on Buddhist meditative traditions: in other words, a different way of providing a new take on a canonical genre.

Before you move on to the main focus of this case study, Adams's opera *Doctor Atomic* (2005), the next activity will give you a flavour of this composer's music.

Activity

Listen now to two short pieces by John Adams, which you can find on the module website: 'For with God no thing shall be impossible', which is from *El Niño*, and an extract from *The Dharma at Big Sur.* Can you say anything about the musical styles of these two pieces?

You should allow about 20 minutes for this activity.

Discussion

There are two different musical styles here. The first is very rhythmic and driving, with repeating patterns. The second is meditative and much more fluid. You will find both of these styles in *Doctor Atomic*.

As with several earlier works by Adams, the subject matter of *Doctor Atomic* is political, in this case focusing on Dr Robert Oppenheimer (1904–1967) and the testing of the first atomic bomb at Los Alamos in New Mexico: the so-called 'Trinity' test. Specifically, you will listen to a musical interpretation by Adams of John Donne's poem 'Batter my heart'.

You should allow about 20 minutes for this activity.

Activity

Read Adams's own account of Oppenheimer below. Why do you think he might have been an attractive subject for a composer writing an opera? You don't need to understand all of the terminology (for example, 'twelve-tone') to get a sense of this.

Oppenheimer, known as 'Oppie' to his friends and students, was certainly a magnetic figure for dramatic treatment. In life he possessed qualities we don't usually associate with scientists. He was highly cultured in all the arts; immensely literate; able to speak fluent German, French, and Dutch; and had a reading command of half a dozen more languages, including Sanskrit, which he learned so that he could read the Bhagavad Gita in its original form. He collected paintings – there was a van Gogh among the family's artworks – and he listened exclusively to classical music. Among his favorite pieces were the late Beethoven quartets, and it is said that in his last years, while living at Princeton, he met Stravinsky and became a fan of that composer's twelve-tone Requiem Canticles. This was not your standard playlist for a physicist. At Harvard, as an eighteen-year-old taking advanced graduate courses in physics and chemistry, he unwound at night by composing sonnets. Some twenty-five years later, in the anxious hours leading up to the test firing of the bomb, he is rumored to have calmed his shattered nerves by reading from a tattered copy of Baudelaire's Fleurs du mal, which he kept as a kind of spiritual vade mecum. He and his youngest brother, Frank, had the benefit of an elite education, the finest tutors, travel, and exposure from a young age to high culture.

(Adams, 2008, p. 274)

Discussion

Perhaps one of the reasons that Adams was drawn to this subject was that Oppenheimer, with his great interest in art, music and literature, offered scope for the composer to draw on these connections. His fascination for languages finds its way into the **libretto**.

Adams's opera is structured in two big acts differentiated by time and emotion. Act 1 is set a few weeks before the bomb is to be tested. Act 2 takes place on the morning of 15 July 1945, the day of the test, and ends just before the bomb is detonated. The key figure in the opera is naturally Oppenheimer himself, with some less important solo roles and a chorus.

Of particular interest is the way in which the opera's libretto was constructed. Peter Sellars (b.1957) created the libretto from an amalgam and adaptation of a number of historical and literary sources such as declassified US government documents and communications between the scientists, government officials and military personnel who were involved in the project. In addition, it quotes extensively from the famous Hindu scripture the *Bhagavadgītā*, from the poetry of Charles Baudelaire (1821–1867) and Muriel Rukeyser (1913–1980), and from the religious poems of John Donne (1572–1631).

Figure 2.6 *Doctor Atomic*, John Adams, London Coliseum, 2009. Photographed by Laurie Lewis. Photo: © Laurie Lewis/Lebrecht Music & Arts

Act 1 concludes with an aria sung by Oppenheimer, the setting of Donne's 'Batter my heart'. The poem is used here as a means of expressing Oppenheimer's crisis of faith in the atomic bomb he has created. The use of the Donne poem in this context has some parallels with the use of *Antigone* in *The Island*, which you will study in Chapter 6.

Donne, the sonnet and 'Batter my heart'

Donne was not only a poet, but ended his career as Dean of St Paul's Cathedral in London, though he was, in fact, born a Catholic. Though Donne's writing is not always agonised, the passionate poem you are about to read is most indicative of his temperament and style. The poem is an example of a sonnet, a popular poetic form that you will meet again in Chapter 5.

The sonnet

A sonnet is a poem usually consisting of fourteen lines linked by a regular rhythm and one of two major **rhyme schemes**. The Italian, or Petrarchan, sonnet falls into two parts. The first eight lines are called the 'octave', comprising two **quatrains**, which rhyme ABBAABBA, and the last six lines, called the 'sestet', usually rhyme CDECDE or CDCDCD. In the English, or Shakespearean, sonnet there are three quatrains rhyming ABABCDCDEFEF, with a concluding rhyming couplet, GG. Traditionally, the sonnet includes a distinctive change of mood or thought, either after the octave or at the start of the closing couplet. This is called the 'turn'.

Activity

You should allow about 20 minutes for this activity.

Read the poem below, then read it aloud, and finally listen to an audio recording of it, which you can find on the module website ('John Donne: "Batter my heart"'). Try to identify the characteristics that make this poem a sonnet. What do you notice about Donne's use of language? Look in particular at the **alliteration** – that is, the way in which Donne emphasises particular words by repeating the same initial sound.

> Batter my heart, three-personed God; for, you
> As yet but knock, breathe, shine, and seek to mend;
> That I may rise, and stand, o'erthrow me, and bend
> Your force, to break, blow, burn, and make me new.
> I, like an usurped town, to another due,
> Labour to admit you, but oh, to no end,
> Reason your viceroy in me, me should defend,
> But is captived, and proves weak or untrue,
> Yet dearly I love you, and would be loved fain,

But am betrothed unto your enemy,
Divorce me, untie, or break that knot again,
Take me to you, imprison me, for I
Except you enthral me, never shall be free,
Nor ever chaste, except you ravish me.

(Smith, 1980, p. 314)

Discussion

Donne's poem has fourteen lines, and the first eight, as you probably
noticed, rhyme ABBAABBA – the Petrarchan form of the sonnet. The turn
comes with the word 'Yet', indicating a new surge of poetic potency. Even
though the rhyme in 'Batter my heart' is quite clear and prominent, it
does not seem to create effects of balance or regularity. One of the main
reasons is that it is prevented from doing so by the comparative force of
the alliterated words, which pull against one another, slowing everything
down in the complicated series of sounds and rhythms in each line. The
way that the sounds of the poem do battle with each other perfectly
complements the emotional, psychological and spiritual battle that the
poem describes between Donne's poetic voice and his God. One word
that may have struck you in particular is 'divorce', when Donne is
describing his desire to be forced apart from 'your enemy' and reunited
with 'you' (God). Highly unusual in this context, it illustrates very well the
tension the poem exploits between earthly, physical attraction and
relationships and a more spiritual love.

Activity

Now watch the performance of '"Batter my heart" from Adams's *Doctor
Atomic*'. You can find the film of this on the module website. It lasts about
7 minutes. In this initial viewing, jot down your thoughts on Adams's
interpretation of this poem. Then watch the film once more.

You should allow about
20 minutes for this
activity.

Discussion

My own feeling is that Adams turns these words into a highly emotional,
personal outpouring of guilt. Oppenheimer sings alone on the stage, the
poetry drawn out into a long soliloquy, with orchestral interjections. You
may have noticed that the orchestral interruptions are very fierce,
injecting an energy into the mainly slow, expressive vocal piece –
expressing the turbulence in Oppenheimer's mind. I hope you spotted
this contrast of musical styles.

You may be interested to read Adams's account, given below, of how he
and Sellars approached this poem. Note that the reference to a D-minor

chord is to the static harmony that underpins the singing, allowing the voice to project the words in a theatre:

> In an inspired decision, Peter placed the famous John Donne Holy Sonnet, 'Batter my heart, three-person'd God,' at the very end of act 1. Oppenheimer was much drawn to the metaphysical poets Donne, Andrew Marvell, and George Herbert. The 'three-person'd God' of Donne's poem provided the stimulus for Oppenheimer's whimsical naming of the test site: Trinity. The image of the physicist, alone at last, contemplating his dark, destructive creation, drew from me a musically strange response, but one that in retrospect seems entirely appropriate. After a whole act of music that teeters on the cusp of atonality, 'Batter my heart' appears as an archaic trope, its D-minor chord sequences projecting a slow, stately gravitas that to me spoke for the poem's content as well as for what must surely have been Oppenheimer's wildly conflicting emotions. How could this supremely intelligent and sensitive man not have peered into the terrible future of what this bomb would bring? How could he not have suspected the horrific, lingering pain and slow agonising death that its radiation would cause for tens of thousands of innocent civilians? The Donne poem is an expression of the keenest spiritual pain, a beseeching, an appeal to God that He physically beat and batter the speaker in order that his divided self might rise up and be made whole again:
>
>> That I may rise, and stand, o'erthrow me, and bend
>> Your force, to break, blow, burn and make me new.
>
> Oppenheimer sings these words in the depth of night while standing alone in front of the sinister plutonium sphere that has been swathed shroud-like in a canvas tent. It was one of the eeriest and most disturbing stage images I'd ever witnessed. When Oppenheimer is done singing and the orchestral coda batters the last of a sequence of D-minor chords, he unfolds a flap of the tent and disappears into it, like a man going back into the womb. Gerald Finley, the Canadian-born baritone for whom I wrote the role, sang this aria with an intensity of feeling that never failed to leave the hall rapt in awe. Rarely had I experienced a moment when the performance of a piece of mine brought so much more to the music than its composer had imagined.
>
> (Adams, 2008, pp. 285–6)

Conclusion

In this chapter you've studied a wide range of musical styles, focusing on the concept of the musical canon. You should have gained from it a sense of some of the canonical genres, such as symphony, opera and oratorio, as well as an awareness of how performers play a part in the creation and development of the canon, as in the examples of Milstein and the Great American Songbook.

References

Adams, J. (2008) *Hallelujah Junction*, London, Faber and Faber.

Anonymous (1818) 'Beethoven's Eighth Symphony', *Allgemeine musikalische Zeitung*, Vienna, 17 January (trans. P. Howard).

Faber, T. (2005) *Stradivarius*, London, Pan Macmillan.

Gupta, R.V. and Roy, B. (n.d.) Linn Records [Online]. Available at http://www.linnrecords.com/artist-robert-vijay-gupta—badal-roy.aspx (Accessed 23 April 2014).

Newbould, B. (1997) *Schubert: The Music and the Man*, Berkeley, CA, University of California Press.

Schonberg, H.C. (1992) 'Nathan Milstein dies at 88: an exalted violin virtuoso', *New York Times*, 22 December.

Schwarz, B. (2007–14) 'Milstein, Nathan', in *Grove Music Online. Oxford Music Online* [Online], Oxford, Oxford University Press. Available at http://www.oxfordmusiconline.com.libezproxy.open.ac.uk/subscriber/article/grove/music/18714 (Accessed 23 April 2014).

Seth, V. (1999) *An Equal Music*, London, Phoenix.

Smith, A.J. (ed.) (1980) *John Donne: The Complete English Poems*, Harmondsworth, Penguin.

Further reading

We suggest two items to help you expand two areas of Chapter 2. The first, by the choirmaster Gareth Malone (2013), will build your general knowledge, picking up some of the themes in the first part of the chapter. The second, by John Suchet, a presenter on the radio station Classic FM who is known for his passion for Beethoven, develops the work in Section 2.2.

Malone, G. (2013) *Gareth Malone's Guide to Classical Music: The Perfect Introduction to Classical Music*, London, William Collins.

Suchet, J. (2012) *Beethoven: The Man Revealed*, London, Elliott & Thompson.

If you are interested in knowing more about the symphony, you might turn to two articles that were written for the Open University's BBC series *Symphony*, first broadcast in 2011. These consider in general terms what happened to the symphony after Beethoven, and how the symphonic canon has evolved. You can find links to the articles on the module website. In the first, 'Musical landscapes: the symphony after 1900', Fiona Richards looks at the symphony around the world during the first half of the twentieth century. In the second, 'Yesterday's genre, or the music of the future', Ben Winters ponders the state of the symphony since 1945.

Reading 2.1 The 'Hallelujah' chorus from *Messiah* (1741)

Source: Music by George Frideric Handel. Transcribed from the audio recording on the module website.

Hallelujah! Hallelujah! Hallelujah!
Hallelujah! Hallelujah!

For the Lord God omnipotent reigneth.
Hallelujah! Hallelujah! Hallelujah! Hallelujah!

For the Lord God omnipotent reigneth.
Hallelujah! Hallelujah! Hallelujah! Hallelujah!
Hallelujah! Hallelujah! Hallelujah!

The kingdom of this world
Is become the kingdom of our Lord,
And of His Christ, and of His Christ;
And He shall reign for ever and ever,
For ever and ever, for ever and ever,

King of kings, and Lord of lords,
King of kings, and Lord of lords,
And Lord of lords,
And He shall reign,
And He shall reign for ever and ever,
King of kings, for ever and ever,
And Lord of lords,
Hallelujah! Hallelujah!

And He shall reign for ever and ever,
King of kings! and Lord of lords!
And He shall reign for ever and ever,
King of kings! and Lord of lords!
Hallelujah! Hallelujah! Hallelujah! Hallelujah!
Hallelujah!

Reading 2.2 'I vow to thee, my country' (1921)

Source: Music by Gustav Holst, words by Sir Cecil Spring-Rice.
Transcribed from the audio recording on the module website.

I vow to thee, my country, all earthly things above,
Entire and whole and perfect, the service of my love;
The love that asks no question, the love that stands the test,
That lays upon the altar the dearest and the best;
The love that never falters, the love that pays the price,
The love that makes undaunted the final sacrifice.

Reading 2.3 'Non più andrai' from the opera *Le Nozze di Figaro* (*The Marriage of Figaro*) (1786)

Source: Music by Wolfgang Amadeus Mozart, words by Lorenzo da Ponte. Transcribed from the audio recording on the module website; English translation by Patricia Howard, 2001.

Non più andrai, farfallone amoroso,	No more will you go, amorous butterfly,
Notte e giorno d'intorno girando;	Night and day wandering around;
Delle belle turbando il riposo,	Disturbing the repose of pretty women,
Narcisetto, Adoncino d'amor.	Little Narcissus, little Adonis of love.
Non più avrai questi bei pennacchini,	No more will you have those fine plumes,
Quel cappello leggero e galante	That hat so light and gay,
Quella chioma, quell'aria brillante,	Those curls, that brilliant air,
Quel vermiglio donnesco color.	That rosy and womanlike complexion.
Tra guerrieri, poffar Bacco!	Among soldiers, God approving,
Gran mustacchi, stretto sacco.	Fierce moustaches, tightest tunic.
Schioppo in spalla, sciabla al fianco,	Shouldered musket, side slung sabre,
Collo dritto, muso franco,	Head erect with frank expression,
Un gran casco, o un gran turbante,	A great helmet or great turban,
Molto onor, poco contante!	Honour huge but little money!
Ed invece del fandango	And in place of the fandango
Una marcia per il fango	Just a march through mud and middens,
Per montagne, per valloni	Through the mountains, through the valleys.
Con le nevi e i sollioni	Through the snows and through the scorchings,
Al concerto di tromboni	To the boom of the trombone,
Di bombarde, di cannoni	And the mortar, and the cannon,
Che le palle in tutti i tuoni	And the cannon-balls whose whistling
All'orecchio fan fischiar.	Sends a shudder through your ear.
Cherubino alla vittoria,	Cherubino bound for glory,
Alla gloria militar.	Bound for glory in the field.

Reading 2.4 'Anything goes' (1934), version 1, sung by Ella Fitzgerald

Source: Lyrics and music by Cole Porter. Transcribed from the performance by Ella Fitzgerald in the audio recording on the module website.

Times have changed,
And we've often rewound the clock,
Since the Puritans got a shock,
When they landed on Plymouth Rock.
If today,
Any shock they should try to stem,
'Stead of landing on Plymouth Rock,
Plymouth Rock would land on them.

In olden days a glimpse of stocking
Was looked on as something shocking,
Now, heaven knows,
Anything goes.
Good authors too who once knew better words,
Now only use four-letter words
Writing prose,
Anything goes.

The world has gone mad today
And good's bad today,
And black's white today,
And day's night today,
When most guys today
That women prize today
Are just silly gigolos.

So though I'm not a great romancer
I know that I'm bound to answer
When you propose,
Anything goes.

Reading 2.5 'Anything goes' (1934), version 2, sung by Caroline O'Connor

Source: Lyrics and music by Cole Porter. Transcribed from the performance by Caroline O'Connor in the audio recording on the module website.

Times have changed,
And we've often rewound the clock,
Since the Puritans got a shock,
When they landed on Plymouth Rock.
If today,
Any shock they should try to stem,
'Stead of landing on Plymouth Rock,
Plymouth Rock would land on them.

In olden days a glimpse of stocking
Was looked on as something shocking,
Now, heaven knows,
Anything goes.
Good authors too who once knew better words,
Now only use four-letter words
Writing prose,
Anything goes.

If saying your prayers you like,
If green pears you like,
If old chairs you like,
If back stairs you like,
If love affairs you like
With young bears you like,
Why, nobody will oppose!

So though I'm not a great romancer
I know that I'm bound to answer
When you propose,
Anything goes.

If driving fast cars you like,
If low bars you like,
If old hymns you like,
If bare limbs you like,
If Mae West you like,

Or me undressed you like,
Why, nobody will oppose!
And every night,
The set that's smart
Is intruding on nudist parties in studios,
Anything goes.

Reading 2.6 'Erlkönig' (1815)

Source: Music by Franz Schubert, words by Johann Wolfgang von Goethe. Transcribed from the audio recording on the module website; English translation by Robert Philip, 2004.

Erlkönig

Wer reitet so spät durch Nacht und Wind?
Es ist der Vater mit seinem Kind;
Er hat den Knaben wohl in dem Arm,
Er fasst ihn sicher, er hält ihn warm.

'Mein Sohn, was birgst du so bang dein Gesicht?'
'Siehst, Vater, du den Erlkönig nicht?
Den Erlenkönig mit Kron und Schweif?'
'Mein Sohn, es ist ein Nebelstreif.'

'Du liebes Kind, komm, geh mit mir!
Gar schöne Spiele spiel ich mit dir;
Manch bunte Blumen sind an dem Strand,
Meine Mutter hat manch gulden Gewand.'

'Mein Vater, mein Vater, und hörest du nicht,
Was Erlenkönig mir leise verspricht?'
'Sei ruhig, bleibe ruhig, mein Kind;
In dürren Blättern säuselt der Wind.'

'Willst, feiner Knabe, du mit mir gehn?
Meine Töchter sollen dich warten schön;
Meine Töchter führen die nächtlichen Reihn
Und wiegen und tanzen und singen dich ein.'

'Mein Vater, mein Vater, und siehst du nicht dort
Erlkönigs Töchter am düstern Ort?'
'Mein Sohn, mein Sohn, ich seh es genau:
Es scheinen die alten Weiden so grau.'

'Ich liebe dich, mich reizt deine schöne Gestalt;
Und bist du nicht willig, so brauch ich Gewalt.'
'Mein Vater, mein Vater, jetzt fasst er mich an!
Erlkönig hat mir ein Leids getan!'

Dem Vater grauset's, er reitet geschwind,
Er hält in Armen das ächzende Kind,
Erreicht den Hof mit Mühe und Not:
In seinen Armen das Kind war tot.

The Erl-King

Who rides at a gallop through night so wild?
It is the father with his dear child.
He grips the boy firmly in his arms,
He holds him safe, he keeps him warm.

'Son, why do you cower so fearfully?'
'Father, the Erl-king! Can you not see?
The dreadful Erl-king with crown and tail?'
'My son, it is mist blown by the gale.'

'You lovely child, come away with me,
We'll play together down by the sea;
Such pretty flowers grow on the shore,
My mother has golden robes in store.'

'My father, my father, oh do you not hear
What the Erl-king whispers into my ear?'
'Be calm, stay calm, it's nothing my child,
But dry leaves blown by the wind so wild.'

'My fine young lad, won't you come away?
My daughters are waiting for you to play;
My daughters will lead the dance through the night,
And sing and rock you until you sleep tight.'

'My father, my father, can you still not see
The Erl-king's daughters waiting for me?'
'My son, my son, I can see quite clear
The moon on the willows, there's nothing else there.'

'I love you my boy, you are such a delight;
And I'll take you by force if you put up a fight.'
'My father, my father, he's gripping me fast!
The Erl-king is hurting! Help me, I'm lost!'

The father shudders, and speeds through the night,
In his arms, he holds the moaning boy tight;
At last he arrives, to home and bed:
In the father's arms the child was dead.

Reading 2.7 'The Vagabond' (1904)

Source: Music by Ralph Vaughan Williams, words by Robert Louis Stevenson. Transcribed from the audio recording on the module website.

Give to me the life I love,
Let the lave go by me,
Give the jolly heaven above,
And the byway nigh me.
Bed in the bush with stars to see,
Bread I dip in the river –
There's the life for a man like me,
There's the life for ever.

Let the blow fall soon or late,
Let what will be o'er me;
Give the face of earth around,
And the road before me.
Wealth I seek not, hope nor love,
Nor a friend to know me;
All I seek, the heaven above,
And the road below me.

Or let autumn fall on me
Where afield I linger,
Silencing the bird on tree,
Biting the blue finger.
White as meal the frosty field –
Warm the fireside haven –
Not to autumn will I yield,
Not to winter even!

Let the blow fall soon or late,
Let what will be o'er me;
Give the face of earth around,
And the road before me.
Wealth I ask not, hope nor love,
Nor a friend to know me;
All I ask, the heaven above,
And the road below me.

Reading 2.8 Beethoven, Third Symphony, opening of third movement

Source: Beethoven, L. van (1951) *IIIe Symphonie in E flat major, 'Héroique', op. 55* (ed. M. Pincherle), Paris, Heugel & Cie.

Reading 2.9 Beethoven, First Symphony, opening of first movement

Source: Beethoven, L. van (1999) *Symphony No. 1 in C major, op. 21* **(ed. J. Del Mar), Kassel, Bärenreiter-Verlag.**

Reading 2.10 Beethoven, Ninth Symphony, opening of first movement

Source: Beethoven, L. van (1999) *Symphony No. 9 in D minor, op. 125* (ed. J. Del Mar), Kassel, Bärenreiter-Verlag.

© 1996 by Bärenreiter-Verlag, Kassel

Reading 2.11 Beethoven, Ninth Symphony, opening of fourth movement

Source: Beethoven, L. van (1999) *Symphony No. 9 in D minor, op. 125* **(ed. J. Del Mar), Kassel, Bärenreiter-Verlag.**

Chapter 3
Art History and the canon

Emma Barker with Gill Perry

Contents

Aims

This chapter will:

- discuss the significance of the concepts of the canon and authority for Art History

- examine some of the ideas that have shaped the canon of art and how these have changed over time

- familiarise you with works of art in different media by Caravaggio and Ai Weiwei

- develop your skills of visual and textual analysis.

Materials you will need

In this chapter, you will be directed to the module website in order to access links to the website of the National Gallery.

Introduction

In this chapter, we shall explore the significance of the idea of the canon for the discipline of Art History. As with Literature and Music, the term is used to refer to a body of works that are considered by the relevant authorities to embody the highest standards of artistic achievement. This statement raises several questions. What are the works that together constitute the canon of art? Which standards of artistic achievement do they embody? Who are these authorities who decide what counts as great art?

These are the questions that we shall try to come to grips with in this chapter. One point that needs to be made before going any further is that what we are talking about here is a canon of western art. If you consult any general survey of art through the ages, or any list of the world's greatest artworks, you will find that it is dominated by a distinctively western tradition of high art centred on painting and sculpture. Most of the names will be those of artists from western Europe and, latterly, the United States, such as Leonardo da Vinci (1452–1511), Rembrandt (1606–1669), Paul Cézanne (1839–1906) and Jackson Pollock (1912–1956). Central to the canon is the idea of the masterpiece, which, in the context of art history, signifies not simply a work by a major figure in this tradition, but also, for the most part, a unique art object, generally a painting (see Figures 3.1–3.4). Such celebrated works are typically to be found in one of the great museums of the western world, like the Louvre in Paris or the Museum of Modern Art in New York (Figures 3.5–3.6).

This chapter will start by examining one of these museums, the National Gallery in London, which houses a famous collection of western European painting. As we shall see, such institutions are not simply the repositories or storehouses of the canon, but also actively shape our perception of what great art is. In other words, they are among the authorities who help to define the canon; other such authorities to be discussed in this chapter include artists, scholars, critics and collectors. We shall go on to look more closely at one of the acknowledged masterpieces in the National Gallery, *The Supper at Emmaus* by Caravaggio (1583–1610). What makes it a particularly interesting example to consider is that this artist's work became canonical only relatively recently; it therefore shows that the canon of art, like other canons, changes over time. We shall go on to explore two issues that have already been addressed elsewhere in this book: first,

Figure 3.1 Leonardo da Vinci, *Mona Lisa*, 1503–06, oil on poplar, 77cm x 53cm. Musée du Louvre, Paris. Photo: © RMN-Grand Palais (Musée du Louvre)/Michel Urtado

Figure 3.2 Rembrandt van Rijn, *The Return of the Prodigal Son*, *c*.1668–69, oil on canvas, 262cm x 205cm. State Hermitage Museum, St Petersburg. Photo: © Hermitage/The Bridgeman Art Library

Figure 3.3 Paul Cézanne, *Mont Sainte-Victoire and the Viaduct of the Arc River Valley*, 1882–85, oil on canvas, 65cm x 82cm. Metropolitan Museum of Art, New York, Acc.n.: 29.100.64. H.O. Havemeyer Collection, Bequest of Mrs H.O. Havemeyer, 1929. Photo: Malcom Varon. Photo: © 2013. Image copyright The Metropolitan Museum of Art/Art Resource/Scala, Florence

the idea of **classicism** and its role in shaping the canon; and, second, the significance of different **genres** and their implications for how we value works of art. Finally, we shall consider how new developments in contemporary art challenge established ideas of what canonical art is, with reference to works of art commissioned in recent years for a particular space in another London museum, Tate Modern.

Figure 3.4 Jackson Pollock, *Number 1, 1948*, 1948, oil and enamel on unprimed canvas, 173cm x 264cm. Museum of Modern Art, New York, purchase Acc. n.: 77.1950. Photo © 2013. Digital image, The Museum of Modern Art/Scala, Florence. © The Pollock-Krasner Foundation ARS, NY and DACS, London 2014

Figure 3.5 Musée de Louvre, Paris. Photo: © Alex Segre/Alamy

Figure 3.6 Museum of Modern Art (MoMA), David and Peggy Rockefeller Gallery Building, New York. Photographed by Gavin Jackson. Photo: © Arcaid Images/Alamy

3.1 Visiting the National Gallery

In order to explore how museums shape our perception of great art, let us consider what we might experience if we were to visit the National Gallery.

Established in 1824, at a time when Britain was the dominant power in the world, the gallery's name identifies it with the public authority of the nation-state. Since 1838 it has been housed in a large building designed for the purpose on the north side of Trafalgar Square, a site chosen because of its central location, which links together different parts of London. Built in the classical style, the façade of the gallery centres on a **portico**, consisting of a row of columns supporting a triangular **pediment**, which served as the original entrance to the building (today it is one of four entrances). Nelson's Column was erected in the middle of the square shortly afterwards to commemorate Admiral Lord Nelson who died at the Battle of Trafalgar in 1805. As the symbolic heart of the capital, the square has historically been used for political demonstrations, though national celebrations and festive gatherings also take place there. Until recently, a road ran along the north side of the square, but the area in front of the National Gallery was pedestrianised and a broad flight of steps down to the middle of the square built in 2003.

Activity

Figure 3.7 shows Trafalgar Square as it is today, with the National Gallery on the far left, the church of St Martin in the Fields in the left background and Nelson's Column to the right.

You should allow about 10 minutes for this activity.

Look at the picture in the light of the information in the previous paragraph and consider what sort of message about the gallery is conveyed by its location and architecture (including the layout of the square). Another way of putting this is to say that you should think about the values (political, religious, social, and so on) that the gallery seems to be associated with.

Discussion

The location in Trafalgar Square suggests that the gallery, like Nelson's achievements, is a source of national pride. The size and grandeur of the square reinforce the message, not least because the gallery appears to be the most important building there, occupying as it does the whole of its upper side. The architecture of the gallery is also grand and imposing, with its large columns and central dome; whether or not you have any

Figure 3.7 Trafalgar Square after redevelopment, with Nelson's Column (1840–43), designed by William Railton, the National Gallery (1832–38), designed by William Wilkins, and St Martin in the Fields (1722–24), designed by James Gibbs. Photo: © Foster + Partners

particular knowledge of classical architecture, you are likely to know that this style of building tends to be used for high-status buildings such as palaces. Moreover, the architecture finds an echo in the portico in front of the church, suggesting that the gallery has an almost sacred significance. At the same time, the central location and transport links (note the buses!) suggest that it is for everyone, not just the elite. Similarly, the wide flight of steps that lead from the middle of the square to the north side offers a direct approach to the gallery, encouraging people to enter. In other words, the values that it is associated with are a combination of patriotic feeling, social prestige, quasi-religious devotion and democratic ideals. The overall message seems to be that the gallery deserves everyone's attention and respect, whoever they are and whatever their values. In sum, we see here an institution strongly imbued with authority, even if in reality by no means everyone would be able or willing to regard it in this way.

Furthermore, the point of all this authority is to encourage us to look at and admire the collection of paintings that the gallery houses. However, since it consists of over 2000 pictures dating from the thirteenth to the nineteenth centuries, it is impossible to take in the whole collection in a single visit. The institution therefore offers a helpful list of 'must see' paintings, the highlights of the collection, on its website. Although some of the individual choices are slightly arbitrary, the list as a whole provides a snapshot of the canon of western painting before 1900.

Activity

For this activity, you need to look at a page of the website of the National Gallery. You can do this by following the link provided on the module website.

You should allow about 30 minutes for this activity.

Once you are on the National Gallery website, you should explore the highlights of the collection. At the time of writing, this consisted of a list of 30 paintings. You can find further information about each one by clicking on it.

What does this list tell us about the canon of art? Is it weighted towards any particular nationalities and/or periods? You might also take note of any particular artists whose names are familiar to you.

Discussion

A clear bias can be discerned towards Italy, which accounts for ten of the thirty paintings. Most of these, moreover, date from the fifteenth and early sixteenth centuries (the period known as the **Renaissance**). You may have recognised some of the artists in this area as canonical: for example, Leonardo, Michelangelo (1475–1564), Raphael (1483–1520) and Titian (active 1506–1576). The next best represented nation is the French, who account for six or seven works (depending on whether or not you count the *Wilton Diptych*). Here, the main emphasis is on the nineteenth century and, in particular, the second half of the century; three paintings date from this era. The name that is most likely to be familiar is Monet, the most famous of the artists known as **Impressionist**s; Cézanne may also be familiar, especially if you have already studied AA100 *The arts past and present*. After the French come the British, with four or five works (again depending on how you count the *Wilton Diptych*). In this case, the emphasis is on the eighteenth and early nineteenth centuries. You might expect the art of Britain to be better represented in its national gallery, so it would be reasonable to assume that British art is not particularly canonical. After that come the Flemish with four works and the Dutch with three, though, given that Flanders (or 'southern Netherlands', broadly equivalent to modern-day Belgium) and Holland are such small countries, this is still an impressive showing, especially given that two of the Dutch artists (Rembrandt and Vincent

Van Gogh (1853–1890)) are among the most famous of all European painters. After that come Spain and Germany, with only one work each.

Now that you have gained an overview of the canon of western art, as it is encapsulated by the list of the highlights of the gallery's collection, you should also be aware that each nation has its own canon, in which certain periods typically predominate. For example, while the canon of Dutch art is dominated by Rembrandt and Van Gogh, it also includes other Dutch artists who are considered to have made a significant contribution to western art. Most of them worked during the seventeenth century, traditionally regarded as the 'golden age' of Dutch painting (just as the mid eighteenth to mid nineteenth century is considered the golden age of British art). Almost all the Dutch pictures on display in the gallery (Van Gogh being the main exception) date from this period. Similarly, the National Gallery displays British paintings dating only from around 1750 to 1850. Particular emphasis is given to the landscape painter J.M.W. Turner (1775–1851), widely regarded as Britain's greatest artist (Figure 3.8).

Figure 3.8 Joseph Mallord William Turner, *The Fighting Temeraire Tugged to Her Last Berth to Be Broken Up*, 1839, oil on canvas, 91cm x 122cm. National Gallery, London. Photo: © The Bridgeman Art Library

In making this selection of 30 paintings that are not to be missed, the National Gallery ensures that they will receive more attention than other works in the collection. Much the same point can be made about the collection as a whole. A painting in the gallery is likely to be better known than one in a less prominent museum or (even more so) one in private ownership. This means that the National Gallery has the power to shape the canon through the decisions it makes about what paintings to acquire and display. More precisely, it is the gallery's director and **curator**s who wield this power, together with the wealthy art collectors who have enriched its collection over the years through gifts and bequests. In 1924, for example, the textile magnate Samuel Courtauld (1876–1947) established a trust fund to acquire French Impressionist and **Post-Impressionist** paintings for the nation, which helped to consolidate the canonical status of these previously controversial modern art movements.

3.2 Looking at painting: Caravaggio's *The Supper at Emmaus*

So what makes a painting a canonical 'masterpiece', aside from the fact of being in the collection of a major museum like the National Gallery? Why do certain 'national schools' (as they are known) predominate? Why are the works of certain periods more valued than those of others? How and why does what counts as great or canonical art change over time?

In order to make a start on answering these questions, we shall take a look at one of the paintings on the National Gallery's list, *The Supper at Emmaus* by Michelangelo Merisi, known as Caravaggio after his birthplace (Figure 3.9). You may already know about this artist and have some idea of what makes his work canonical, but, for the moment, we are going to focus on this one picture, dating from 1601, which hangs today in the room devoted to seventeenth-century Italian painting in the National Gallery. Before going any further, however, it is important to register that what we have in front of us is a reproduction in a book, which inevitably fails to convey many of the things that might strike you if you saw the actual painting on the walls of a gallery.

Activity

You should allow about 15 minutes for this activity.

Read the caption to Figure 3.9. What is the purpose of the additional information about the painting that it provides, and how does the painting compare in these respects to others reproduced in this chapter?

You might also like to check out how the picture looks on the walls of the National Gallery by taking a virtual tour of the room in which it hangs. You can find a link on the module website.

Discussion

Besides the name of the artist, the title of the picture and the date it was painted, the caption tells us that it is made of oil paint on canvas and that its dimensions are 141cm x 196cm. It thereby reminds us that a painting is not just an image (like a photograph) but also a material object. More precisely, it reveals that *The Supper at Emmaus* is typical of the western tradition in the way that it is made, since most of the pictures reproduced in this chapter are also painted in oil on canvas. It contrasts in this respect with the earliest examples (Figures 3.1 and 3.12) and the latest (Figure 3.4). Furthermore, the caption reveals that it is a fair-sized

Figure 3.9 Caravaggio, *The Supper at Emmaus*, 1601, oil on canvas, 141cm x 196cm. National Gallery, London. Photo: © The Bridgeman Art Library

painting, larger than Figures 3.1 and 3.14, for example, but smaller than Figures. 3.4 and 3.12. If you took the virtual tour, you will have a better sense of what the experience of viewing the picture would be like; features you may have noted include the elaborate frame around it and how it compares in size with others in the same room.

Let us now explore what is going on in Caravaggio's painting. The subject is taken from the Bible, as was often the case at the time even for pictures that, like this one, were not painted for a church. More precisely, it depicts an episode from the Gospel according to Luke, one of four books in the New Testament that record the life and teaching of Jesus of Nazareth. The episode in Luke's Gospel concerns Jesus's first appearance to his followers following his death by crucifixion and subsequent resurrection. Two of his disciples encounter him on the road to the village of Emmaus, but do not recognise him until he sits down with them for the evening meal, presumably at an inn, when he blesses bread and breaks it as he did at the Last Supper (the final meal that he shared with his followers before his death). For Jesus's followers, this event reveals him as the Messiah or 'Christ', that is, the promised deliverer of the Jewish people and redeemer of mankind prophesied in the Hebrew Scriptures (or Old Testament).

Activity

You should allow about 20 minutes for this activity.

You will find Luke's account of this episode reproduced as Reading 3.1. Read this through now and consider what the overall emphasis of the text is, with respect to the thoughts and feelings of the two disciples about Jesus's crucifixion and resurrection.

Discussion

The text emphasises the disciples' sense of wonder and bewilderment at the events of the last few days, which do not fit in with what they expected of him whom they believed to be the Christ or Redeemer. They talk things over to try to make sense of them, but do not yet grasp that Jesus has risen from the dead. The sense of mystery is reinforced by the way in which Jesus's identity is somehow hidden from them when they cnoountor him on the road. When they recognise him as the risen Christ, the sense of wonder only increases since he vanishes before their eyes.

Next we need to take a closer look at the painting itself. A particularly effective way of establishing what is distinctive about almost any work of art is to compare it with a similar work, especially one depicting the same subject. In this case, a useful point of reference is provided by Titian, whose painting of *The Supper at Emmaus* is fairly typical of the way that artists painted this subject before Caravaggio (Figure 3.10).

Figure 3.10 Titian, *The Supper at Emmaus*, *c.*1530, oil on canvas, 169cm x 244cm. Musée du Louvre, Paris. Photo: © RMN-Grand Palais (Musée du Louvre)/Stéphane Maréchalle

Activity

Compare Caravaggio's *The Supper at Emmaus* with Titian's version, taking account of the following:

You should allow about 20 minutes for this activity.

1 The basic **composition**, that is, the format (vertical or horizontal) and the overall arrangement of figures and other elements in the picture space.

2 Other compositional features, such as the relative scale of figures and background, the means that the artist uses to create an illusion of space and depth, and the viewpoint from which we appear to view the scene.

3 Pose, gesture and expression.

4 Colour, light and shade.

5 Overall effect.

Discussion

1   Caravaggio follows Titian in employing a horizontal format and in placing Jesus in the centre of the composition, with the two disciples seated at the table on either side of him; in both cases, a man, identifiable as the innkeeper, stands to the left of Jesus and a white cloth is spread over a carpet on the table.

2   However, in Caravaggio's painting the figures are both fewer in number (there is only the one onlooker, not two) and larger in scale relative to the background, which is quite plain, whereas Titian depicts smaller figures in a more elaborate setting, which includes a landscape in the distance. By contrast, in Caravaggio's painting the space appears very shallow, with only the diagonal formed by the table edge to suggest depth. The viewpoint is both quite high and close in, such that we look down at the food and drink on the table, while the legs of figures and table are hidden from view. Again, this is different from Titian's painting, where the viewpoint is lower down and further away, allowing us to see the dog under the table.

3   The body language of Caravaggio's figures is far more forceful: Jesus does not just raise his hand in blessing, but stretches out his arm; the right-hand disciple flings out both arms; while the left-hand one pushes back his chair as if about to jump to his feet. Their astonishment is heightened by contrast with the innkeeper, who stands with his hands on his belt, as in Titian's painting, while looking at Jesus with an apparently baffled expression on his face.

4   Caravaggio's colours are much warmer and earthier, mostly brown and red, with no blue at all, and the contrasts of light and dark are much stronger, so that the whole scene seems more vividly present and more intensely dramatic.

5   The overall effect is one of great naturalism and immediacy by comparison with the more dignified and distant scene depicted by Titian, not least because everything in Caravaggio's painting, from the roast chicken on the table to the hole in the left-hand disciple's sleeve, seems much more concrete and down to earth. Also significant in this respect is the way that the actions of the two disciples and the basket of fruit projecting over the table edge seem to burst out of the picture space into the real world.

Now that we have read the text from which the subject is taken and analysed what is distinctive about Caravaggio's treatment of it, we are in a position to consider the meaning or message of the picture. The important point to register here is that the meaning of any work of art is not the same as its subject or content, but depends on the effect made on the viewer by formal elements such as the composition, use of colour, and so on. You can put it like this: **form** + content = meaning.

Activity

1   How does Caravaggio's treatment of the subject (including the appearance of Jesus) convey the significance of the Gospel text to the viewer?

2   How does the viewer's reaction to the painting contribute to its meaning?

You should allow about 20 minutes for this activity.

Discussion

1   By depicting the supper at Emmaus in such a dramatic and naturalistic way, Caravaggio conveys the wonder of the disciples at the resurrection of Jesus from the dead, which is given so much emphasis in the Gospel, and gives the impression that these holy events are happening in front of our own eyes, so that we become witnesses to or even participants in them. This is reinforced by the unconventional appearance of Jesus, who is shown beardless, with a youthful, fleshy face. It helps us to grasp the significance of the subject, because it makes it understandable that the disciples did not recognise him until he blessed the bread.

2   Since it may take us a moment to work out who the central figure is, we share the same experience of recognition as the disciples. The meaning of the picture thus concerns not simply what happened at Emmaus or even the miracle of Jesus's resurrection, but also the viewer's acceptance of him as the Christ or Redeemer. In other words, the burden of responsibility for making the picture meaningful lies with us.

Finally, let us consider *The Supper at Emmaus* as a work by Caravaggio. Originally commissioned by a Roman nobleman, Ciriaco Mattei, it was soon acquired by one of the leading art collectors of the period, Cardinal Scipione Borghese (1577–1633), demonstrating how highly regarded the artist was at the time. Today, Caravaggio is one of the most popular of all the 'old masters', thanks not just to his dark and dramatic paintings but also to his equally dramatic, not to say sensational, life story. He is the subject of a steady stream of articles, books and television programmes; there is even a feature film about him, directed by Derek Jarman (*Caravaggio*, 1986). Temporary loan exhibitions of his work attract large audiences, as, for example, did the National Gallery's exhibition *Caravaggio: The Final Years* (2005), which featured pictures painted after the artist fled from Rome in 1606 in order to avoid being tried for murder.

However, Caravaggio has not always been so highly regarded. His reputation was at a low ebb in the nineteenth century, when *The Supper at Emmaus* entered the National Gallery's collection. It was donated by the fifth Baron Vernon in 1839, a few years after he tried unsuccessfully to sell it at auction: nobody was willing to meet the asking price. Although Caravaggio's work started to be reassessed around 1900, it is only since 1951, when a major exhibition devoted to his work and that of his followers was held in Milan, that the artist has gained his current canonical status. Nowadays, any securely attributed painting by the artist (that is to say, agreed by experts to be from his own hand rather than by a follower) that did come up for sale on the open market would sell for millions.

3.3 Classicism and the canon of art

To explain the shifts in Caravaggio's status, we need to explore some of the broader factors that have historically shaped people's thinking about what great art is. In order to do so, we first need to appreciate the central role that classicism has played in the formation of the canon of western art. Classicism, it should be noted, is a term that broadly refers to works of art inspired by the models provided by ancient Greece and Rome. It is also associated with such principles as order, harmony, proportion and balance. In other words, the term has a more precise significance in Art History than it does in Music or Literature, where it tends to be used more loosely.

In order to explore this connection, it is helpful to note that the word 'canon' originated in ancient Greek as a term for a measuring stick and later took on the meaning of a rule or law. It also signified a standard against which something could be judged. Thus, in the fifth century BCE, the Greek sculptor Polykleitos wrote a now lost treatise known as the *Canon* in which he set out his mathematically based principles for creating a perfectly proportioned and balanced human figure. These principles were exemplified in one of his sculptures, also therefore called *Canon*; this was probably the *Doryphoros* ('Spear Bearer'), which is now known only from later copies made in the Roman empire (Figure 3.11). This commitment to representing ideal bodies, devoid of flaws, was shared by other fifth-century Greek artists, whose works have been completely lost. The painters Zeuxis and Parrhasios, for example, are both reported by ancient writers to have used several models for a single figure, selecting the most beautiful parts of each in order to achieve a perfection not to be found in nature. What made the surviving traces of Greek art so compelling for later generations of artists and writers is not simply the beauty it embodied, however, but also its identification with some kind of higher reality, such as was theorised by the philosopher Plato (427–347 BCE). That is to say, it was believed that these ideal forms were the physical manifestation of abstract qualities such as reason, truth and virtue. As such, they were considered to have a timeless, universal validity.

As a result, the canon in the Greek sense of a standard of perfection has helped to shape the western canon in the modern sense of a body of great works of art. As we saw in considering the highlights of the National Gallery's collection, the art of the Italian Renaissance constitutes the core of the canon and it was during this period, in the

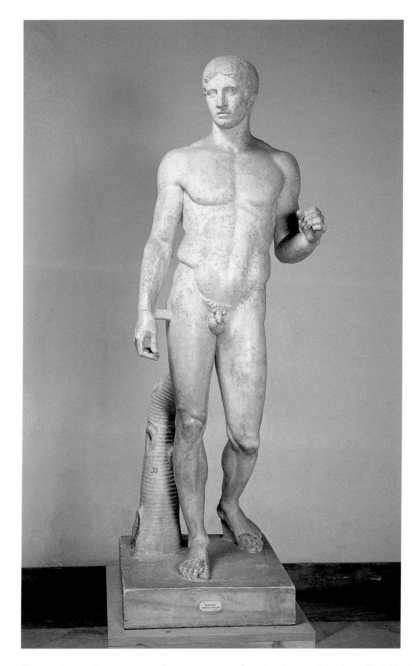

Figure 3.11 *Doryphoros*, Roman copy after the lost original by Polykleitos, marble, height 200cm. Museo Archeologico Nazionale, Naples. Photo: © Museo Archeologico Nazionale/The Bridgeman Art Library

fifteenth and sixteenth centuries, that a major revival of interest in the legacy of classical antiquity took place. It is for this reason that the period has since become known as the Renaissance, meaning 'rebirth'. The canon of Renaissance art has largely been shaped by the Italian artist and art historian Giorgio Vasari (1511–1574), who, in his highly influential *Lives of the Most Excellent Painters, Sculptors and Architects*, first published in 1550, argued that art had been brought to a new perfection in recent times, thanks above all to the achievements of Leonardo, Raphael and Michelangelo. According to Vasari, what enabled Italian artists of his own era to make the crucial breakthrough, leaving behind what he called the dry and stiff manner of the recent past, was the rediscovery of the art of antiquity, as exemplified by recently rediscovered statues, such as the Laocoön and Apollo Belvedere, most of which were then (and remain) on display in the sculpture court erected for the purpose in the Vatican: 'all possessing the appeal and vigour of living flesh and derived from the finest features of living models' (Vasari, 1965, p. 251). Regarded as the standard against which all other works of art should be judged, these sculptures quickly became known across Europe through plaster casts and prints. They remained an inspiration for artists and a magnet for tourists until the nineteenth century, when it was recognised that they were not Greek originals but Roman copies.

Now let us explore how Caravaggio fared when judged against the classical ideal. In order to do so, we shall consider the views of the antiquarian and art historian Giovanni Pietro Bellori (1613–1696), who played a highly influential role in forming the canon of seventeenth-century art. His *Lives of the Modern Painters, Sculptors and Architects*, first published in 1672, contains accounts of the lives and works of a small selection of artists, whom he considered the most important of recent times. In writing the *Lives*, Bellori followed the example of Vasari, whose canon of Renaissance art he endorsed, though they differed in their assessments of its most important figures; whereas the earlier writer revered Michelangelo above all, Bellori believed that Raphael was the greatest artist since antiquity. His own canon was also dominated by Italian artists, though it did include two Flemish painters, Peter Paul Rubens (1577–1640) and Anthony van Dyck (1599–1641), and a French one, Nicolas Poussin (1594–1665). The book is prefaced by an essay upholding the importance of the ideal in art; 'noble painters and sculptors', Bellori argues, 'form in their minds an example of higher beauty, and, by contemplating that, they emend nature without fault of colour or line' (2006, p. 57).

Realism

Although this section focuses on classicism, it is necessary to say something here about another term used by writers on art. Any work of art that offers a convincing representation of the way things look to us in the world around us may be called 'realist'. However, Realism more strictly refers to a nineteenth-century French art movement; artists associated with it depicted contemporary life among ordinary people in a down-to-earth, unidealised style. In Reading 3.3, when Caravaggio is described as 'the first realist', he is being linked to this movement. The word 'realism' also appears in Reading 3.2, which is a modern translation of a seventeenth-century text; in fact, the word in the original Italian is *naturale* (naturalness). Words such as 'naturalism' and 'naturalistic' have a similar but looser meaning, without such specific connotations as 'realism'.

Activity

You should allow about 20 minutes for this activity.

Reading 3.2 is an extract from Bellori's life of Caravaggio (from his *Lives of the Modern Painters, Sculptors and Architects*). Read it through now and answer the following questions:

What does Bellori think of Caravaggio's work and what are his reasons for his assessment? What does his account suggest about the artist's canonical status?

Discussion

For Bellori, Caravaggio's art is deficient because of his failure to select the most beautiful forms in nature. In so doing, he rejects the canon as it existed in his own period, that is, the example of the antique and of Raphael, who, as already mentioned, Bellori regarded as the greatest artist of the Renaissance. Instead, he claims, Caravaggio depicts nature exactly as he sees it in the world around him, without idealising his models at all. Bellori gives as an example a painting of Mary Magdalen, which, he says, is really just a likeness of a girl drying her hair. He suggests that the artist relied so closely on his models and vaunted his debt to nature because he had no real knowledge of art and was unable to do anything other than copy what he saw ('The moment the model was taken from him, his hand and his mind became empty'). However,

Bellori is not entirely critical of Caravaggio; he admires his use of colour, which he describes as 'truthful'. More generally, he suggests that the artist's naturalism had a beneficial effect on art in so far as it countered an opposite tendency at the time towards a too artificial style ('*maniera*'). Furthermore, the very fact that Bellori chose to include Caravaggio in his book demonstrates that he regarded him as one of the most important artists of modern times. Nevertheless, Bellori's final assessment is negative; he regards Caravaggio as setting a bad example, leading astray other artists, who ought to have known better than to copy him. From this, it follows that his work cannot be truly canonical since, so far from setting the standard for other artists, Caravaggio represents a danger to art.

If you think back to *The Supper at Emmaus*, you will realise that what Bellori says cannot be strictly true. Caravaggio did not just paint what he saw, without reference to the art of the past or any mental effort on his part. Although the picture appears very down to earth, like a scene taking place in real life, the similarities to Titian's version of the subject make clear that Caravaggio was aware of the precedents provided by earlier artists. Moreover, he must carefully have calculated all of the elements of the composition in order to achieve the desired effect. X-ray photographs of his paintings demonstrate that, though he did not make preparatory drawings like other artists, he worked out his compositions on the canvas, often changing his mind radically as he worked. Nevertheless, his refusal to take ancient sculpture as models for imitation, combined with the darkness against which his figures stand out so forcefully, means that his paintings appear utterly different from the most revered masterpieces of the Renaissance, such as Raphael's great fresco in the Vatican known as *The School of Athens* (Figure 3.12), with its balanced arrangement of graceful and dignified figures set within a vast airy architectural space. Consequently, Bellori was not alone in considering Caravaggio a menace. Poussin, for example, reportedly said that he 'had come into the world in order to destroy painting' (quoted in Warwick, 2009, p. 13). As a result of such hostile assessments, the artist's success in his own lifetime gave way to centuries of neglect.

Figure 3.12 Raphael, *The School of Athens*, *c.*1510–11, fresco, 500cm x 770cm. Stanza della Segnatura, Vatican Museums and Galleries, Rome. Photo: © Scala, Florence

Activity

You should allow about 15 minutes for this activity.

Now read what a later authority, the British artist and critic Roger Fry (1866–1934), has to say about Caravaggio. Reading 3.3 is an extract from Fry's notes to his 1905 edition of the *Discourses* (lectures) delivered by Sir Joshua Reynolds to the students of the Royal Academy. Read it through now and answer the following questions:

How does Fry's view of Caravaggio differ from Bellori's? What standards does he use to evaluate the artist's work? What does this suggest about Caravaggio's relationship to the canon?

(Note that the artists not previously mentioned in this chapter to whom Fry refers are the French painter Édouard Manet (1832–1883) and the Spanish painter Diego Velázquez (1599–1660).)

Discussion

In contrast to Bellori's critical account of Caravaggio, Fry offers a highly favourable one. The aspects of the artist's work that the earlier writer found problematic are precisely the things Fry admires. Whereas Bellori criticised Caravaggio's failure to respect the great artists of the past, Fry praises his defiance of authority and tradition, which makes him 'the first modern artist'. Moreover, whereas Bellori saw Caravaggio as arrogant in his disdain for earlier art, Fry praises the artist for being true to himself; his art is based on 'his own temperamental attitude', and, as a result, is characterised by 'sincerity' and 'originality'. Similarly, whereas Bellori deplored Caravaggio's failure to idealise, Fry celebrates him as 'the first realist', though his application of the rather disdainful word 'squalid' to Caravaggio's work suggests that he still retains something of the classical hostility to unidealised art. The standard against which Fry assesses Caravaggio is that of the art of his own era, as exemplified by Manet, but his reference points also include two other seventeenth-century artists, Velázquez and Rembrandt, neither of whom featured in Bellori's canon but with whom Fry obviously expects his reader to be familiar, so they must have been canonical by 1905. Overall, this passage demonstrates that, in order for Caravaggio to enter the canon, it was necessary for the dominance of the classical ideal to give way to a new set of artistic values.

In other words, Fry's assessment of Caravaggio helps us to see how much the basis of the canon has changed since the time of Bellori. The new set of artistic values that he gives expression to here had developed during the nineteenth century, as artists, scholars and others challenged the authority of classicism. At least in part they did so because of the rapid political, economic and social change of the period, which undermined its status as an ideal valid for all times. Since then, nineteenth-century artists have been assessed first and foremost on the basis of a distinctively modern concern with originality, self-expression and innovation. As a result, the canon of western art has expanded to include many artists who were neglected and even disdained while classicism held sway because their work did not conform to its standards. Modern art now has its own canon, extending from Manet in the later nineteenth century to Pollock in the mid twentieth century and beyond. Nevertheless, the legacy of classicism continues to shape the canon. Not only do the great artists of the Italian Renaissance retain a central position, but the canonical status of some modern artists also partly depends on classical values; a case in point is Cézanne, whose work (as you may know from your study of AA100 *The arts past and present*) contains significant classical elements.

3.4 The hierarchy of genres and the canon of art

In exploring the role that classicism has historically played in shaping the canon of western art, we have largely been concerned with the form or style of art. That is to say, we have focused on *how* artists painted their pictures rather than *what* they painted. However, the subject matter of works of art has also played an important role in determining judgements of artistic value. In order to explore this issue, we shall need to consider the issue of genre and, more particularly, what is known as the hierarchy of genres. The crucial point is that, as you have seen with music and will go on to see with Literature, some types or genres of artistic production are valued more highly than others.

The hierarchy of genres was outlined by André Félibien (1619–1695), a scholar and administrator, in his preface to the *Conferences of the Royal Academy of Painting and Sculpture*, published in 1669. Founded in Paris in 1648, the Royal Academy was an official institution of the then immensely powerful French monarchy and, as such, highly authoritative. Like earlier academies of art in Italy, it aimed to raise the status of the artist by defining art as a serious-minded intellectual activity. To this end, it provided its members with opportunities for theoretical debate about art, together with training for young (male) artists. This training centred on drawing after the naked human form, both on the basis of live models and of casts and copies after antique sculptures, in order to equip them with the skills they needed to produce classically idealised works of art (Figure 3.13).

Activity

Read the extract from André Félibien's preface, which is reproduced as Reading 3.4. You are being asked to read this passage because it is a crucial source text; every subsequent account of the hierarchy of genres depends on it. However, it is quite difficult, so don't worry if you have trouble grasping the meaning. After you have read the passage, answer the following questions:

You should allow about 20 minutes for this activity.

1 What types of painting does Félibien value most highly and what are his reasons for his view?

2 What are Félibien's reasons for considering other kinds of picture inferior and why does he place them in the order that he does?

Figure 3.13 Charles-Joseph Natoire, *The Life Class at the Royal Academy of Painting and Sculpture*, 1746, pen, black and brown ink, grey wash and watercolour and traces of graphite over black chalk on laid paper, 45cm x 32cm. Courtauld Institute of Art, London, D.1952.RW.3973. Photo: © The Samuel Courtauld Trust, The Courtauld Gallery, London

Discussion

1   The types of painting that Félibien values most highly are those that
depict 'historical and legendary subjects', along with 'subjects treated
by poets': that is, pictures that tell a story taken from an existing
textual source. Although the 'pleasing' poetic subjects he refers to
presumably include stories about love, he especially values paintings
in which the narrative has a moral or religious character ('the virtues
of great men and the most elevated mysteries'). He also refers to
'allegorical compositions', that is, pictures that use complex
symbolism or allegory to convey their message. His reason for
valuing such text-based paintings most highly is that they are both
'difficult and noble'. By 'difficult', he primarily seems to refer to the
intellectual effort required for their creation, though he also suggests
that they involve a technical challenge since they involve depicting
groups of figures, rather than just one. 'Noble' seems to mean both
moral and social superiority, since an artist who paints such subjects
is said to distance himself from what is 'common and base'. Félibien
is very emphatic that this is the only kind of picture that counts as
great art, given his repetition of the word ('great actions', 'great
painter', 'greatness of his art').

2   He considers other types of picture inferior on the grounds that they
are less intellectually demanding and instead primarily require manual
skill. The artist who paints them does not create 'pictures in the mind'
or achieve 'beauty' and 'perfection', but merely copies the
appearance of nature. In other words, the distinction between higher
and lower types of picture can be mapped on to the distinction we
have already encountered between the classical ideal and a
naturalistic approach. (Remember that Bellori said that Caravaggio
painted from the model because he had nothing in his mind.) In
addition, other kinds of picture are inferior because they depict lower
aspects of God's creation. Portraiture is relatively dignified, because it
depicts human beings, who are described as 'God's most perfect
work on earth'. Landscapes and animal paintings are placed next,
since they still involve painting living, moving nature, while artists who
paint 'fruit, flowers or shells', that is, what we now call **still life**, come
bottom on the grounds that this type of picture depicts only dead
matter.

Although Félibien sets out the basic rationale for the hierarchy of
genres, his account needs a few clarifications. First, it should be noted
that the narrative pictures that he identifies as the highest genre are

usually known as history paintings. It is worth bearing in mind that this category includes not just historical subjects in the literal sense, but also mythological and religious scenes. Thus, for example, Caravaggio's *The Supper at Emmaus* can be counted as a history painting, whether or not you believe that the event depicted in the painting actually took place. However, Félibien would still not have rated the painting very highly, because of the unidealised way that the sacred subject is depicted. His other writings make clear that he had a very low opinion of Caravaggio's work.

Second, Félibien omits another important genre of western painting, that is, scenes of everyday life, as exemplified by the work of Dutch seventeenth-century painters such as Pieter de Hooch (1629–1684) (Figure 3.14). This type of picture rather confusingly became known in the late eighteenth century as **genre painting**. It was ranked beneath history painting on the grounds that it involved nothing more than mere copying of the world around us. However, because it was not mentioned in Félibien's codification of the hierarchy of genres, it did not have a fixed place. Genre painting could be considered superior to portraiture on the grounds that it involved depicting groups of figures in fictional scenarios, like history painting, whereas portraits merely recorded the likeness of particular individuals. However, it seems also to have been regarded as inferior to portraiture, presumably because it typically showed anonymous figures of humble status whereas portraits traditionally commemorated the great and powerful, in accordance with the logic that the value of a painting depends on the status of the subject it depicts.

The hierarchy of genres can thus be summarised as follows:

- history painting
- portraiture/genre painting
- landscape
- animal painting (often omitted from the list)
- still life.

What needs to be emphasised here is that the hierarchy of genres and the distinctions between the various genres provided a theoretical framework that never entirely corresponded to artistic practice. As we have seen, the hierarchy of genres depended on the distinction between high-minded idealisation and lowly naturalism, which reflected the priorities of artists in Italy and France where history painting was widely

Figure 3.14 Pieter de Hooch, *The Courtyard of a House in Delft*, 1658, oil on canvas, 74cm x 60cm. National Gallery, London. Photo: © The Bridgeman Art Library

practised between the sixteenth and the nineteenth centuries. It was of much less relevance to other countries with very different artistic traditions. In Britain, for example, where a Royal Academy of Arts was founded in 1768, the institution's first president, Sir Joshua Reynolds (1723–1792), delivered regular lectures in which he upheld academic values, including the hierarchy of genres. However, like most British artists at the time, he actually earned his living as a portrait painter. Moreover, even in Italy and France artists regularly produced paintings that did not fit neatly into one category but blurred the boundaries between different genres. In other words, it is not always easy to determine which genre a picture belongs to, with the result that it is also difficult to know exactly what status such a picture would have had in the hierarchy of genres.

Figure 3.15 Caravaggio, *Penitent Magdalen*, *c*.1594–95, oil on canvas, 123cm x 99cm. Palazzo Doria-Pamphilj, Rome. Photo: © akg-images. Mary Magdalen (St Mary of Magdala) is traditionally supposed to have been a prostitute who repented of her sins and became a follower of Christ

Activity

Take a look at Figures 3.15–3.18. In each case, you should take care to note the title of the painting and any supporting information given in the picture caption. You should also refer back to what has been said about each artist earlier in this chapter, particularly the period in which they worked.

You should allow about 25 minutes for this activity.

Now try to work out in which genre to place each picture and which other genre(s) it also overlaps with. How high or low do you think its status would have been in the hierarchy of genres?

Pay particular attention to the subject matter, the number of the figures, their identity and scale.

You should be aware that there are no definitive answers! The point of this activity is to show how difficult it can be to place particular pictures in the hierarchy of genres.

Discussion

Figure 3.15: Caravaggio, *Penitent Magdalen*

The subject matter qualifies the picture as a history painting; Mary Magdalen was, after all, a saint. However, Félibien specifically states that history paintings depict several figures, whereas here there is only one, as in a portrait. Moreover, we have seen that Bellori dismissed this painting as simply a depiction of a girl drying her hair, which would make it a scene of everyday life. It can be assumed that it would have ranked beneath other history paintings in the hierarchy of genres – though this would hardly have mattered to Caravaggio himself, since he was working before the hierarchy was formalised.

Figure 3.16 Nicolas Poussin, *Landscape with the Ashes of Phocion Collected by His Widow*, 1648, oil on canvas, 117cm x 179cm. Walker Art Gallery, Liverpool. Photo: © Walker Art Gallery, National Museums Liverpool/The Bridgeman Art Library. Phocion was an ancient Athenian general and statesman who was executed after being falsely accused of treason

Figure 3.16: Poussin, *Landscape with the Ashes of Phocion Collected by His Widow*

In this case, too, the subject matter qualifies the picture as a history painting; it is concerned with a hero of classical antiquity. However, its title identifies it primarily as a landscape, presumably on the grounds that the figures are tiny in relation to the total picture space. Nevertheless, the narrative element would allow it to rank higher in the hierarchy of genres than a landscape that showed only anonymous figures and even more so than one with none at all. Given that Poussin was admired by Bellori and himself disapproved of Caravaggio, we can assume that it would have been important to Poussin to elevate a relatively lowly genre.

Figure 3.17 Joshua Reynolds, *Garrick between Tragedy and Comedy*, 1760–61, oil on canvas, 147cm x 182cm. Waddesdon, The Rothschild Collection (Rothschild Family Trust), on loan since 1995, 102. 1995. Photo: Mike Fear © The National Trust, Waddesdon Manor. David Garrick was the most famous British actor of the eighteenth century, renowned for his versatility in different types of drama

Figure 3.17: Reynolds, *Garrick between Tragedy and Comedy*

Since it depicts a particular individual, this has to be a portrait. However, it is more ambitious than the vast majority of portraits; not only does it contain three figures, but those of Tragedy and Comedy are allegories or personifications of abstract qualities, such as Félibien saw as being one of the most elevated features of history painting. Given Reynolds's academic credentials, it can be assumed that he too sought to elevate the status of his work in the hierarchy of genres, even if the picture seems quite light-hearted in its mood, as Garrick grins apologetically at the stern figure of Tragedy while being dragged away by Comedy.

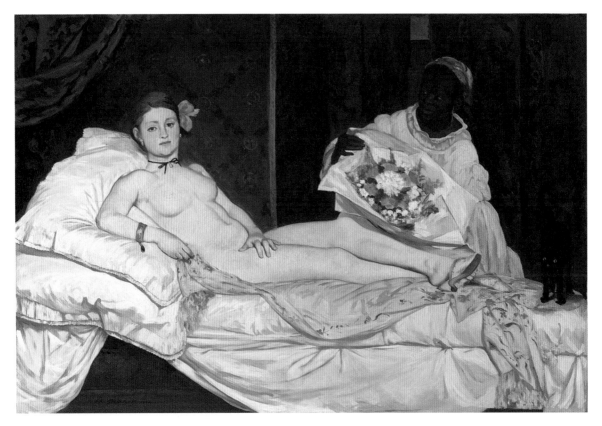

Figure 3.18 Édouard Manet, *Olympia*, 1863, oil on canvas, 131cm x 190cm. Musée d'Orsay, Paris. Photo: © RMN-Grand Palais (Musée d'Orsay)/Hervé Lewandowski. The title, 'Olympia', can be assumed to be the name of the principal figure depicted in this painting, which is, however, not a portrait of any known individual

Figure 3.18: Manet, *Olympia*

The title of this painting sounds rather grandly classical and it depicts a naked figure, such as young artists were trained to draw in the Academy. However, the details suggest that it does not actually depict a classical subject – the black maid on the right is wearing modern dress – and nor does the painting seem to have much in the way of a narrative: the maid seems to be bringing some flowers to the woman. On this basis, it could be identified as a genre painting, except that it is much larger than genre paintings usually are. Moreover, the way that the main figure looks out of the picture at the viewer makes it look a bit like a portrait. Overall, it seems to push at the boundary between history and the lower genres. Since, unlike Caravaggio, Manet lived when the hierarchy of genres was well established, he must have been deliberately challenging it.

As we have already seen, the nineteenth century challenged the dominance of classical idealism, which had provided the rationale for the hierarchy of genres in the first place. As a result, history paintings ceased to be automatically ranked above other types of picture. It was during this period, for example, that a portrait by Leonardo, the *Mona Lisa*, became one of the most famous pictures in the world. A more direct challenge to the hierarchy of genres came from the new political and social values that developed during the nineteenth century. Artists and critics increasingly rejected the idea that a great work of art was one that depicted a high-status subject such as a king or a saint. Part of the reason that Rembrandt entered the canon when he did, for example, was because he was regarded as a democratic artist, who showed sympathy for the poor and suffering in his work. With the development of modern art and, in particular, the emergence of abstract art, the focus on subject matter as a key factor in determining how a work of art should be valued came to seem even less convincing.

Arguably, however, the hierarchy of genres still helps to shape what is today understood as 'high art'. We still tend to expect great works of art to have a serious purpose or a profound message. More light-hearted works are seldom accorded the same status. For example, it may not matter to us that Caravaggio's *The Supper at Emmaus* qualifies as a history painting because of its biblical subject matter, but its sombre tone and solemn mood nevertheless make it seem more important than a less weighty scene. These expectations even seem to affect the evaluation of abstract art. Jackson Pollock's canonical status, for instance, surely has something to do with the vast size and often subdued colours of his pictures, which help to identify them as high art in the tradition of history painting. However, it gets more complicated when it comes to contemporary artists, who have moved away from the western tradition of painting and sculpture to engage with a much wider range of media.

3.5 Hallowed objects in modern spaces: canons and contemporary art

Gill Perry

Over the last few decades the visual arts in Britain, especially modern and contemporary art, have experienced a remarkable growth in popularity, encouraged by a major programme of investment in several high-profile national galleries with new or spectacular architectural spaces. You saw in the first section of this chapter how the imposing location and architectural structure of the National Gallery, with its classical portico, helped to give the gallery a quasi-sacred status. As we shall see, the positioning and shape of several galleries of modern art have performed similar functions. In 2000 a new museum of modern and contemporary art, Tate Modern, on the south bank of the River Thames near Blackfriars Bridge in London, was opened with a great celebratory fanfare. A converted power station with a massive central Turbine Hall had been gutted and redesigned by the architectural partnership Herzog & De Meuron. The original hall, emptied of its huge power-generating turbines, was opened out into a massive entrance area and exhibition space (Figures 3.19 and 3.20).

Figure 3.19 Tate Modern, south of the River Thames, London. Photographed by Nicholas Kane. Photo: © Arcaid Images/Alamy

Figure 3.20 Turbine Hall, Tate Modern, London. Photo: © Tate, London 2013

Tate Modern was expected to attract an impressive figure of around 2 million visitors a year. Since then it has actually attracted between 5 and 6 million visitors annually, helping to position modern and contemporary art at the forefront of the UK's cultural identity and its thriving tourist economy. In this section I shall explore the various ways in which this major cultural institution and its spaces of display have helped both to consolidate and to expand our ideas of what might constitute modern canon(s) of art.

'Tate'

Tate Bankside is at the heart of a recently established network of Tate galleries across England. Apart from the original Tate Gallery in London in its extended building by the Thames at Millbank (established in 1897; renamed 'Tate Britain' in 2000), Tate Liverpool opened in the renovated Albert Docks in Liverpool in 1988, followed by Tate St Ives in Cornwall in 1993, in a building designed by architects Evans and Shalev on the site of an old gasworks overlooking Porthmeor beach. The more recent Turner Contemporary, partnered with Tate, is also positioned on the coast on the raised seafront at Margate, Kent, in a striking three-storey building designed by the architect David Chipperfield; it opened in 2011 (Figure 3.21). It is no coincidence that all of these gallery sites are waterfronts offering dramatic vistas, either overlooking the Thames or on the English coast, where they stand as evocative landmarks symbolising the best of British art, exemplified by the famous paintings of Turner (Figure 3.8), as they look out to sea – to those countries and cultures beyond the UK's national borders.

'Tate', then, is a confederation of museums which display the nation's collection of British and modern and contemporary art. Tate Britain houses British art from 1500 to the present day, while Tate Modern shows British and international modern and contemporary art. Tate Liverpool and Turner Contemporary have similar functions, but on a smaller scale, while Tate St Ives displays modern art by artists who have connections with the local area. The Tate brand and its satellites command a wide range of imposing national sites and have increasingly come to be seen as a storehouse of the modern canon. As I shall argue, such high-profile architectural spaces provide dramatic and spectacular physical environments that merge with the power of the brand to confer special status on the objects exhibited within them.

But as we saw in the preceding sections of this chapter, canon formation is a complex process, involving many considerations, including institutional, social and economic factors. Association with a particular prestigious national gallery (such as the National Gallery or Tate) can be critical, but some galleries can also help to institute new – or socially and geographically diverse – canons. In fact many recent writers reject the idea of 'the' canon, instead arguing for the existence of multiple canons in our increasingly globalised culture, which are produced at 'different times and in different geographic locations by individuals, groups, and institutions pursuing at times very different

Figure 3.21 Turner Contemporary, Margate, Kent, 2011. Photo: © Manu/ Alamy

agendas' (Brzyski, 2007, p. 3). Although women artists have featured much less prominently than men within the western canon of the last four centuries, in the twenty-first century they are among those 'groups' that are increasingly becoming visible within galleries of contemporary art, reflecting broader cultural shifts in modern society. Although outnumbered by commissions by men, several women have designed large-scale **installations** for the Tate Turbine Hall since 2000, including the inaugural commission of Louise Bourgeois's *Maman* (1999) (Figure 3.22) and Rachel Whiteread's *Embankment* (2005). And installation art, which usually consists of a group or assemblage of objects or sculptural forms and is often large-scale, has become one of the most visible and successful new 'genres' of modern art.

Tate Modern also sees itself as an institution in touch with global and transnational art practices that circulate around the many international exhibitions and biennales, from Havana to Istanbul to Venice, which now dominate the art world calendar. The growing economic and cultural importance of countries such as China and Brazil, together with African nations, has also been reflected in some of Tate Modern's recent curatorial decisions. In 2007, for example, the Brazilian artist Hélio Oiticica (1937–1980) was given a major retrospective; in 2010–11 the Chinese artist Ai Weiwei (b.1957) was commissioned to create his

Figure 3.22 Louise Bourgeois, *Maman*, 1999, steel and marble sculpture, 927cm x 892cm x 1024cm. Turbine Hall, Tate Modern. Photo: © Tate, London 2013. © The Easton Foundation/DACS

installation *Sunflower Seeds*, covering much of the floor space of the Turbine Hall (Figure 3.23); and in 2013 the Benin artist Meschac Gaba (b.1961) curated his 'Museum of Contemporary African Art' in the gallery. In making such curatorial decisions, the Tate network seeks to use its influence in setting the agenda for the broader art world to

Figure 3.23 Ai Weiwei, *Sunflower Seeds*, installation October 2010–May 2011, porcelain, dimensions variable. Turbine Hall, Tate Modern. Photo: © Tate, London, 2013. © Ai Weiwei

loosen the dominance of what (as you have seen) is broadly labelled the 'western canon' in major British institutions of contemporary art.

As you can see from Figure 3.20, the Turbine Hall runs the length of the gallery, with the entrance space sloping down to the main concourse; the very high ceilings and natural sunlight from overhead windows contribute to a striking entrance to what is now deemed (on the basis of visitor numbers) the most popular art gallery in the world. Artists who have won commissions in this space are guaranteed wide international media coverage; their status and visibility within the global art world are inevitably enhanced by both the context and the requirement to create a work that can somehow interact with this extraordinary architectural frame – which, it has often been suggested, is reminiscent of the towering, sacred space of a cathedral. As such it presents challenges to artists; it is difficult not to respond to its spectacular dimensions with the fear of being overwhelmed by its vastness.

Ai Weiwei

Sunflower Seeds has been one of a series of ambitious commissions for this enormous hall since it opened in 2000. In 2010–11 Ai Weiwei created an extraordinary landscape of over 100 million porcelain sunflower seeds. Each seed was unique, individually hand-sculpted and painted by craftsmen in the Chinese city of Jingdezhen, famous for its imperial pottery. The artist wanted visitors to literally immerse themselves in the installation, by walking or sitting on the carpet of seeds, even building sandcastles or putting these porcelain kernels in their mouths. However, following the enthusiastic response of the first visitors to *Sunflower Seeds*, the gallery became concerned that these baked clay seeds were emitting a potentially harmful dust that could contravene health and safety laws. Although Ai Weiwei had intended this work to be an interactive installation, involving the physical participation of the viewer, it was decided to cordon it off, so that it could be viewed only from behind a barrier. The floor of the Turbine Hall, which appeared densely carpeted in a mass of tiny grey kernels, was now out of bounds.

Activity

You should allow about 15 minutes for this activity.

Now turn to Reading 3.5, which is a description of Weiwei's *Sunflower Seeds* drawn from the Tate website. It includes a statement by the curator, Juliet Bingham. Read this through and have a look back at Figure 3.20. Then answer these questions:

How does the viewer experience this work? How do the context and the changed conditions for viewing influence the way you read the work? How might these objects be seen to be 'thought-provoking'?

Discussion

In its early intended form, Ai Weiwei's porcelain field offered an original and engaging approach to the space of the Turbine Hall, inviting both physical and cultural responses. It both echoed and countered the dramatic scale of the space. It was designed for the viewer to move around, to be experienced through direct and close physical contact, echoing a key characteristic of installation art. This is rather different, of course, to the viewing conditions required for two-dimensional paintings, which, as you saw in the preceding sections, have dominated the western canon up until at least the early twentieth century.

One might even argue that by cordoning off the carpet of seeds to avoid the spread of dust, the curators distanced us from the work, contributing to the sense of wonder that this massive architectural space, and its hallowed contents, can convey. This change has also encouraged us to view the seeds from more limited and restricted viewpoints, making the experience closer to that involved in viewing a tableau or a two-dimensional painting.

Bingham describes *Sunflower Seeds* as a 'thought-provoking sculpture' full of 'narrative and personal content'. She is referring here to the cross-cultural references in the use of millions of hand-crafted porcelain seeds from Jingdezhen, and their capacity to encourage us to think about the geopolitics of cultural and economic exchange. This major Tate commission provided work for many skilled Chinese workers. When seen in this way, these material objects can offer some rich associations, histories and meanings to the artwork. And the fact that each of the porcelain seeds is different adds to the unique – and even extraordinary – nature of the work. Apart from the cathedral-like setting, the sheer quantity and scale of these handmade objects, and the labour involved, add to our sense of awe and surprise on viewing it.

In terms of Tate's developing relationship with contemporary Chinese art and culture, and the institution's contribution to the establishment of multiple canons, there are some other stories to tell here. Ai Weiwei is probably one of the most famous artists in the world today. Like many other successful artists working in modern China, he has been influenced in his work by aspects of western conceptual art (he lived in the USA from 1981 to 1993), and his work draws on hybrid sources and ideas. The increasing international visibility of Chinese art might be seen to echo the dramatic rise of Chinese global power and economic success. But Ai Weiwei has a complicated relationship with Chinese culture; he is a social activist concerned with human rights. Arrested at Bejing airport in April 2011, during the period in which *Sunflower Seeds* was shown at Tate Modern, he was held for 81 days by the Chinese government without official charges being filed, although he was subsequently accused of tax evasion. He and his movements are now closely monitored by the Chinese authorities. Meanwhile, the appeal of his art to a western audience has continued to thrive. In 2013 his work was among the most visible at the Venice Biennale, widely seen as the most prestigious event in the art world calendar. Apart from his major commission for the German Pavilion inside the main Biennale space, titled *Bang* (2010–13), which was made up of 886 wooden Chinese stools (Figure 3.24), he also made two other projects for locations across Venice.

One of these, in the Zuecca Project Space on the island of Giudecca, was an expanded version of his work *Straight*, comprising tonnes of steel bars recovered from the schools that collapsed during the Sichuan earthquake in China in 2008. Over 5000 children perished in these schools. Another piece, *SACRED*, exhibited in the church of Sant'Antonin, consisted of six large iron boxes, with peepholes for viewing. Inside there were sculptures, re-creating miniature scenes from

Figure 3.24 Ai Weiwei, *Bang*, 2013, 886 antique stools, dimensions variable. German Pavilion, Venice Biennale 2013. Photo: © Felix Hoerhager/dpa picture alliance/Alamy. © Ai Weiwei

Ai Weiwei's detention. He is shown sleeping, eating, on the lavatory or in the shower, always with two guards. Positioned in an actual ecclesiastical setting, *SACRED* has led some critics to suggest that the artist is positioning himself as a saint or martyr, contributing to his own canonisation (Higgins, 2013). Although his work has been defended as 'just being honest' about his experiences, it could be argued (as we have seen) that spectacular settings add to the awe-inspiring status that we accord this work of art.

Activity

Specific objects loaded with cultural, historical or personal meanings are also important themes in these works at the Venice Biennale. Look again at Ai Weiwei's *Bang* (Figure 3.24), a crowded display of antique three-legged stools that can be found in most Chinese family homes.

You should allow about 15 minutes for this activity.

How would you describe the content of this installation (that is, the objects that compose it and how they are arranged)? What literal and symbolic meanings does the work suggest? What does it tell us about developments in the modern canon(s) of art?

Discussion

Familiar domestic objects have been reconceived in a crowded mass of piled, hanging and linked stools, with the occasional coloured one breaking the sense of confusing repetition. (The wooden three-legged stool was a remarkably uniform object used by all sectors of Chinese society for centuries, until plastic and metal became standard materials for furniture construction after the Cultural Revolution.)

In the context of this installation, the wooden stool could be seen as a metaphor for the individual of the past, jostling for space in a crowded postmodern world. Each stool is also a material object carrying traces of a private domestic history, of everyday family lives in China.

Collected and reconceived within the context of the German Pavilion at the prestigious Venice Biennale, these stools provide vivid examples of the changing artistic forms, objects and ideas that are part of the multiple canons of contemporary art. As we have seen, the historical notion of the western canon now coexists with a variety of works that display a much wider range of media, geographical contexts and cultural histories.

Conclusion

This chapter has extended your exploration of the canon to Art History. As we have seen, since the Renaissance the canon of art has been shaped and reshaped by the relevant authorities, that is, artists, art historians, curators, critics and collectors, in response to cultural, institutional, political, economic and other factors. Today, it has expanded to include a much more diverse array of artists and artworks than ever before, to the extent that many now prefer to speak of multiple canons. Nevertheless, what counts as canonical art continues to be shaped by influential authorities responding to similar factors.

Moreover, the core of the western canon remains largely unchallenged, so that it still makes sense to talk of 'the canon'. The modern preference for individualism and innovation has modified many of the value judgements of the past, but our ideas about great art continue to be shaped by the legacy of classical antiquity. In Chapter 5 you will explore the significance of this legacy in connection with a canonical work of literature, Homer's *Iliad*. You might therefore like to reflect on possible connections or differences between classicism as it has been discussed in this chapter and the exploration of related issues in the context of the discipline of Classical Studies.

References

Bellori, G.P (2006) *The Lives of the Modern Painters, Sculptors and Architects* (trans. A. Sedgwick Wohl), New York, Cambridge University Press.

Brzyski, A. (ed.) (2007) *Partisan Canons*, Durham, NC and London, Duke University Press.

Caravaggio (1986) Directed by Derek Jarman [Film]. London, British Film Institute.

Caravaggio: The Final Years (2005) Exhibition held at the National Gallery, London, 23 February–22 May 2005 [Exhibition catalogue].

Higgins, C. (2013) 'Portrait of the artist as a detainee', *Observer*, 31 May.

Vasari, G. (1965) *Lives of the Artists* (trans. G. Bull), Harmondsworth, Penguin (reissued as *Lives of the Artists*, vol. 1, in 1987).

Warwick, G. (ed.) (2006) *Caravaggio: Realism, Rebellion, Reception*, Newark, DE, University of Delaware Press.

Further reading

One of the most famous and popular introductions to the history of art is E.H. Gombrich's *Story of Art*, first published in 1950. It is still well worth reading, but you should be aware that it is heavily biased towards the art of western Europe and the legacy of the classical tradition. For a more recent introduction that aims to redress the balance, you are advised to take a look at John Fleming and Hugh Honour (2009). If you would like to read more about Caravaggio, a good place to start is Andrew Graham-Dixon (2011). You might also like to check the Tate website for further discussion and more photographs of Ai Weiwei's *Sunflower Seeds*, as well as a video of the artist talking about the work.

Fleming, J. and Honour, H. (2009) *A World History of Art*, 7th edn, London, Laurence King.

Gombrich, E.H. (1995) *The Story of Art*, 16th edn, London, Thames & Hudson (pocket edn published 2006).

Graham-Dixon, A. (2011) *Caravaggio: A Life Sacred and Profane*, London, Penguin.

Tate (2010) 'The Unilever Series: Ai Weiwei: Sunflower Seeds' [Online]. Available at http://www.tate.org.uk/whats-on/tate-modern/exhibition/unilever-series-ai-weiwei-sunflower-seeds (Accessed 7 April 2014).

Reading 3.1 Luke, Chapter 24

Source: Luke, Chapter 24, 13–31 (New Revised Standard Version).

13 Now on that same day two of them were going to a village called Emmaus, about seven miles from Jerusalem,

14 and talking with each other about all these things that had happened.

15 While they were talking and discussing, Jesus himself came near and went with them,

16 but their eyes were kept from recognizing him.

17 And he said to them, 'What are you discussing with each other while you walk along?' They stood still, looking sad.

18 Then one of them, whose name was Cleopas, answered him, 'Are you the only stranger in Jerusalem who does not know the things that have taken place there in these days?'

19 He asked them, 'What things?' They replied, 'The things about Jesus of Nazareth, who was a prophet mighty in deed and word before God and all the people,

20 and how our chief priests and leaders handed him over to be condemned to death and crucified him.

21 But we had hoped that he was the one to redeem Israel. Yes, and besides all this, it is now the third day since these things took place.

22 Moreover, some women of our group astounded us. They were at the tomb early this morning,

23 and when they did not find his body there, they came back and told us that they had indeed seen a vision of angels who said that he was alive.

24 Some of those who were with us went to the tomb and found it just as the women had said; but they did not see him.'

25 Then he said to them, 'Oh, how foolish you are, and how slow of heart to believe all that the prophets have declared!

26 Was it not necessary that the Messiah should suffer these things and then enter into his glory?'

27 Then beginning with Moses and all the prophets, he interpreted to them the things about himself in all the scriptures.

28   As they came near the village to which they were going, he walked ahead as if he were going on.

29   But they urged him strongly, saying, 'Stay with us, because it is almost evening and the day is now nearly over.' So he went in to stay with them.

30   When he was at the table with them, he took bread, blessed and broke it, and gave it to them.

31   Then their eyes were opened, and they recognized him; and he vanished from their sight.

Reading 3.2 Bellori on Caravaggio

Source: Hibbard, H. (1983) *Caravaggio*, **New York, Harper & Row, pp. 361–73.**

It is said that the ancient sculptor Demetrios was such a student of life that he preferred imitation to the beauty of things; we saw the same thing in Michelangelo Merisi, who recognized no other master than the model, without selecting from the best forms of nature – and what is incredible, it seems that he imitated art without art. [...] he began to paint according to his own inclinations; not only ignoring but even despising the superb statuary of antiquity and the famous paintings of Raphael, he considered nature to be the only subject fit for his brush. As a result, when he was shown the most famous statues of [the ancient sculptors] Phidias and Glykon in order that he might use them as models, his only answer was to point toward a crowd of people, saying that nature had given him an abundance of masters. [...] Since Caravaggio aspired only to the glory of color, so that the complexion, skin, blood, and natural surfaces might appear real, he directed his eye and work solely to that end, leaving aside all the other aspects of art. Therefore, in order to find figure types and to compose them, when he came upon someone in town who pleased him he made no attempt to improve on the creations of nature. He painted a girl drying her hair, seated on a little chair with her hands in her lap. He portrayed her in a room, adding a small ointment jar, jewels and gems on the floor, pretending that she is the Magdalen [see Fig. 3.15 in the text]. She holds her head a little to one side, and her cheek, neck, and breast are rendered in pure, simple, and true colors, enhanced by the simplicity of the whole figure, with her arms covered by a blouse and her yellow gown drawn up to her knees over a white underskirt of flowered damask. We have described this figure in detail in order to show his naturalistic style and the way in which he imitates truthful coloration by using only a few hues. [...]

Without doubt Caravaggio advanced the art of painting, for he lived at a time when realism was not much in vogue and figures were made according to convention and *maniera* [manner], satisfying more a taste for beauty than for truth. Thus by avoiding all pettiness and falsity in his color, he strengthened his hues, giving them blood and flesh again, thereby reminding painters to work from nature. [...] Moreover, he claimed that he imitated his models so closely that he never made a single brushstroke that he called his own, but said rather that it was nature's. Repudiating all other rules, he considered the highest achievement not to be bound to art. For this innovation he was greatly acclaimed, and many talented and educated artists seemed compelled to follow him [...] Such praise caused Caravaggio to appreciate himself alone, and he claimed to be the only faithful imitator of nature. Nevertheless he lacked *invenzione* [invention], decorum, *disegno* [drawing or design], or any knowledge of the science of painting. The moment the model was taken from him, his hand and his mind became empty.

Nonetheless many artists were taken by his style and gladly embraced it, since without any kind of effort it opened the way to easy copying, imitating common forms lacking beauty. Thus, as Caravaggio suppressed the dignity of art, everybody did as he pleased, and what followed was contempt for beautiful things, the authority of antiquity and Raphael destroyed. [...]

Just as certain herbs produce both beneficial medicine and most pernicious poison, in the same way, though he produced some good, Caravaggio has been most harmful and wrought havoc with every ornament and good tradition of painting.

Reading 3.3 Fry on Caravaggio

Source: Fry, R. (1905) Introduction and notes to Sir Joshua Reynolds, *Discourses to the Student of the Royal Academy*, London, Seeley, p. 170.

[…] there is hardly any one artist whose work is of such moment as his [Caravaggio's] in the development of modern art. […] the art of the nineteenth century is continually marked by an unconscious return to his point of view. Manet, for instance, goes back rather to him than to Velasquez [sic]. He was, indeed, in many senses the first modern artist; the first artist to proceed not by evolution but by revolution; the first to rely entirely on his own temperamental attitude and to defy tradition and authority. Though in many senses his art is highly conventional (the peculiar illumination, though possible under certain conditions, giving us a sense of strangeness and unnaturalness in the whole effect) he was also the first realist, in the most limited sense of the word, as emphasising the commonplace – not to say the squalid – even in scenes of heroic and poetical significance. For all this, his force and sincerity compel our admiration, and the sheer power of his originality makes him one of the most interesting figures in the history of art. His peculiar illumination, with its polarised light and complete suppression of reflected light, was a great invention […] In spite of a superficial resemblance, his notion of **chiaroscuro** differs *toto coelo* [entirely] from Rembrandt's.

Reading 3.4 Félibien on the hierarchy of genres

Source: Félibien, A. (1669) Preface to the *Conferences of the Royal Academy of Painting and Sculpture*, in Edwards, S. (ed.) (1999) *Art and its Histories: A Reader*, New Haven, CN and London, Yale University Press, p. 35.

As the pleasure and instruction we receive from the works of painters and sculptors derive not only from their knowledge of drawing, the beauty of the colours they use or the value of their materials, but also from the grandeur of their ideas and from their perfect knowledge of whatever they represent; it follows that there is a particular kind of art quite separate from the artisan's manual skill and physical materials, involving the prior creation of pictures in the mind, without which a painter and his brush cannot create a perfect work. This art is not like those in which hard work and manual skill alone can create beauty.

It is precisely this grand art and this intellectual knowledge which can be learned from these lectures […]

[Painting] generally applies itself to all kinds of ways of representing natural forms [   ]

That part of the representation of a natural form which consists simply of drawing lines and mixing colours is considered to be work of a mechanical kind. It therefore follows that, as different practitioners of this art apply themselves to various subjects, the more difficult and noble their choice of subject, the further they move away from what is common and base, and the more they distinguish themselves by a more illustrious kind of work.

Thus, the artist who does perfect landscapes is superior to another who paints only fruit, flowers or shells. The artist who paints living animals deserves more respect than those who represent only still, lifeless subjects. And as the human figure is God's most perfect work on earth, it is certainly the case that the artist who imitates God by painting human figures, is more outstanding by far than all the others. However, although it is a real achievement to make a human figure appear alive, and to give the appearance of movement to something which cannot move; it is still the case that an artist who paints only portraits has not yet achieved the greatest perfection of art and cannot aspire to the honour bestowed on the most learned of his colleagues. To achieve this, it is necessary to move on from the representation of a single figure to that of a group; to deal with historical and legendary subjects and to represent the great actions recounted by historians or the pleasing subjects treated by poets. And, in order to scale even greater heights, an artist must know how to conceal the virtues of great men and the most elevated mysteries under the veil of legendary tales and allegorical compositions. A great painter is successful in ventures of this kind. Herein lie the force, nobility and greatness of his art.

Reading 3.5 Ai Weiwei at Tate Modern

Source: Tate (2010) 'The Unilever Series: Ai Weiwei: Sunflower Seeds' [Online]. Available at http://www.tate.org.uk/whats-on/ tate-modern/exhibition/unilever-series-ai-weiwei-sunflower-seeds (Accessed 7 April 2014).

About the exhibition

Sunflower Seeds is made up of millions of small works, each apparently identical, but actually unique. However realistic they may seem, these life-sized sunflower seed husks are in fact intricately hand-crafted in porcelain.

Each seed has been individually sculpted and painted by specialists working in small-scale workshops in the Chinese city of Jingdezhen. Far from being industrially produced, they are the effort of hundreds of skilled hands. Poured into the interior of the Turbine Hall's vast industrial space, the 100 million seeds form a seemingly infinite landscape.

Porcelain is almost synonymous with China and, to make this work, Ai Weiwei has manipulated traditional methods of crafting what has historically been one of China's most prized exports. *Sunflower Seeds* invites us to look more closely at the 'Made in China' phenomenon and the geo-politics of cultural and economic exchange today.

Update: Friday 22 October 2010

The landscape of sunflower seeds can be looked upon from the Turbine Hall bridge, or viewed at close range in the east end of the Turbine Hall on Level 1. It is no longer possible to walk on the surface of the work, but visitors can walk close to the edges of the sunflower seed landscape on the west and north sides.

Although porcelain is very robust, we have been advised that the interaction of visitors with the sculpture can cause dust which could be damaging to health following repeated inhalation over a long period of time. In consequence, Tate, in consultation with the artist, has decided not to allow members of the public to walk across the sculpture.

Sunflower Seeds is a total work made up of millions of individual pieces which together [form] a single unique surface. In order to maintain and preserve the landscape as a whole, Tate asks visitors not to touch or remove the sunflower seeds.

Juliet Bingham, Curator, Tate Modern

Ai Weiwei's Unilever Series commission, *Sunflower Seeds*, is a beautiful, poignant and thought-provoking sculpture. The thinking behind the work lies in far more than just the idea of walking on it. The precious nature of the material, the effort of production and the narrative and personal content create a powerful commentary on the human condition. *Sunflower Seeds* is a vast sculpture that visitors can contemplate at close range on Level 1 or look upon from the Turbine Hall bridge above. Each piece is a part of the whole, a commentary on the relationship between the individual and the masses. The work continues to pose challenging questions: What does it mean to be an individual in today's society? Are we insignificant or powerless unless we act together? What do our increasing desires, materialism and number mean for society, the environment and the future?

Chapter 4
The Protestant Reformation and iconoclasm

Ole Peter Grell with Fiona Richards and Kim Woods

Contents

Aims

This chapter will:

- investigate the symbolic power of objects as reflected in iconoclasm: the religiously motivated destruction of images
- introduce you to the different forms that iconoclasm took during the Reformation period
- present you with some of the contemporary writings about images and the rationale for their rejection
- help you to develop your skills in the use of texts and images as primary sources
- explore issues of historical interpretation in examples related to the Reformation.

Materials you will need

In this chapter, you will need to listen to the following audio recordings, which can be found on the module website:

- Ein feste Burg
- J.S. Bach, 'Ein feste Burg'.

You will also be directed to the module website for an online activity and to access the online edition of the *Oxford English Dictionary*.

Introduction

In the second half of this book we continue our exploration of the idea of authority, but from a different angle. Having considered how certain cultural products acquire and maintain authoritative status, we shall now turn to some examples of cultural authority being challenged, or appropriated in entirely new contexts. As you may remember from the introduction to this book, the range of academic disciplines widens here to include History, Classical Studies and Literature, but you will also find examples from Art History and Music, linking back to your work on the first half of the book. In addition, the crossovers between Classical Studies and Literature in Chapters 5 and 6 further reinforce Book 2's interdisciplinary approach to the idea of authority.

The current chapter is presented mainly from the historian's perspective, using, as you'll see, images and texts as sources (of information) about the past; but it is also an aspect of religious history that we are focusing on here. You will recall from Chapter 1 that music can play a part in the study of religious practice, and here we shall see how it can complement the study of religious history. More recently, in Chapter 3, you were introduced to some examples of religious art, and here you will be able to extend your skills in visual analysis as you examine works of religious art in their original contexts. Overall, this is a chapter in which the concepts of voices, texts and material culture are closely intertwined, via the topic of iconoclasm.

You may not be familiar with the term 'iconoclasm', but you have probably come across the word 'icon', referring to painted or mosaic pictures of Christ or the saints in the Greek Orthodox or Russian Orthodox Churches. And you will undoubtedly be familiar with an adjective derived from this word – describing something as 'iconic' has become common usage. The second half of the term 'iconoclasm' is based on a Greek word for 'breaking', and you may know what it means when someone is described as being 'an iconoclast': such a person attacks established beliefs, values or respected institutions because they are considered flawed or harmful. An iconoclast, then, challenges authority in one way or another.

Activity

Look up the word 'iconoclasm' in the online version of the *Oxford English Dictionary*. Remember that you can find the *OED* by following the link in

You should allow about 10 minutes for this activity.

the 'Databases' section of the OU Library website – or by following the direct link provided on the Study Planner of the module website.

What do you think are the important features of this word?

Discussion

Among a number of examples of its historical use, you will find that the *OED* defines iconoclasm as the act of breaking or destroying images, especially pictures and sculptures set up as objects of veneration.

The reference to objects might remind you of your study of material culture in the first book of the module, *The Lives of Objects*. Our historical case study in this chapter will pick up some of the ideas you encountered earlier.

So, this chapter focuses on iconoclasm during a particular period of European history known as the **Reformation**, a movement covering most of the sixteenth century which challenged the authority of the Catholic Church and the papacy. Iconoclasm played a part in this challenge and, in turn, helped to establish the authority of the Reformed churches. Over the last thirty or so years historians and art historians have taken a particular interest in iconoclasm during the Reformation period and produced a wealth of literature on the subject. They have been baffled and fascinated by the fact that the late medieval period, and especially the last decades of the fifteenth century, saw an explosion of religious art and religious activity that was followed by an iconoclastic reaction just a few decades later, occasionally even involving some of the very people who had previously donated artworks or money for the same causes. The historian Sergiusz Michalski has described the term iconoclasm as 'a both forceful and somewhat ambiguous expression' when used within Reformation history (1993, p. 75).

But before we plunge into sixteenth-century history, it is worth remembering that acts of ritual destruction and desecration performed for religious reasons have evoked strong passions in all ages, including our own. In 1992, for example, a group of militant Hindus demolished the Babri Mosque in Ayodhya in India. Television images of the mob's destruction of the 500-year-old mosque, which had been built on the site of an earlier Hindu temple, shocked the rest of the world. However, such actions have a long pedigree. Superimposing one's place of worship on that of another, defeated faith has been a feature of the religious history of the world since the earliest times. In Britain, for instance, the early Christians frequently built their new churches on the former sites of pagan worship.

Another contemporary example of iconoclasm is the destruction of giant Buddhist statues in Bāmiyān, Afghanistan by supporters of the Taliban in 2001. Again, these actions were widely reported in newspapers and on television. The reasons for the Taliban's destruction of these particular sculptures provide an interesting mixture of a religious, political and propagandist rationale which bears comparison with some of the examples you will encounter in the Reformation period. Even the Taliban leader at the time, Mullah Mohammed Omar, admitted that **idolatry**, or the danger of it, was not the main reason why the Muslim Taliban proceeded to destroy these statues. There are in fact hardly any Buddhists left in Afghanistan today. Instead, it was the 'western' obsession with preserving these sculptures or artefacts which made them a tempting target for the Taliban, who through this act of destruction were able to show defiance towards the west while simultaneously achieving publicity for the present-day Islamic hostility towards the use of religious **iconography**. In this instance, as well as in earlier periods such as the Reformation, it is important to realise that the destruction of such objects may represent a symbolic protest or act against what the actors involved consider an unacceptable set of beliefs and values.

4.1   Iconoclasm and the Reformation

The Reformation was a series of debates, movements and conflicts about the nature of Christianity that took place in the fifteenth and sixteenth centuries. It will be familiar to you if you have studied AA100 *The arts past and present*, but it may be worth briefly recapping some of the core teachings of Christianity that were being tested during the Reformation.

Christian beliefs

- The central Christian beliefs relate to Jesus of Nazareth (*c.*4 BCE– *c.*29 CE), regarded by his followers as the Messiah or 'Christ'.
- For Christians, Jesus is both fully human and fully divine. He was resurrected from the dead after being crucified, thus overcoming the power of sin and death.
- As the sinless 'Son of God', Jesus is the essential means of reconciliation between God and humankind.
- Jesus's teachings, recorded in the New Testament of the Bible, have unique spiritual and moral authority.
- Christians seek to attain forgiveness of sins and eternal life ('salvation') through faith in Jesus Christ, and to live by his teachings.

While these core beliefs are more or less shared, Christians have differed on how to interpret them and, crucially during the Reformation period, on who can interpret the word of God. Without touching on the finer points of the theology of the reformers, all of them broadly believed, in contrast to the Catholic Church, that 'salvation depended primarily on personal faith rather than participation in the rituals of the church, that believers could legitimately draw direct spiritual inspiration from God rather than being dependent on a hierarchy of priests and bishops, and that ultimate authority lay in the original text of the Bible rather than in church traditions' (Wolffe, 2008, p. 78). Inevitably, this shift also led to different views about how objects associated with Christian worship (such as church furnishings, images and even the Bible itself) should be treated.

Images and objects

As you study this chapter, you will encounter the religious language of images and icons. For Protestant reformers of the sixteenth century, what was termed an 'image' was often in fact an 'idol' – an object of worship. 'Images' might therefore include altarpieces, statues, paintings or any object that was seen as being associated with inappropriate veneration (such as oil lamps and service books). As you will see, Protestant hostility towards such images was expressed in terms of 'abolishing', 'removing' or 'destroying' them – actions that were intended to effect the reform not only of their churches but also of their beliefs. The rhetoric of idolatry was not all there was to it, though. We have already seen that iconoclasm could be a symbolic protest against a set of values, and this was certainly so in the Reformation.

At a distance of 500 years, it may seem odd that during the Protestant Reformation objects and images became the focus of what was, after all, essentially a religious conflict. Why should they have been considered so important when there were fundamental theological differences at stake? Nowadays we are probably used to looking at works of art for their aesthetic qualities, and at objects primarily in terms of their use. In order to grasp the emotive theme of iconoclasm, we need to understand that religious authority might be invested in both works of art and some liturgical objects – that they exercised power in terms of their symbolism, functions and meanings. This is what put them at the very heart of religious conflict: they were not minor details; they really mattered.

Since the time of the early Christian Church, art had had a recognised function as a means of visualising religious narratives and beliefs for the benefit of those without access to written texts. The principle that visual images served a purpose equivalent to the written or spoken word was articulated by one of the key figures of authority in the early church, Pope Gregory the Great (*c.*540–604), and his statements were much quoted in succeeding centuries. Protestant reformers emphatically rejected this equivalence and recognised the authority only of the word – the written word of the Bible and the spoken word of authoritative sermons. Pope Gregory had also claimed that visual images were capable of inspiring devotion, worship and emulation, while

Protestant reformers saw in them only the lure of idolatry. In rejecting the role of images in the Christian Church, the Protestants were overthrowing centuries of authority.

The issue of religious images provoked a variety of reactions among Protestants, from popular violence and destruction to the controlled intervention of Protestant preachers and local authorities which resulted in all or some of the images being removed – but not necessarily destroyed.

AA100's discussion of the Reformation centred on changes in English Christianity. This chapter is concerned with the Reformed churches in Germany, Switzerland and the Netherlands (see Figure 4.1) that were inspired by the theology of Martin Luther (1483–1546), Heinrich Zwingli (1483–1531) and later John Calvin (1504–1564). The word 'Protestant' is used to broadly describe those who were opposed to the pope and the Catholic Church. This term is derived from the objection – 'the *protestatio*' – presented at the **Diet** (meeting) of Speyer in 1529 by supporters of the German reformer Luther who were opposed to the decisions taken by its Catholic majority. The word 'evangelical' was also used by sixteenth-century Protestant reformers to describe their reliance on Jesus's teachings in the New Testament, as 'evangelist' is the name sometimes given to the authors of the four books (the Gospels) in the New Testament that recount the life and teachings of Jesus. But although the reformers shared much common ground in their opposition to the Catholic Church and the pope, there was not one unified Protestant church and the Reformation had a different character in different parts of Europe. We shall see some of these differences played out in relation to iconoclasm.

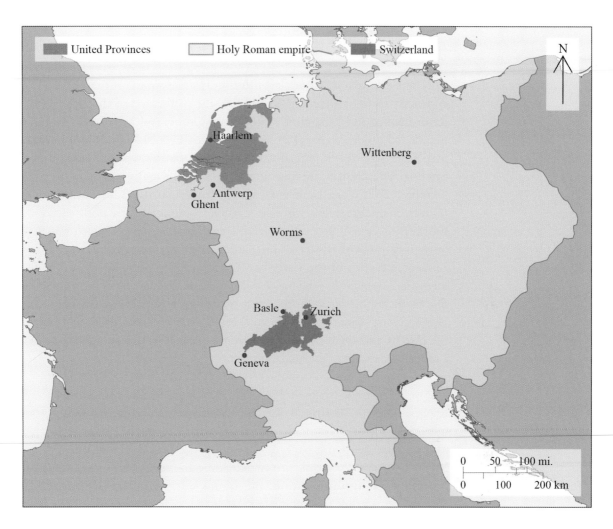

Figure 4.1 Map showing the loose confederation of German states known as the Holy Roman empire in the sixteenth century. The United Provinces, part of the Netherlands, separated from the Holy Roman empire in 1581, and the Swiss Confederation, although nominally part of the Holy Roman empire until 1648, was in effect independent

4.2 The Wittenberg iconoclasm

The first example of iconoclasm during the Reformation period very appropriately took place in Wittenberg, the birthplace of the Reformation, and as such it represents an important case study. It was here that Luther (Figure 4.2) had inadvertently started the Reformation and from here that it spread across Europe via the new technology of printing. Traditionally the beginning of the Reformation is dated to 31 October 1517, when Luther is supposed to have nailed his 95 theses (points of disagreement with the Catholic Church) to the door of the Castle church in Wittenberg, thereby starting the process which resulted in the break-up of western Christianity. Over the next few years Luther's criticism of the Catholic Church and the pope developed and intensified, while his polemical writings went through endless printruns due to their popularity. Luther and his fellow reformers at the new University of Wittenberg were supported and protected by their patron, the elector and duke of Saxony, Frederick the Wise (elector 1486–1525). Luther was excommunicated by the pope in January 1521 and a few months later he was summoned by the head of the Holy Roman empire, Charles V (reigned 1519–56), to appear before him at the imperial Diet of Worms. Before he allowed Luther to attend this meeting, Elector Frederick secured guarantees from the emperor for his safe passage there and back. Luther attended the Diet of Worms between 16 and 26 April, firmly defending his religious position despite his recent **excommunication**. But on his way back from Worms to Wittenberg, Luther was 'abducted' by agents of Frederick the Wise. The elector clearly feared for the safety of his most prominent theologian, despite the guarantees of the emperor. Luther subsequently stayed under armed protection at Wartburg Castle, which belonged to Frederick, until events in Wittenberg necessitated his return.

Andreas Karlstadt in Wittenberg

Meanwhile, events in Wittenberg unfolded rapidly. Andreas Karlstadt von Bodenheim (1480–1541), who had started out as a colleague of Luther's at the University of Wittenberg, began to assume a position of influence in Luther's absence during the autumn of 1521. Karlstadt (Figure 4.3) had been a supporter of Luther since 1517 and was among his closest collaborators in the early years of his Wittenberg career. Having already in 1521 published pamphlets arguing against clerical celibacy and monastic vows, Karlstadt, with the support of Philip

Figure 4.2 Lucas Cranach the Younger, *Martin Luther*, *c*.1546, woodcut. H7400, Germanisches Nationalmuseum, Nuremberg. Photo: Germanisches Nationalmuseum, Nuremberg

Figure 4.3 Unknown artist, *Andreas Karlstadt*, *c.*1540, copper engraving, 12cm x 8cm. Photo: akg-images

Melanchthon (1497–1560), another of Luther's close collaborators, sought to implement Protestant reforms in Wittenberg during the last months of that year. By December Karlstadt had, through his sermons, encouraged the Wittenbergers to take direct action and bring about a physical reformation of their church. Inspired by Karlstadt, a group of students and townspeople forced their way into the city church on 3 December, driving the Catholic priests away from the altar and destroying the missals (books which contained the complete services for the Masses said throughout the year).

Why were the missals chosen for destruction, rather than something more significant from an iconoclastic perspective, such as the altar or side altars? Possibly because the latter action might have been considered too risky at this point – altars were, after all, costly items often given by named donors, whereas missals were cheaper and could be replaced. At the same time missals carried great symbolic and theological significance, closely linked as they were with the Catholic Mass which the evangelicals found particularly objectionable.

Figure 4.4 Georg Braun and Frans Hogenberg, *View of the City of Wittenberg*, c.1558, copper engraving. Photo: akg-images

The following day another crowd attacked the Franciscan monastery in the town. Here the rioters demonstrated their willingness to escalate their actions by destroying the altar. This action set in motion a series of iconoclastic events in Wittenberg. Elector Frederick the Wise initially decided not to intervene, merely issuing orders for the preservation of the Catholic Mass. Meanwhile popular demand for religious change grew, and in mid December a meeting of the city council was interrupted when a crowd stormed into the council chamber and demanded that the Mass be suspended and replaced with an evangelical service. Finally, on Christmas Eve rioters broke into the city church, intimidating the priests and smashing lamps.

This choice of item by the iconoclasts would strike most of us today as an odd one – what could be offensive to evangelicals about oil lamps? Why were they considered idols? Notably, these lamps were described as 'oil gods' (idols who consume oil) in some of the contemporary polemical literature. They often burned before images, and as eternal lights – burning continuously – they were considered typical of the conspicuous consumption of the Catholic Church, using up pious bequests which could be spent more profitably on the poor, in particular. Breaking them therefore had significant symbolic value for the evangelicals.

Figure 4.5 Interior of the *Stadtkirche* (city church), St Mary's church. Photo: akg-images/ullstein bild. Typically for a Lutheran church, attention here focuses on a triptych by Lucas Cranach the Elder (1472–1553) depicting the Last Supper. Note also the prominence of the pulpit (to the right), and the implicit suggestion that preaching the word of God is more important than the worship of things

On Christmas Day 1521, with the permission of the city council, Karlstadt celebrated an evangelical service in the city church, addressing the congregation dressed as a layman while distributing **Communion** in both forms (wine and bread) to the laity. This was a revolutionary event of great symbolic value, for in the Roman Catholic tradition ordinary people received only the bread. For the first time, an evangelical service had taken place in the city.

The city council openly demonstrated its support by issuing a decree on 24 January 1522, calling (among other things) for Duke Frederick to remove all offending images from the local churches as quickly as possible. Only a few days later Karlstadt published his influential pamphlet 'On the Abolition of Images', emphasising the need for magistrates to take the lead in such matters if they wanted to avoid God's anger and punishment. Despite the council setting a date by which images were to be removed, a band of local iconoclasts decided to take matters into their own hands. Led by the preacher Gabriel Zwilling (1487–1558), who early on had joined Luther in the Augustinian college in Wittenberg, the iconoclasts pulled down and destroyed images within the Wittenberg churches. Reports reached Frederick the Wise to the effect that Karlstadt and Zwilling were responsible for this, having worked the crowd to a fury by their turbulent preaching and saying that if the magistrates proved unwilling to act then the common people had the right to remove the images. Events in Wittenberg clearly set a revolutionary precedent, empowering the common people to destroy offending images or idols in their locality if the authorities proved slow or reluctant to take action.

Activity

Reading 4.1 is a short extract from Andreas Karlstadt's pamphlet 'On the Abolition of Images'. This pamphlet was published in 1522, at the time of the events it refers to, so it is a primary, or contemporary, historical source. Read the extract through and then answer the following questions:

You should allow about 20 minutes for this activity.

1 What is Karlstadt's view of images?

2 According to Karlstadt, who is responsible for the removal/destruction of images?

Discussion

1   Karlstadt is adamant that the use of images is forbidden and should be banned. They invariably lead to idolatry and therefore cannot be tolerated, because God has forbidden their use.

2   When it comes to who is responsible for removing and/or destroying the images which have been introduced into the churches, Karlstadt is less clear. He has no doubt that the images must be destroyed, using biblical references to urge the overthrowing, breaking and burning up of such objects, but it is not clear who should take the initiative here. Initially Karlstadt refers to 'Christians' (in other words, everyone) as being responsible for this; then he emphasises that the removal of images should be undertaken by the 'highest authorities' (central government); finally, he informs his readers that the 'magistrates' (city councils) are obliged to act. What matters to Karlstadt is to take immediate iconoclastic action; he is less concerned about who is going to authorise such action.

However, when Karlstadt published his treatise 'Whether One Ought to Behave Peacefully and Spare the Feelings of the Simple' two years later, he was adamant that responsibility for immediate iconoclastic action rested with every Christian and every community. He firmly rejected Luther's argument that the abolition of images had to be postponed until the whole community had established a common policy – winning over those whom Luther termed the 'weaker brethren'. Karlstadt saw no need for adjusting the pace of reform to make sure that the weaker brethren were on board. By 1524 Karlstadt had fully accepted revolutionary iconoclastic violence. For him it was a Christian duty to remove images from the local community's place of worship, even if this was opposed by other members of this community, because it was God's will that all idols should be destroyed.

The iconoclastic disturbances quickly came to an end in Wittenberg due to the intervention of Frederick the Wise. Luther, by then deeply worried about the turn of events, returned from Wartburg Castle on 7 March 1522, once more to take charge of the evangelical movement in the city.

Luther's response to Karlstadt

Before the iconoclastic events in Wittenberg, Luther had had little to say about the use of images within places of worship. In his 'Sermon on Usury' in 1520 he had condemned what he termed unnecessary expense on church decoration. Such money was, according to him, better spent on the poor and needy. Later, in 1521, he included the visual arts in his attack on **indulgence**s (remissions for the punishment of sins after death) and his rejection of the cult and collection of **relic**s. He portrayed religious art and images as a deplorable effort by individual believers and communities to earn their salvation through 'good works'. According to Luther, salvation could be achieved only through faith and grace. As he put it in his 'Sermon on Good Works', people donated money to churches or images only because they mistakenly thought that they could buy their way into heaven (Michalski, 1993, pp. 7–8).

Luther immediately set to work on his return from Wartburg Castle and delivered a series of Lenten sermons in the city church between 9 and 17 March 1522. All eight sermons were published the following year, but the sermon 'On Images' was published instantly and was reprinted seven times within the next 12 months. Evidently Luther considered this the central part of his Lenten sermons and it had to be disseminated without delay.

Activity

You will find an extract from one of Luther's Lenten sermons (delivered on 9 March 1522) reprinted as Reading 4.2. Read it through now and then answer the following questions:

You should allow about 20 minutes for this activity.

1 What is Luther's view of images?

2 What does he propose to do with them?

Discussion

1 Luther considers images to have no importance – they are 'nothing and […] no service is done to God by erecting them'. Images are neither good nor bad on their own, but only become evil, as Luther puts it, because of the idolatry they attract – as images, they are of no significance.

2 Luther rejects any form of compulsion. He will happily preach against the use of images, but rejects all forms of direct action (iconoclasm) initiated by those who are opposed to their use.

Luther further developed his argument that images were of little or no consequence over the next couple of years, culminating in his pamphlet of 1525, 'Against the Heavenly Prophets'. Here he accused Karlstadt of proposing that the destruction of religious artworks was an obligation for all good Christians, thereby endangering Christian freedom and attaching religious importance to material objects – suggesting a kind of 'good works in reverse', or, in other words, that iconoclasm would lead to salvation. Against Karlstadt's demand for the removal or destruction of images from churches, Luther stated that it was only through the Word of God that idolatry could be removed from the hearts of Christians. Only then would images become truly harmless. Images could be removed, according to Luther, only when a communal consensus had been reached, and even then they could be removed by the proper authorities alone. Anything which smacked of public disorder which could lead to riots and social and political breakdown had to be avoided.

Music in Lutheran churches

Fiona Richards

While Luther believed images to be unimportant, he clearly recognised that the manner of their removal or destruction could be dangerous, both for the church and for society. In contrast, he saw music as a means of promoting religious and social cohesion. He viewed singing in church as both a social activity and part of the ritual of worship, and encouraged domestic hymn-singing as part of his belief in the sanctity of the Christian home. It should be said that music in church was by no means a new idea, but Luther turned it from a lavish, ornate spectacle performed by professionals into something that was scaled down, but a communal activity. More than other church reformers, Luther gave music an important role, to such an extent that in 1523 the Nuremberg poet Hans Sachs described him as 'the Wittenberg nightingale'. In 1524 his tract 'To the Councilmen of All Cities in German Lands, that They Erect and Maintain Christian Schools' emphasised the importance of music with the words: 'I speak for myself; if I had children and found it within my power to do so, I would insist that they study not only languages and history, but also learn to sing and become acquainted with music and the entire field of mathematics' (Brandt, 1962, p. 347).

Luther was himself a singer and lutenist and was largely responsible for the evolution of the German hymn, or 'chorale'. Hymns have been an important part of Protestant worship since the Reformation, beginning as melodies sung in unison, and subsequently harmonised. The first Protestant hymn book, for use in church, in the home and in schools, was published in Wittenberg in 1524 by Johann Walter (1496–1570), a church musician and assistant to Luther. Luther wrote the foreword to this *Geistliches Gesangbüchlein* ('Little Sacred Songbook') and composed 23 of its 38 hymns. One of the best-known was 'Ein feste Burg' ('A mighty fortress'). Figure 4.6 shows its original version. Although it doesn't look quite like modern musical notation, you might be able to trace the shape and contour of the melody.

Activity

You can find an audio recording of 'Ein feste Burg' on the module website. Listen to it now. How are the words set to the music? Before you start, you might like to think back to the hymn, 'I vow to thee, my country', you listened to in Chapter 2.

"Ein' feste Burg."

Figure 4.6 'Ein feste Burg' ('A mighty fortress'), original manuscript with Luther's signature

Discussion

The hymn is metrical, simple and repetitive, with the words set syllabically. Luther believed in the pre-eminence of the text, therefore this setting favours declamation over florid or complex word-setting.

'Ein feste Burg' was also, however, one of the most significant hymns of the Reformation on account of its stirring text ('A mighty fortress is our God, a bulwark never failing'). Luther's hymns not only had significance in his own time, but had long-lasting consequences, underpinning subsequent German Protestant music and eventually migrating beyond Europe.

Two centuries after Luther wrote his simple hymn, J.S. Bach (1685–1750), one of the great composers of the Baroque period, worked it into a more lavish version for voices and orchestra. Fittingly, his cantata was written for Lutheran celebrations on Reformation Day (31 October).

Activity

You can find an audio recording of an extract from J.S. Bach's 'Ein feste burg' on the module website. Listen to it now before reading on. The tune is easiest to pick out at the beginning of the extract.

As an aside, you might note that John Calvin, whose religious views you will encounter later in this chapter, had a very different attitude to music in church, allowing only the singing of psalms, with no instrumental accompaniment. So with regard to music as well as images the Protestant Reformation generated a range of views, with no single authority dominating.

4.3 Iconoclasm in Zurich

We turn now to iconoclastic events in Zurich during the early years of
the Reformation, which proved more radical and dramatic than those
that had taken place in Wittenberg. Although Zurich was neither a
commercial nor an educational centre, at the start of the sixteenth
century it was considerably bigger than Wittenberg, with a population of
around 5700 people. Rather than just a city, it was a city-state
controlling tracts of land outside the city walls with a population of
over 58,000 people. The Zurich iconoclasm, which influenced other
towns and cities in southern Germany and Switzerland in particular, was
characterised by an extreme aversion to any use of images in places of
worship. This hatred of images is termed **iconophobia**.

Heinrich Zwingli and controlled iconophobia

Like Andreas Karlstadt, the two most prominent leaders of the
Reformed Church – Heinrich Zwingli and John Calvin – were
iconophobes. Zwingli (Figure 4.7) began preaching against the cult of the
saints shortly after his arrival in Zurich in 1519. By January 1523 the
evangelical movement in Zurich, under the leadership of Zwingli, was
quickly gaining the upper hand. By the time that iconoclastic acts
occurred in the city in the autumn of 1523, Zwingli and his fellow
evangelical preachers had been preaching against the use of images for
many months. One of Zwingli's colleagues, Ludwig Haetzer (c.1500–
1529), published a small pamphlet in the autumn of 1523, 'A Judgement
of God Our Spouse Concerning How One Should Regard All Idols and
Images'. Written in German, Haetzer's pamphlet consisted of a collection
of passages from the Bible, primarily selected from the most outspoken
Old Testament condemnations of idolatry (You have encountered a few
such Old Testament texts in Reading 4.1, from Karlstadt's 'On the
Abolition of Images'.) Not only did this pamphlet provide those inclined
towards taking iconoclastic action with the necessary tools from the Bible
to justify their action, but it also contained a section praising and
glorifying those who had destroyed images. The pamphlet undoubtedly
added to the fire already generated by evangelical sermons and served to
encourage direct action by individual evangelicals. Not surprisingly, a
number of iconoclasts took action and were later apprehended by the city
council and briefly imprisoned for what remained illegal acts, but their
action forced the issue of whether or not images should continue to be
tolerated in Zurich's churches.

Figure 4.7 Hans Asper, *Heinrich Zwingli*, 1531, oil on parchment, 35cm x 24cm, 133, Winterthur Kunstmuseum, Switzerland. Photo: akg-images

One such iconoclast was Lorenz Hochrütiner, a weaver and occasional lay preacher, who in the autumn of 1523, together with two other men, entered the St Nicholas chapel in the Fraumünster church, where they removed and destroyed the lamps which hung in front of the pulpit. Hochrütiner and his companions then sprinkled each other with holy water, pretending to take an oath together. Hochrütiner, when questioned, referred to the lamps as idols: the fact that the expensive oil for the lamps which burned day and night was financed by church income and tithes, which could have been spent on the deserving poor, would from an evangelical perspective have given them a significant emblematic value, symbolising what was wrong with the Catholic Church. The business with the holy water served to deride what the evangelicals considered superstition and demonstrated the water's lack of power, but it also reflected gestures and behaviour linked to **Carnival** and the associated rites of what was known as 'the world turned upside down', which allowed people to make fun of dignitaries and institutions.

Only two weeks after the city council had found him guilty of this offence, Hochrütiner was engaged in yet another attack on a religious object. This time he helped to bring down a large wooden crucifix at a crossroads just outside one of the city gates. Not only did Hochrütiner and his collaborators find the crucifix offensive, they had planned to sell the wood and donate the money to the poor.

These issues were all dealt with by the Second Zurich Disputation, one of two large-scale meetings in 1523 organised by the Zurich city council and involving both clergy and laymen. The meeting debated the use of images and the Mass, before condemning both. Even so, disagreement emerged among the evangelical preachers about the need for the immediate removal of all images from churches. When the city council stated its position on 27 October, it warned that no one was allowed to remove or alter any image in the churches, except those who had donated them. Images which had been commissioned and paid for by the congregation could only be removed with 'the entire congregation's knowledge and will' (Palmer Wandel, 1994, p. 82).

Activity

You should allow about 20 minutes for this activity.

Now read the evangelical preachers' 'Advice Concerning the Mass and Images' (10–19 December 1523), which is reproduced as Reading 4.3. Then answer the following questions:

1   How does this 'Advice' compare with the decision of the Second Zurich Disputation to get rid of images?

2   Do the evangelical preachers endorse popular and spontaneous iconoclasm?

Discussion

1   This falls well short of the outright condemnation of images issued by the Second Zurich Disputation. The first paragraph simply encourages some of the images, such as the retables (altarpieces or panels resting on the altar itself), to remain closed or covered, while discouraging the use of silver and gold images in processions at church festivals and weddings. Only those who have donated images have the right to remove them, while a local majority is needed to remove images paid for by the individual congregation or parish.

2   No. Even where a democratic decision about removing images has been reached, removal has to be done in an orderly manner, causing as little offence as possible. Evangelical preachers who encourage members of their flock to undertake iconoclastic acts on their own initiative should first be discouraged from making such statements, then fined, and finally stripped of their benefices if they persist.

The lack of agreement among the preachers and the magistracy about what action to take guaranteed that the 'Advice' had to be cautious. Consequently, individual acts of iconoclasm continued and intensified. The city council then appointed yet another committee in the spring of 1524 to explore what to do about images and the Mass. This time the verdict was to eliminate all images from the churches and to introduce a Reformed Communion. The council followed this advice and ordered all images to be removed on 8 June 1524, but once again emphasised that this should be done with consideration for others and without causing offence. Private donors were given a week to remove images that they had donated, while a consensus among the congregation still had to be secured before images paid for by parish funds could be removed. Even at this stage the council was not motivated by evangelical faith, but by its concern to protect private property and to retain peace and consensus within the wider community.

A week later the Zurich magistracy finally legislated in favour of iconoclasm. They concluded that since God had forbidden images and idols, Zurich would 'do away with the images or idols in all places', so that people could turn away from them and instead worship 'God through Our Lord Jesus'. They would also allocate all the money hitherto spent on such images to the poor, 'who are a true image of God' (Palmer Wandel, 1994, pp. 96–7). This sudden decisiveness was due to the change in the balance of power within the council, as two of its leading conservative, Catholic members had just died. Private donors were still granted permission to remove images donated by them and their families, but what was left behind or had been paid for by the local communities were to be removed by a committee appointed by the council on 2 July. Over the next ten days this committee moved from church to church in Zurich, took down sculptures and images and smashed them up. Paintings and altarpieces were destroyed in bonfires lit in front of the churches, while objects made of precious metals and stones were broken up, the metal melted down and all of it sold for the benefit of the poor in particular.

The events in Zurich show how iconoclasm could be sanctioned and organised by the authorities, but not all cases were like this. The iconoclasm of the sixteenth century took many forms, including violent destruction associated with the riots of French Protestants, known as **Huguenots**, in 1560–61, and the so-called Wonder Year in the Netherlands in 1566–67.

4.4   John Calvin and Geneva

John Calvin's name was linked with that of Zwingli in the last section as a key iconophobic reformer. However, Calvin (Figure 4.8) was unusual among the early reformers in that he did not have to quickly develop a religious response to images under the pressure of iconoclastic events, for the city in which he spent most of his adult life, Geneva, had already abolished all religious art before he arrived there. Calvin had originally fled his native France for Basle and was on his way to Strasbourg in July 1536 when he broke his journey in Geneva. Encouraged by the local reformer William Farel (1489–1565), Calvin stayed on in the city for two years until falling out with the magistracy in 1538. The clash was over the question of ecclesiastical discipline. Calvin and Farel's unwillingness to accept the magistracy's claim to supremacy over the clergy in ecclesiastical affairs resulted in their dismissal and exodus. Calvin then settled temporarily in Strasbourg until he was recalled by the Genevan magistracy in 1541. He wrote extensively and repeatedly about images, not only in his major work, the *Institutes of the Christian Religion* (first published in 1536 and gradually expanded until the final version was published in 1559), but also in a number of pamphlets and letters.

Activity

You should allow about 25 minutes for this activity.

Read the extract from Chapter 11 of John Calvin's *Institutes of the Christian Religion*. This is reprinted as Reading 4.4. Why, according to Calvin, should there be no paintings and sculptures in churches?

Discussion

Calvin begins with a historical argument, questioning why latter-day Christians have found a need for images when the church fathers and the ancient church had no call for them. He emphasises that images or 'visible representations' only entered the church 500 years after its foundation, at a time when, as he puts it, 'the purity of the ministry had somewhat degenerated'. Clearly the church fathers had made a conscious and rational decision to exclude images from the church because of the risk they carried for weaker souls who might easily be led into superstition and idolatry. That this is so has, according to Calvin, been proved by recent developments within the Catholic Church. The only images Calvin will allow are, as he puts it, 'those living symbols which the Lord has consecrated by his own word': baptism and Communion.

Figure 4.8 Unknown artist, *John Calvin*, *c*.1555, oil on wood, 28cm x 20cm. Museum Boymans-van Beuingen, Rotterdam. Photo: akg-images

Calvin traced the origin of idolatry to **the Fall** (Adam and Eve's lapse from innocence to sinfulness in the Garden of Eden). Since then, he believed, humankind's spiritual shortcomings had magnified as a result of this original sin. In this state of corruption, humankind was constantly in danger of losing its bearings. The root of idolatry, according to Calvin, lay not in images or the material world, but within humankind itself, which is constantly tempted to seek God on its own terms rather than on the Creator's.

Calvin therefore wanted no images, sculptures or crucifixes in churches. The only decorations he would allow were inscriptions from the Bible. He wanted to see the law of God in writing, with inscriptions from the Bible painted on the walls of churches in the same way as pictures had been used. This, however, was not to be done to justify the believers as if they were trying to pay off God in some way. Calvin considered such inscriptions to be the manifestations of God's voice, serving to enhance the faith of the congregation. His directives proved hugely influential on the interior decoration of Calvinist churches across Europe.

While Calvin developed his theology and his reformation of Geneva he was under no pressure from followers taking direct iconoclastic action. However, during the last decade of his life he was appalled to hear news of the Huguenots' great iconoclastic campaigns in France. Having established a rigidly controlled theocracy in Geneva, Calvin considered the disorder and destruction linked to these events in France totally unacceptable. In 1561 he wrote to the Calvinist pastor in Sauve in France, pointing out what a foolish act the burning of idols and the destruction of the cross in the town had been. He took issue with the pastor not only for not having tried to restrain the activists, but – even worse – for actually having encouraged them in his sermons. There was, according to Calvin, no justification for such disorder: 'God has never commanded the casting-down of idols, except to each in his own house, and in public to those he arms with authority' (Bonnet, 1858, pp. 205–6).

Calvin's insistence on an orderly, authority-led solution to the Huguenot drive to cleanse their local churches of idols and images had, as he was to learn, little or no effect, and he became increasingly bitter towards his co-religionists in France.

4.5 Iconoclasm in the Netherlands

Iconoclasm came relatively late to the Netherlands and neighbouring areas, beginning in 1566 as part of a wider process of economic, religious and political protest caused by local hostility to the rule of the

Figure 4.9 Map showing the division of the Low Countries following the secession of the northern provinces from Habsburg-Spanish rule in 1581

Spanish **Habsburgs**. Protestantism, in the shape of Calvinism, was to play a vital role in the process whereby the seven northern provinces known as the United Provinces (the modern-day Netherlands) acquired full independence from Spanish rule. Calvinist theologians, for example, turned upside down traditional dogmas that taught that it was unlawful and unchristian to resist and overthrow divinely ordained rulers, even if they behaved like tyrants. At the same time, they provided a form of justification for those towns and cities that wished to remove all traces of Catholic worship by legitimising acts of vandalism and destruction aimed at local churches.

The *Beeldenstorm*

Iconoclasm began in west Flanders on 10 August 1566 when crowds, having attended a Calvinist sermon, attacked a local Catholic convent and smashed its religious images. The *Beeldenstorm* (literally, 'image' or 'statue' storm), as it became known locally, was undoubtedly inspired by the increasingly aggressive sermons given by a growing number of Calvinist preachers. They clearly found a receptive audience for their message, and an iconoclastic rage spread first across Flanders and then on to other provinces such as Brabant, Zeeland, Holland, Utrecht, Friesland and Groningen. The iconoclasts comprised local people assisted by organised bands of 'professional' iconoclasts, many of whom had been recruited from the exiled Dutch and Walloon (French-speaking people from the southern Netherlands) Calvinist communities in England and Germany.

Ten days later the iconoclast wave hit Antwerp. It coincided with the city's annual fair, which attracted many visitors. The city council was aware of the potential danger of iconoclastic attacks on the city's churches and took precautionary measures by arming the militia and removing a large image of the Virgin Mary, which was normally displayed prominently during the fair. On 20 August, serious disorder broke out in and around the Church of Our Lady, with groups of young men playing football inside the church and throwing stones at the altars, and the city council made a concerted effort to clear the church and close it off. This failed, however, and by evening a large crowd had taken control of the church, breaking, robbing and plundering. First they smashed the image of the Virgin Mary which the city council had sought to protect and preserve. Then they attacked statues, pictures and altars, not to mention the famous organ. According to the Jesuit historian Famiano Strada (1572–1649):

> They cast down or plundered these with such vehemence and headlong insolence that before midnight they had reduced one of the largest, most glorious and splendidly adorned churches in Europe with its seventy altars to an empty and ghastly hulk. No locks were strong enough to protect the treasures entrusted to them.

(Quoted in Duke et al., 1992, p. 150)

Activity

Look carefully at Figure 4.10, which shows an etching by Frans Hogenberg (1540–c.1590), *The Iconoclasm*, published in 1570. (Remember you can view the image in more detail on the module website.) Hogenberg was clearly inspired by the dramatic events in the Church of Our Lady in Antwerp, as you can see from the fact that he put the date 20 August 1566 at the bottom of the etching.

But ignoring the text under the etching for now, note down what you think is going on in the image.

You should allow about 20 minutes for this activity.

Figure 4.10 Frans Hogenberg, *The Iconoclasm*, *c.*1570, etching, 21cm x 28cm. First published by Frans Hogenberg, Cologne. Rijksprentenkabinet, Rijksmuseum Amsterdam. Photo: Rijksmuseum, Amsterdam

Discussion

You will have noted that the church is presented in a stylised way, suggesting that Hogenberg did not seek to depict a specific event or place. Inside the church, a number of people are busy pulling down statues. Further back, a couple of people are smashing up a side altar and **triptych** with their axes, while two others are tearing up religious vestments. To the right of the picture, one man is standing on a table while destroying an image on the wall with his pickaxe. Closer to the foreground, another man has scaled a ladder to smash a window – obviously a stained-glass window depicting some religious event or figure. At the foot of the ladder, another man is chopping up a wooden statue. A couple of soldiers are visible in front of the church, where a number of people are making off with large bundles of goods.

Activity

Now turn to Readings 4.5 and 4.6, which are extracts from two recent interpretations of Hogenberg's etching. The first (Reading 4.5) is by the art historians James Tanis and Daniel Horst; the second (Reading 4.6) is by the art historian Mia Mochizuki. Read them through now. You will find that they offer two very different interpretations of this image. Which one do you find most convincing, and why?

(Before you answer the question, remember to read the text under Hogenberg's etching – reproduced at the start of Reading 4.5.)

You should allow about 40 minutes for this activity.

Discussion

Both interpretations are valid and offer valuable insights into our understanding of this image.

Mochizuki's interpretation (in Reading 4.6) is that the iconoclasm depicted in the etching represents 'an organized and orderly endeavor'. Her view is that what Hogenberg shows is a methodical destruction of images controlled and directed by the civic authorities. She sees it as an event which hardly interrupts the daily business of the city, and where the soldiers in front of the church calmly direct events with no sign of procedures being out of control or violent.

Tanis and Horst (in Reading 4.5), on the other hand, take note of the verse under the etching, which clearly indicates that the total destruction involved in the iconoclasm was inspired by Calvinist preaching. They notice that the event is taking place at night. Unlike Mochizuki, they emphasise the scale and diversity of the destruction and the fact that looters are using the opportunity to benefit. They also see the soldiers or militia guards in front of the church in a totally different light – not directing events, but 'rather helplessly' pointing towards the men leaving the church carrying clubs, possibly on their way to the next church.

These readings illustrate the difficulties historians and art historians encounter when trying to interpret an image from the past, especially when relying exclusively on that image. However, if you accept that Hogenberg was inspired by the events in Antwerp, as evidenced by his inclusion of the date of 20 August 1566, then Mochizuki's interpretation of the iconoclasm in the image as an 'orderly' event controlled and directed by the civic authorities becomes difficult to accept. Furthermore, close inspection of the image reveals that the event took place at night and was accompanied by extensive looting. This would indicate that it was a far more volatile and disorderly event, along the lines suggested by Tanis and Horst.

St Bavo's cathedral in Haarlem

The city of Haarlem had been fortunate to avoid having its churches disturbed by iconoclasts, first during the *Beeldenstorm* in 1566–67 and later in 1573 when Calvinist citizens had attempted, but failed, to take over St Bavo's, the city's cathedral. But five years later, on 29 May 1578, St Bavo's eventually experienced a violent iconoclasm. It happened on the day of Corpus Christi (a day when Catholics celebrate the institution of the **Eucharist**), immediately after Catholic clergy and believers had finished their procession through the city. According to one of the Catholic members of the Haarlem city council who witnessed the attack on St Bavo's, soldiers had already begun to behave disrespectfully during the Mass; during the last hymn large numbers of soldiers entered the church with their swords drawn, while making a lot of noise. Many people were hurt and one of the priests killed while the building was plundered. Meanwhile, soldiers outside the church threatened members of the congregation with their weapons. During the chaotic events of that day in St Bavo's, a number of valuable pieces of devotional art either disappeared or were destroyed.

One of the objects that disappeared from St Bavo's was a sculpture of Christ on a donkey. The work depicted in Figure 4.11 is, of course, not the object from St Bavo's, but a similar figure which has been preserved in the Netherlands. Such life-sized figures or objects painted in naturalistic tones to give the impression of a living being are typical of late medieval Catholic art, and were intended to create a real affinity between the figure and the believer. This particular figure would have been brought out for the Palm Sunday procession and wheeled up through the nave to the altar of St Bavo's by the Haarlem Jerusalem Brotherhood, whose members had the honour of accompanying the statue in the procession re-enacting Christ's entry into Jerusalem. For Catholics, such statues had a defined purpose in visualising the Easter narrative. For the Calvinists in Haarlem, however, this image would have symbolised some of the worst idolatry in the Catholic Church and therefore would have been a prime target for destruction.

Some items survived the iconoclasm and were presumably later dismantled, such as Our Lady of the Sun, a so-called **Marianum** (Figure 4.12) (this is a representation of Mary holding the Christ child, with golden rays of the sun behind her and a serpent representing Satan

Figure 4.11 Unknown artist, *Christ on a Donkey*, late fifteenth to early sixteenth century, paint on limewood, 185cm x 91cm x 87cm. Rijksmuseum Twenthe, Netherlands. Photo: R. Klein Gotink, Collection Rijksmuseum Twenthe, Enschede

Figure 4.12 Unknown artist, view of the Marianum, crucifixion and apostle cycle (on columns), early sixteenth century. St Lambertus's Church, Neeroeteren, Belgium

Figure 4.13 Pieter Janszoon Saenredam, *The Interior of St Bavo, Haarlem*, 1628, oil on panel, 39cm x 48cm. Getty Museum, Los Angeles. Photo: The J. Paul Getty Museum, Los Angeles. Digital image courtesy of the Getty's Open Content Program

under her feet). Evidently, as can be seen from Pieter Janszoon Saenredam's painting from 1628 (Figure 4.13), St Bavo's was totally cleansed of images in accordance with the most stringent Calvinist principles and instead, as particularly recommended by Calvin himself, decorated with biblical texts on pillars, boards and altars.

The Ghent altarpiece

Kim Woods

As you have seen in this chapter, historians traditionally use objects, images and texts as sources for understanding big events in history such as the Reformation. Other approaches start with the objects themselves, and for our final example in this chapter we shall use some of the strategies of the art historian to explore one of the most spectacular artworks that survived the iconoclasm in the Low Countries during the Reformation. This is a monumental fifteenth-century painting known as the Ghent altarpiece (Figures 4.14 and 4.15). The *Beeldenstorm* reached

Figure 4.14 Hubert and Jan van Eyck, *The Ghent Altarpiece*, closed position showing the right and left panels, including the Annunciation (top) and the donors, Joos Vijd and his wife Elisabeth Borluut (bottom left and right, respectively), 1432, oil on panel. St Bavo's cathedral, Ghent. Photo: © Hugo Maertens/Lukas – Art in Flanders VZW

Figure 4.15 Hubert and Jan van Eyck, *The Ghent Altarpiece*, open position, 1432, oil on panel 375cm X 520cm. St Bavo's cathedral, Ghent. Photo: © Hugo Maertens/Lukas – Art in Flanders VZW

the Flemish city of Ghent on 22 August 1566, when, according to one eyewitness source, a band of 'rogues', mostly apprentices and clothworkers from outside the city, began to ransack the city's churches in the name of Protestant reform. The eyewitness recounts that at the Cathedral of St Bavo the various panels of a famous fifteenth-century painted altarpiece of the Holy Lamb (sometimes called the Mystic Lamb) had been taken up into the tower of the church a few days before for safekeeping. Concealed there, they escaped destruction and survive to this day, apart from one panel stolen in 1934 and never recovered. What was so important about a painted altarpiece that warranted its destruction? And what was so special about this particular altarpiece that made the church authorities go to such lengths to protect it?

The Ghent altarpiece is a huge, very complicated but powerful **polyptych**, a work of art made up of several different panels. A cryptic inscription on the frame reveals that it was painted by two brothers, Hubert and Jan van Eyck, and completed in 1432. The outer panels fold in to cover the fixed central panels, creating two very different states of viewing. In its closed state (Figure 4.14), which is how the altarpiece would have been for much of the year, we see the narrative of the Annunciation, where the angel Gabriel announces to the Virgin Mary that she will conceive and bear a son, Jesus Christ. Above Gabriel and Mary are biblical and classical figures thought to have foretold the coming of Christ: the biblical prophets Zechariah and Micah and between them the Erythraean and Cumaean sibyls (ancient mythical secular prophets). Below Gabriel and Mary are the two people who paid for the altarpiece, Joos Vijd and his wife Elisabeth Borluut. Between them are simulated statues of John the Baptist and John the Evangelist. These were not just saints venerated by the couple: before becoming the Cathedral of St Bavo in the sixteenth century the church had been dedicated to St John the Baptist, as was the city of Ghent itself.

When these shutters are opened (Figure 4.15), no fewer than 12 panels are revealed. In the centre of the upper storey is the seated figure of Christ with his mother the Virgin Mary and John the Baptist, accompanied on either side by musical angels and on the outer edges by Adam and Eve, the first humans and those responsible for the first sins committed. In the lower storey is a vision of heaven populated by all the worthy people – or saints – of the past. 'Reading' the painting like a page, from left to right, the two left shutters show the just judges and the knights of Christ; in the centre panel are prophets and patriarchs, apostles and clergy with further saints in the background, including female martyrs; in the two right shutters are hermits and pilgrims, foremost among them a giant St Christopher. In the very centre of this lower storey is a lamb on an altar, a symbolic representation of Jesus Christ, and a fountain in front of it, the symbolic fountain of life mentioned in the biblical Book of Revelation. From the fountain a stream of water seems to flow out of the front of the frame into the space of the viewer – in actual fact, on to the very altar on which the altarpiece was placed, bringing together the divine imagery of the painting and the religious rituals associated with the altar. All of this subject matter is quite difficult to decipher, and you may agree with the Protestant reformers that words would do a more useful job.

Activity

Look carefully at the altarpiece in its closed state and then in its open state (Figures 4.14 and 4.15). (Remember that you can view these images in more detail on the module website.) What are the main differences between the two in terms of colour, perspective and the scale of the figures? What effect do these differences have?

You should allow about 10 minutes for this activity.

Discussion

When closed, the Ghent altarpiece is quite sober in colour; the figures are quite largescale and seem to be placed close to the viewer (near the front edge of the picture); the sense of recession into space is limited and a little odd. The effect is quite immediate, and good in terms of visibility.

When open, the altarpiece is much more colourful. The upper storey is not unlike the outer shutters in that its large-scale figures are set as if close to the viewer. The lower storey is much more complicated, with its various small-scale figure groups and ambitious landscape setting. It is very impressive and more festive, but the details on the lower storey are harder to pick out.

The Ghent altarpiece would have been opened on Sundays and at times of celebration in the church calendar, so the differences you have noticed are quite deliberate: the open view was intended to look splendid. This altarpiece was placed on an altar dedicated to All Saints and would have been opened on that church festival, which helps to explain the subject matter. While saints had a very important role in the Catholic Church, their validity was challenged by the Protestant reformers and their feast days no longer celebrated.

Although the reformers identified idolatry as the overwhelming risk inherent in religious art, this judgement also implied a complete rejection of art's traditional role of visualising, instructing or inspiring worship or good behaviour. It could be argued that the altarpiece when closed visualised the crucial biblical narrative of the Annunciation, and when open inspired worship as well as reminding the viewer of doctrine (the original sin of Adam and Eve). The religious authority of art was fundamentally challenged by the reformers. In the case of the Ghent altarpiece, however, there was another authority at stake as well.

By the mid sixteenth century the Ghent altarpiece was a famous and canonical early Netherlandish painting that cultured visitors to the Low Countries made a point of seeing. The German artist Albrecht Dürer (1471–1528) visited it during a trip to the Low Countries in 1521 and described it as 'a most precious painting, full of thought' (quoted in Dhanens, 1973, p. 13). The diarist and historian Marcus van Vaernewyck (1516/18–1569), the eyewitness who described the image breaking of 1566, eulogised the painting, comparing Van Eyck to the legendary ancient Greek painters of the past such as Apelles and Zeuxis, the highest accolade an artist could be given at the time. The altarpiece was 'a heavenly thing to behold', he declared, and 'You would search in all Christendom for a work comparable to this one' (Van Vaernewyck, 1872–81, vol. I, part 2, pp. 144–5). An anthology of poems by the Ghent painter and writer Lucas de Heere (c.1534–1584) compiled in 1565 included an ode written 'in praise' of the Ghent altarpiece (De Heere, 1969, p. 29).

What these sources show is that only a few years before the iconoclasm, the Ghent altarpiece had attained a kind of authority as an example of excellence. There appears to have been a clear consensus among commentators on art that Jan van Eyck was a founder figure in the development of early Netherlandish painting and that the Ghent altarpiece was a crucial work in its history, with an artistic importance that went far beyond its original function as the altarpiece of a family chapel. As such, the possibility that the Ghent altarpiece should be destroyed by iconoclasts must have been unthinkable: the Low Countries would have lost a work of art perceived to be fundamental to its cultural heritage.

We have already seen in Chapter 3 that the canon of Renaissance art was largely Italian, established by the influential Italian artist and art historian Giorgio Vasari (1511–1574) in his *Lives of the Most Excellent Painters, Sculptors and Architects*, first published in 1550 and in an enlarged edition in 1568, just two years after the iconoclasm. The writings of De Heere and Van Vaernewyck show that a distinctively Netherlandish canon was also beginning to emerge, perhaps in reaction to Vasari, whom Van Vaernewyck mentions by name. A series of engraved *Portraits of Some Celebrated Artists of the Low Countries* was published just after the iconoclasm, in 1572, by the humanist writer Dominicus Lampsonius (1532–1599), completing the work begun by the publisher Hieronymus Cock (c.1510–1570).

It is clear from all of this that art became controversial in religious circles at precisely the same time as it was gaining authority in terms of cultural heritage. The history of the Ghent altarpiece reveals the collision between these two systems of value. To end this section we need to consider what was so special about this altarpiece.

Figure 4.16 Hubert and Jan van Eyck, *Adam*, detail from the left wing of *The Ghent Altarpiece*, 1432, oil on panel. St Bavo's cathedral, Ghent. Photo: © Hugo Maertens/Lukas – Art in Flanders VZW

Figure 4.17 Hubert and Jan van Eyck, *The Adoration of the Mystic Lamb*, panel from *The Ghent Altarpiece*, 1432, oil on panel. St Bavo's cathedral, Ghent. Photo: © Hugo Maertens/Lukas – Art in Flanders VZW

Activity

You should allow about 15 minutes for this activity.

Look very closely at the panels of Adam and of the Adoration of the Holy Lamb (Figures 4.16 and 4.17), then think about the altarpiece as a whole. What possible reasons can you think of as to why this altarpiece was singled out for such admiration? What do you admire about it? Make sure that you check the dimensions of the altarpiece to get a sense of its size.

Discussion

There are several points that you might have noticed, such as the sheer size, ambition and complexity of the altarpiece with its many panels. When the altarpiece is open the five panels of the lower storey read as one continuous picture, and this is difficult to do across more than 5 metres. It is the unified landscape setting that makes this work. The artists use a very high viewpoint, as if we are looking down on the scene, and this makes it easier to represent the sweep of landscape into the distance. For 1432, this is sophisticated landscape painting and clever setting of figure groups within that landscape.

You may also have thought about the lifelike qualities of the panels: there are lots of naturalistic details: the identifiable bushes in the landscape of the Adoration of the Holy Lamb; the flower-strewn grass; the falling water in the fountain of life and the ripples where the drops meet the transparent surface of the water below. Adam's anatomy and gestures are also very convincing, and his feet create the illusion that he is about to step out of the picture. You may also have considered the plausible light and shade on the body, which makes him look three-dimensional even though this is a flat painting, or details such as the faint hairs on his chest, his musculature and the undulation in his flesh – look at the dimple in his right thigh, for example. This is real virtuoso painting.

Interestingly, De Heere and Van Vaernewyck also commented on these lifelike qualities in their various writings. Convincing detail and the illusion of life were features admired then as now. Ways of seeing and systems of value change markedly from one context and period to the next, so it is interesting to note that there can also be these continuities.

This study of the Ghent altarpiece has encouraged you to look carefully at a work of art not just as a document of history but as an object in its own right. Some of the questions it raises about the meaning and significance of images will be considered again in Book 4.

Conclusion

This chapter has introduced you to the power of things regarded as so objectionable or dangerous that they had to be destroyed in acts of iconoclasm. They were considered symbols of a Catholic Church which a growing number of evangelicals across Europe believed needed to be cleansed and reformed during the Reformation period. Encouraged by their preachers, these evangelicals often took matters into their own hands in order to bring about religious change by attacking and destroying statues, images and other objects in their local Catholic churches. In some cases the iconoclasts were either assisted or restrained by local authorities and their evangelical leaders, as you have seen in the cases of Wittenberg and Zurich; while other iconoclastic undertakings were driven forward by popular force, as you have seen in the examples from the Netherlands in general and Haarlem in particular. Although the Protestant Reformation was a movement that spread rapidly across Europe (and, eventually, beyond), it took different forms in different places, as illustrated by our focus on iconoclasm. And, as we have seen, the Reformation's challenge to the authority of the Catholic Church also impacted on various kinds of religious art, including music and paintings.

We have attempted to trace these changes mainly from the perspective of the historian, using contemporary (or primary) sources, both written texts and visual images. In the case of the etching by Frans Hogenberg showing iconoclasts in action, we have also considered different scholarly interpretations of this source. Since the historian's task involves not merely assembling texts and objects from the past but also interpreting them in the quest to understand that past, we can see from these examples how careful the historian's analysis needs to be. In building up our understanding of the past, we also need to have as broad an awareness as possible of the contexts within which our sources were created – a theme we shall return to in the historical case study that forms the first part of Book 4 of this module.

Activity

Meanwhile, to broaden out your study of iconoclasm and connect it back to some of the topics you were introduced to in Book 1, you may want to work through the online activity 'Interview with Christopher Pinney', which you can find on the Study Planner of the module website.

References

Bonnet, J. (ed.) (1858) *Letters of John Calvin*, vol. 4, London, David Constable.

Brandt, W.I. (ed.) (1962) *Luther's Works: Christian in Society II*, Luther's Works series, vol. 45, Calgary, Augsburg Fortress Press.

De Heere, L. (1969) *Den Hof en Boomgaerd der Poesien*, ed. W. Waterschoot, Zwolle, W.E.J. Tjeenk Willink.

Dhanens, E. (1973) *Van Eyck: The Ghent Altarpiece*, London, Allen Lane.

Duke, A., Lewis, G. and Pettegree, A. (eds) (1992) *Calvinism in Europe 1540–1610: A Collection of Documents*, Manchester, Manchester University Press.

Michalski, S. (1993) *The Reformation and the Visual Arts: The Protestant Image Question in Western and Eastern Europe*, London, Routledge.

Palmer Wandel, L. (1994) *Voracious Idols and Violent Hands: Iconoclasm in Reformation Zurich, Strasbourg, and Basel*, Cambridge, Cambridge University Press.

Van Vaernewyck, M. (1872–81) *Van die beroerlicke tijden in die Nederlanden, en voornamelijk in Ghendt 1566–1568*, ed. F. Vanderhaeghen, 5 vols, Ghent, C. Annoot-Braeckman.

Wolffe, J. (2008) 'Tradition and Dissent in English Christianity', in Price, C. (ed.) *Tradition and Dissent* (AA100 Book 2), Milton Keynes, The Open University.

Further reading

If you would like to read more about the Reformation in general, Patrick Collinson's paperback book is a good place to start. For a more specific focus on iconoclasm in the Reformation, Carlos Eire's *War Against the Idols* is an older but still readily available text.

Collinson, C. (2003) *The Reformation*, London, Phoenix.

Eire, C.M.N. (1986) *War against the Idols: The Reformation of Worship from Erasmus to Calvin*, Cambridge, Cambridge University Press.

Reading 4.1 Karlstadt, 'On the Abolition of Images'

Source: 'Karlstadt: On the Abolition of Images and that There Should Be No Beggars among Christians (January 27, 1522)' in Lindberg, C. (ed.) (2000) *The European Reformations Sourcebook*, Oxford, Blackwell, p. 57.

See how God forbids all kinds of images, ... God says you shall not worship them, you shall not even honor them. Therefore, God forbids all veneration [of images] and breaks down the papist refuge which by their agility always does violence to the Scriptures and makes black white and evil good. Notwithstanding, one of them may say: Indeed, I do not worship images. I do not honor them for their sake, but rather for the sake of the saints whom they represent. God answers briefly and with few words. Thou shalt not worship them. Thou shalt not honor them. Gloss as you can, you shall in fact not worship them. You shall not bend your knee before them; you shall not light candles before them. ...

Now I will and shall say to pious Christians that all of you who stand in fear of an image have idols in your hearts. ...

Thus shall you deal with them, says God (Deut. 7:5): You shall overturn and overthrow their altars. You shall break their images to pieces. You shall hew down their pillars and burn up their carved images. We have no godly altars but rather heathen or human ones, as noted in Ex. 20:4. Therefore Christians shall abolish them. ... The highest authorities should also abolish images. ...

[O]ur magistrates should not wait until the priests of Baal purge out their wooden vessels and required hindrances. For they will never begin to do it. The highest civil authorities should command and do this. ...

I say to you that God has forbidden images no less nor with less purpose than murder, stealing, robbery, adultery, and the like. ...

Reading 4.2   Luther, 'The Lenten Sermons'

Source: 'Luther: The Invocavit Sermons (March 9, 1522)' in Lindberg, C. (ed.) (2000) *The European Reformations Sourcebook*, Oxford, Blackwell, pp. 62–3.

The summons of death comes to us all, and no one can die for another. Every one must fight his own battle with death by himself, alone. We can shout into another's ears, but every one must himself be prepared for the time of death, for I will not be with you then, nor you with me. Therefore every one must himself know and be armed with the chief things which concern a Christian. And these are what you, my beloved, have heard from me many days ago.

In the first place, we must know that we are the children of wrath, and all our works, intentions, and thoughts are nothing at all. …

Secondly, that God has sent his only-begotten Son that we may believe in him and that whoever trusts in him shall be free from sin and a child of God, …

Thirdly, we must also have love and through love we must do to one another as God has done to us through faith. For without love faith is nothing, … And here, dear friends, have you not grievously failed? …

Fourthly, we also need patience. …

[…]

Love, therefore, demands that you have compassion on the weak, as all the apostles had. …

In short, I will preach it, teach it, write it, but I will constrain no man by force, for faith must come freely without compulsion. Take myself as an example. I opposed indulgences and all the papists, but never with force. I simply taught, preached, and wrote God's Word; otherwise I did nothing. And while I slept [see Mark 4:26–9], or drank Wittenberg beer with my friends Philip and Amsdorf, the Word so greatly weakened the papacy that no prince or emperor ever inflicted such losses upon it. I did nothing; the Word did everything. Had I desired to foment trouble, I could have brought great bloodshed upon Germany; indeed, I could have started such a game that even the emperor would not have been safe. But what would it have been? Mere fool's play. I did nothing; I let the Word do its work. …

Therefore it should have been preached that images were nothing and that no service is done to God by erecting them; then they would have fallen of themselves. That is what I did. …

Now, although it is true and no one can deny that the images are evil because they are abused, nevertheless we must not on that account reject them, nor condemn anything because it is abused. This would result in utter confusion. God has commanded us in Deut. 4 [:19] not to lift up our eyes to the sun [and the moon and the stars], etc., that we may not worship them, for they are created to serve all nations. But there are many people who worship the sun and the stars. Therefore we propose to rush in and pull the sun and stars from the skies. No, we had better let it be. Again, wine and women bring many a man to misery and make a fool of him [Ecclus. 19:2; 31:30]; so we kill all the women and pour out all the wine. Again, gold and silver cause much evil, so we condemn them. Indeed, if we want to drive away our worst enemy, the one who does us the most harm, we shall have to kill ourselves, for we have no greater enemy than our own heart. …

Reading 4.3 'Advice Concerning the Mass and Images', 10–19 December 1523

Source: Quoted in Palmer Wandel, L. (1994) *Voracious Idols and Violent Hands: Iconoclasm in Reformation Zurich, Strasbourg, and Basel,* **Cambridge, Cambridge University Press, p. 82.**

First, it is our opinion that the retables should be immediately closed and not opened again until further notice. They are closed anyway during times of fasting, and the other images are covered. The silver, gold, or otherwise bejeweled images should no longer be brought out, either for weddings or for other days, but instead the highest treasures [*schatz*] of the Word of God should be carried in the hearts of human beings, not the idols before their faces.

2. Next we hold to the most recently issued order, namely that no one is to take any image whatsoever either into or out of the temples, unless he had put them therein before or the majority of an entire congregation decided itself to remove them, and that all removals should be without disgrace, sport, or wickedness, or any wanton manner that might anger anyone.

3. Last: Since it has now been discovered through the Word of God that the mass is not a sacrifice, and also that one should not have images, and since certain pastors in our city moreover agitate constantly against them, with rebellious, irritating, and unfounded words, it is our opinion, to speak to them in that or this form, [to use] fines or the stripping of their benefices, that they do not bring God's Word to nothing.

Reading 4.4 Calvin, 'On Images'

Source: Calvin, J. (1994 [1559]) *Institutes of the Christian Religion*
(trans. H. Beveridge), Grand Rapids, MI, William B. Eerdmans,
pp. 101–2.

But [...] let us here consider, whether it is expedient that churches
should contain representations of any kind, whether of events or human
forms. First, then, if we attach any weight to the authority of the
ancient Church, let us remember, that for five hundred years, during
which religion was in a more prosperous condition, and a purer
doctrine flourished, Christian churches were completely free from visible
representations [...] Hence their first admission as an ornament to
churches took place after the purity of the ministry had somewhat
degenerated. I will not dispute as to the rationality of the grounds on
which the first introduction of them proceeded, but if you compare the
two periods, you will find that the latter had greatly declined from the
purity of the times when images were unknown. What then? Are we to
suppose that those holy fathers, if they had judged the thing to be
useful and salutary, would have allowed the Church to be so long
without it? Undoubtedly, because they saw very little or no advantage,
and the greatest danger in it, they rather rejected it intentionally and on
rational grounds, than omitted it through ignorance or carelessness. This
is clearly attested by [St] Augustine in these words [...] 'When images
are thus placed aloft in seats of honour, to be beheld by those who are
praying or sacrificing, though they have neither sense nor life, yet from
appearing as if they had both, they affect weak minds just as if they
lived and breathed,' &c. And again, in another passage [...] he says,
'The effect produced, and in a manner extorted, by the bodily shape, is,
that the mind, being itself in a body, imagines that a body which is so
like its own must be similarly affected,' &c. A little farther on he says,
'Images are more capable of giving a wrong bent to an unhappy soul,
from having mouth, eyes, ears, and feet, than of correcting it, as they
neither speak, nor see, nor hear, nor walk.' This undoubtedly is the
reason why John (1 John v.21) enjoins us to beware, not only of the
worship of idols, but also of idols themselves. And from the fearful
infatuation under which the world has hitherto laboured, almost to the
entire destruction of piety, we know too well from experience that the
moment images appear in churches, idolatry has as it were raised its
banner; because the folly of manhood cannot moderate itself, but
forthwith falls away to superstitious worship. Even were the danger less

imminent, still, when I consider the proper end for which churches are erected, it appears to me more unbecoming their sacredness than I well can tell, to admit any other images than those living symbols which the Lord has consecrated by his own word: I mean Baptism and the Lord's Supper, with the other ceremonies. By these our eyes ought to be more steadily fixed, and more vividly impressed, than to require the aid of any images which the wit of man may devise. Such, then, is the incomparable blessing of images – a blessing, the want of which, if we believe the Papists, cannot possibly be compensated!

Reading 4.5 Tanis and Horst on Hogenberg's *The Iconoclasm*

Source: Tanis, J. and Horst, D. (1993) *Images of Discord: A Graphic Interpretation of the Opening Decades of the Eighty Years' War,* **Grand Rapids, MI, Bryn Mawr College Library, William B. Eerdmans, p. 41.**

Nach wenigh Predication
Die Calvinsche Religion
Das bildensturmen fiengen an
Das nicht ein bildt davon bleib stan
Kap, Monstrantz, kilch, auch die altar
Und wess sonst dort vor handen war
Zerbrochen all in kurtzer stundt
Gleich gar vil leuten das ist kundt

After a little preaching
Of the Calvinist religion,
The breaking of images commenced
Which left no statue standing.
Cowl, monstrance, goblet, also the altar
And all else that was at hand,
All was broken in short time
As many people soon learned.

[…]

Hogenberg uses a conveniently dissected church to show all the possible forms of destruction of the church decorations. The destruction takes place at night, as is indicated by the various persons bearing torches. Statues are being pulled from their pedestals and chopped to pieces and stained glass windows are being broken. Further back in the church a man with an ax attacks a triptych standing on the altar, while two others tear liturgical garments to pieces. The two guards in the foreground do not seem able to take any action to prevent the iconoclasts from carrying out their business. Both point rather helplessly towards two men leaving the scene bearing torches and clubs, presumably heading towards their next target.

The text under Hogenberg's print refers to the preaching of the Calvinists, shortly after which the destruction started. The print shows also those less driven by religious fervor: two women leaving the scene with their aprons bulging with goods, while on the right two men carry away bags and a large basket. Behind them a man descends the stairs of the sacristy beside the church, hunched under an enormous sack, no doubt also filled with looted goods. Through the windows of the sacristy several of the perpetrators can be seen helping themselves to food and drink, while in the cellar wine gushes from the bashed wine barrels.

Reading 4.6 Mochizuki on Hogenberg's *The Iconoclasm*

Source: Mochizuki, M.M. (2008) *The Netherlandish Image after Iconoclasm, 1566–1672: Material Religion in the Dutch Golden Age*, Aldershot, Ashgate, pp. 106–8.

A scene like Hogenberg's now frequently cited vision of Netherlandish iconoclasm presents another view of image removal, but this time as an organized and orderly endeavor, more in line with what happened in the days following iconoclasm in Haarlem. Part of a series printed in Cologne, where the Mechelen born artist had fled after being banned from the city by the Duke of Alva, the engraving was intended to refer to any Netherlandish church interior of the sixteenth century. Like a cross-section of a living organism prepared for microscopic analysis, Hogenberg presents the church frontally with the wall parallel to the picture plane removed, the viewer placed in the center of a symmetrical building. A row of men are arranged along a diagonal recession, their solidity and solidarity not unlike the sturdy columns, united in their effort to pull down statues atop each of the columns. Others are at work detaching triptych wings, removing graphic images and preparing to break the stained glass windows. Outside the church men and women depart with bundles and baskets filled to overflowing, while some chat or continue to go about their daily business uninterrupted and unalarmed. A soldier, a symbol of civic authority, stands just off-center in the foreground directing participants. This is not an image of violence or an expression of uncontrollable rage. The whole scene is more reminiscent of a well-orchestrated demolition. Townsmen and women, the majority not in the militia, seem joined in their work and not particularly surprised or even overly interested in the events of the day. This is a synchronized and sanitized version of iconoclasm. Only the slightest trace of potential violence is implied by the men with the raised clubs and a statue in the center foreground that has been decapitated and relieved of its lower limbs.

Chapter 5

Homer's *Iliad*: gods, heroes and the authority of ancient Greece

James Robson

Contents

Aims

This chapter will:

- help you to reflect further on the concepts of authority and canon by introducing you to Homer's epic poem, the *Iliad*
- introduce you to the theme of 'remaking authority' by looking at the afterlife of Homer's poetry alongside the poem 'Ceasefire' by Michael Longley
- give you an insight into the particular challenges of working with ancient Greek texts
- allow you to practise and develop skills of close listening and close reading.

Materials you will need

In this chapter, you will need to listen to the following audio recordings, which can be found on the module website:

- Homer's Iliad, Book 24: Priam and Achilles
- Homer's Iliad, Book 22: Achilles and Hector
- Homer's Iliad, Book 6: Hector and Andromache
- Michael Longley, 'Lapsed classicist'.

Introduction

In this chapter you will study part of one of the most canonical products of ancient Greek civilisation, Homer's *Iliad*, alongside the work of the modern Northern Irish poet Michael Longley, a number of whose poems have been inspired by Homeric material. As you work through the material in this chapter, you will gain an introduction to Homer and his world and consider further the themes of authority and the literary canon. Your studies will involve reading Longley's poetry and short extracts from Homer in detail, as well as listening to recordings of longer passages of the *Iliad*.

The chapter also extends your work with the discipline of Classical Studies. This is a broad subject area which can include the study of a number of aspects of the ancient worlds of Greece and Rome. In Book 1 you considered some of the physical remains of these civilisations, notably by exploring an archaeological perspective on the city of Pompeii and through a study of Greek vases. Classical Studies is also concerned with other aspects of ancient Greece and Rome, including languages, history, philosophy and literature (an aspect of which forms the subject of this chapter). One prominent branch of Classical Studies is what is known as Reception Studies, which is the study of the reuse and reconfiguration of classical literature, art and ideas by later artists and thinkers (namely, the way Greek and Roman culture has been 'received'). In this chapter, for example, you will look at the way in which a modern poet (Michael Longley) has reused and reconfigured a passage from Homer's *Iliad* in his poem 'Ceasefire'. The study of Longley's work will also lead you to consider broader questions about how the authority of a text is appropriated and renegotiated by later writers and cultures.

5.1   An Irishman's Homer: Michael Longley's 'Ceasefire'

On 3 September 1994 *The Irish Times* published a poem on its front page written by the Belfast-born poet Michael Longley (b.1939). The poem took as its inspiration an episode from Homer's **epic poem** the *Iliad*, in which the king of Troy, Priam, secretly travels across enemy lines at night to the hut of one of the Greeks who are fighting to take his city: the great warrior-hero Achilles. The two men are bound together by a grim fate: Achilles has recently killed Priam's son, Hector, and maltreated his corpse – in revenge for Hector's killing of Achilles' beloved companion, Patroclus. King Priam pleads for the return of his son's body, while Achilles is filled with thoughts of his own fate. For he knows that he, too, will soon die at Troy, far from his native land and his beloved father.

Here is Longley's poem in full:

Ceasefire

I

Put in mind of his own father and moved to tears
Achilles took him by the hand and pushed the old king
Gently away, but Priam curled up at his feet and
Wept with him until their sadness filled the building.

II

Taking Hector's corpse into his own hands Achilles
Made sure it was washed and, for the old king's sake,
Laid out in uniform, ready for Priam to carry
Wrapped like a present home to Troy at daybreak.

III

When they had eaten together, it pleased them both
To stare at each other's beauty as lovers might,
Achilles built like a god, Priam good-looking still
And full of conversation, who earlier had sighed:

IV

'I get down on my knees and do what must be done
And kiss Achilles' hand, the killer of my son.'

(Longley, 2006, p. 225)

For readers of *The Irish Times* that day, the poem's title and subject matter would have had a special resonance. As you will later hear if you listen to Longley's own account of his poem on the module website, 'Ceasefire' was written amid rumours that the Irish Republican Army (IRA) was on the verge of declaring a cessation of hostilities at a time when the 'Troubles' in Northern Ireland were the focus of considerable public and political attention. The IRA ceasefire came into effect at midnight on Wednesday, 31 August 1994, prompting *The Irish Times* to publish Longley's sonnet in its Saturday edition.

The Troubles

The 'Troubles' was originally the name given to a violent period of Irish history, 1919–23, when the struggle for independence from Britain led to a bitter civil war. The same name was later used about a period of conflict in Northern Ireland, dating from the late 1960s onwards. The issue at stake was the constitutional status of Northern Ireland, with Nationalists (or Republicans: largely Roman Catholic) looking for Northern Ireland to become part of a united Irish state, and Unionists (or Loyalists: mostly Protestant) wanting the province to remain part of the United Kingdom. The conflict was largely resolved by the Northern Irish peace process of the 1990s, which culminated in the Good Friday Agreement of 1998. However, political and social tensions – as well as sporadic violence – have continued into the twenty-first century.

One of the hugely interesting aspects of a poem like 'Ceasefire', I think, is the way that it has such firm roots in two very different contexts – the ancient and the modern – and how these two contexts play off each other. For me, reading the poem with the 1990s Irish political and social context in mind lends a poignant and striking relevance to its themes of death, grief, empathy and the painful realities of coming to terms with one's (former) enemies. But the poem is also a reworking of a famous moment from an ancient poem – a sequence of 200 or so lines of verse from Book 24 of Homer's *Iliad* – and so evokes a very different world, too: the epic poetry of ancient Greece, with its tales of godlike heroes and monumental battles. The poem therefore brings together the mythical past and the tangible present in what for me is a hugely stimulating way, with the two contexts illuminating each other.

The canonical poetry of Homer is thus integrated with contemporary events, the authority of the Greek text providing a parallel to Northern Ireland's memorable recent history.

Activity

You should allow about 20 minutes for this activity.

I'd now like you to perform a brief activity regarding 'Ceasefire'. One point that struck me is that the day it was published there must have been a great variation among the readers of *The Irish Times* in the extent to which they were familiar with Homer's poem: for some readers this would have been the first time they had encountered the story of Priam and Achilles (as it might now be for you), whereas others would have been more or less familiar with the events of this episode of the *Iliad*. I should like you to think about how the reactions of these two different groups of readers might have varied, by considering the following questions:

1   How comprehensible is the poem to someone encountering the figures of Achilles and Priam for the first time?

2   What might a reader familiar with the *Iliad* have gained from the poem that another reader (one unfamiliar with the poem) might not?

To help you with this, you might like to refer back to the opening paragraph of this section, where some key events of the *Iliad* are summarised.

Re-read 'Ceasefire' now and reflect on these questions before moving on to the discussion.

Discussion

1   As a student of the ancient world, I found it challenging to think myself into the position of someone who had never encountered the *Iliad* before. Looking at 'Ceasefire' from this perspective, however, I was struck by the way in which Longley selects and introduces the characters and events of his poem. In addition to the mention of the city of Troy, we find only three proper names there – Achilles, Priam and Hector – and by the end of the poem we are left in no doubt as to who these people are and what their relationship is to each other. We are told twice that Priam is an 'old king' (lines 2 and 6) and his age is also alluded to in lines 1 (where he reminds Achilles of 'his own father') and 11 (where he is described as 'good-looking still'). The mention of 'father' in line 1 also helps to establish Achilles' age relative to Priam's, and in the last line – if the reader has not worked it out before – we are made painfully aware of the relationship between the two men: Achilles is the killer of Priam's son, Hector.

Longley is also careful to leave the context of the encounter fairly
open: few details of time or place are evoked, and so in one respect it
doesn't matter whether the reader knows where Troy is or that the
setting is ancient (tellingly, the hut in which the action of this episode
of the *Iliad* takes place is referred to simply as a 'building' (line 4);
and did you note how a subtle nod was also given to the military
context by the use of the word 'uniform' in line 7?).

2   I have already begun to allude to some of the elements which a
reader familiar with the *Iliad* might have noted about 'Ceasefire', such
as how some features of the Priam–Achilles episode are made less
specific than in the original poem – like the use of the word 'building'
in place of 'hut'. Another detail I spotted was the ritual washing of
Hector's corpse. The washing of the body was an important element
of burial ritual in the ancient Greek world and could be thought of as
being especially necessary in the case of Hector's body: in the *Iliad*,
Achilles defiles the corpse by attaching it to his chariot each day and
dragging it around the burial mound of his dead companion,
Patroclus. Interestingly, the washing of the body also plays an
important role in the Irish funerary tradition, and so here we have a
good example of Longley finding a communality between the two
cultures. The night-time setting of the encounter is also evoked ('at
daybreak': line 8), as is the frequent description of Achilles in the *Iliad*
as 'godlike' (in line 11 he is 'built like a god'). Perhaps more striking
still is the final rhyming couplet (that is, the last two lines) of the poem
where Priam kisses Achilles' hand. In Book 24 of the *Iliad*, we are told
right at the beginning of the episode that Priam kisses Achilles' hand
as he enters his tent, whereas in 'Ceasefire' the description of the
kiss is postponed. In Longley's poem, then, special emphasis is
placed on Priam's act of supplication, with the powerful two-line
speech which ends the poem expressing what for a contemporary
audience must have been highly challenging and uncomfortable ideas
about the process of reconciliation.

Don't worry if your answer to the second question wasn't as full as
mine: even if you have encountered Homer before, you are not
expected to remember every detail of his poem. Later on in this chapter
you will get a chance to look at a translation of the original Homeric
sequence from the *Iliad* and therefore to make your own comparisons
between the two texts.

So far we have been concentrating on how the details of the poem both
correspond to and subtly reconfigure various elements of Book 24 of
the *Iliad* – a far longer sequence that Longley has compressed into 14

lines. But to look at the wood and not just the trees for a moment, part of the excitement of 'Ceasefire' for me as someone familiar with the *Iliad* is that it breathes fresh life into Homer by showing the Priam–Achilles episode in a new light, full of raw emotions and contemporary resonances. As I intimated above, I think that the modern and ancient contexts illuminate each other in 'Ceasefire' in a truly dynamic way – though perhaps you have your own views about a piece of poetry which is, after all, designed to appeal to the emotions as much as the intellect.

This poem is also interesting to consider from the point of view of authority. What difference does it make that 'Ceasefire' is based on a sequence from such a canonical poem as the *Iliad*? Personally, I find this an extremely difficult question to answer. For me as a classicist, the Homeric theme certainly captured my attention – and it also, perhaps, lends the poem an air of authority that it might otherwise not possess. But by inviting comparison with such a canonical work of literature as the *Iliad*, Longley could be said to have made his job difficult: the poem has a lot to live up to! For me, the circumstances of the poem's publication created a further set of expectations, too. The fact that it was published on the front page of *The Irish Times* at a key stage in Northern Ireland's history influenced the way that I read the poem, making me expect that it would be 'important' in some way.

5.2 Introducing the *Iliad* – Book 24: Priam and Achilles

So far we have been considering Homer's *Iliad* somewhat in the abstract, as a text with which some people are familiar and others not. Part of the purpose of this chapter, however, is to introduce you to the *Iliad* – both as a work of art in its own right and also as a poem that holds a key place in the literary canon and has exercised huge influence over western literature.

The *Iliad* was originally composed in a form of ancient Greek (a language which has much in common with the language spoken in Greece and Cyprus today) and so to engage with the poem today means working with a translation of it. There is a large range of English-language translations of the *Iliad* to choose from, but for your work in this chapter you will be listening to (and reading) a version by the British/Canadian scholar Ian Johnston – a translation which has been chosen for its clarity and liveliness. The fact you are working in translation shouldn't worry you unduly, although it does inevitably mean missing out on the rhythm and other sound effects of the original, such as alliteration. Please note that it is the line numbers of the translation (and not the original poem) that are routinely given in this chapter.

> **Translating ancient texts**
>
> Translation Studies is a rich and complex area of scholarship. Historically, distinctions have often been made between translations that capture the 'letter' of the original text ('literal' translations) and those that convey the text's 'spirit' (and many translators aim to convey both the 'letter' and the 'spirit', of course). You may recall, for example, that in the translation of the *Metta Sutta* you read in Chapter 1, the translator, Saddhatissa, prioritised maintaining the 'spirit' over adhering to the rhythm of the original text.
>
> One way in which the translation of the *Iliad* you are working with in this chapter clearly differs from the original Greek is that long sentences are often broken up, so there are fewer words in each line of verse. And so, in one sense, the translation might be said not to be faithful to the 'letter' of the Greek, since the rhythms of the original have been altered. But, in another sense, it could be argued that the 'spirit' has been preserved, with these shorter lines helping to convey something of the pace and flow of the original poem.

Activity

You should allow about 20 minutes for this activity.

As an initial encounter with Homer's poetry, I should like you to listen to an audio recording of the sequence from Book 24 of the *Iliad* on which Longley's 'Ceasefire' is based. You can find this recording, entitled 'Homer's *Iliad*, Book 24: Priam and Achilles', on the module website.

The purpose of listening to this audio recording is simply for you to enjoy the poem and to accustom yourself to Homeric idiom (albeit in translation). Note that the text does not appear in your printed materials: for the moment you should focus on listening to the poem – which means you will experience it in a similar way to the original audience who, as we shall see, would also have heard rather than read Homer's poetry.

Before you begin, a brief word on the context of this passage. Both Achilles and Priam have been sent messages from the gods: Achilles has been instructed to return Hector's body, and Priam has been told that he will receive safe passage if he visits the Greeks, who are encamped near their ships. On his journey from Troy, Priam encounters a handsome Greek who guides him to Achilles' hut. On arrival, this young man reveals to Priam that he is in fact the god Hermes, sent to provide a divine escort.

You will also find it helpful to know that in this extract Greece is referred to as 'Achaea' and the Greeks as 'the Achaeans', whereas Troy is also called by its alternative name, Ilion (from which the word 'Iliad' derives: that is, the poem about Troy).

Listen to the audio recording now.

Discussion

I hope you enjoyed listening to the passage and that you were able to spot the details you had already encountered in Longley's poem. I hope, too, that you were able to get to grips with all the people and places mentioned in these lines: unfamiliar proper names can seem daunting at first, as can some of the other features of Homeric poetry which are perhaps less familiar to modern readers, such as repetition of lines and phrases or the preponderance of (often lengthy) speeches. You will look in more detail at some of the distinctive features of Homer's style later on, but for now it will be useful for you to gain a brief overview of the context in which the *Iliad* was composed and to consider the place of Homeric poetry in the literary canon.

Figure 5.1 Priam in the presence of Achilles. Athenian red-figure *skyphos* by the Brygos Painter, *c*.480 BCE, height 25cm. Found at Cerveteri, Italy. Kunsthistorisches Museum, Vienna, Inv.3710.ARV 380.171. Photographed by Erich Lessing. Photo © akg-images/Erich Lessing

5.3 Homeric poetry and the literary canon

By any measure, the *Iliad* is an extraordinary poem. Composed some time towards the end of the eighth century BCE (perhaps *c*.720–700 BCE, but maybe slightly later), it is commonly viewed as the earliest surviving work of European literature, slightly pre-dating the *Odyssey* (the other epic poem attributed to Homer). Its age alone gives it a unique place in the western literary canon and no doubt goes part of the way to explaining the authority with which it has been invested by subsequent generations and civilisations. Despite many later traditions concerning who 'Homer' was, very little is known about the author – including, as a matter of fact, whether the composition of the poems can really be attributed to one individual. This is largely because the poems date from a period in Greek history about which we know relatively little and from which few written records survive: indeed, this is an era when writing was far from widespread in mainland Greece. This fact is also important for understanding the poems themselves, since there is every reason to believe that the *Iliad* and *Odyssey* were composed without the aid of writing. And so the poems are said to be the product of 'oral composition', which in turn has consequences for how we talk about them: Homer is a 'poet' or 'author', not a 'writer'; and students of Homer talk of the *Iliad* and *Odyssey* as having been 'composed', not 'written'.

Given that these poems were either largely or entirely composed without the aid of writing, perhaps one of the most remarkable features about the Homeric epics is their length: the *Iliad* is a poem of some 15,000 lines, whereas the *Odyssey* stands at around 12,000 lines. The sheer scale of these poems would suggest, then, that in Homer's day a mature poetic tradition already existed, on which the author(s) of the *Iliad* and *Odyssey* were able to build. And this indeed seems to have been the case, since we have evidence of other epic poems dating from the Greek Dark Ages (*c*.1110–*c*.800 BCE), known to later Greeks but now lost. So it turns out that Homer was not the 'first' western poet: but, importantly, the *Iliad* is the oldest poem to have survived.

A further point I should like to draw your attention to is the context in which the poems would originally have been performed. Epic poetry was composed to be sung or chanted to the strain of a **lyre** (which would probably have provided musical support rather than full-blown melodic accompaniment). The traditional Homeric performer would have been a 'bard' (of whom we meet two examples in the *Odyssey*), who would have recited large chunks of poetry as entertainment in contexts such as religious festivals and banquets (each performance presumably covering only a section of a poem).

The last point I want to discuss in this section is the afterlife that the *Iliad* and *Odyssey* enjoyed. Homeric epic held an extremely influential position among later generations of Greeks and formed a keystone of their joint cultural heritage – something particularly significant given that 'Greece' was not a single political entity in ancient times, but rather a patchwork of city-states, which were often at war with one another. Episodes from Homeric poetry continued to be alluded to and reworked by later writers and artists: some of the illustrations in this chapter show vase-paintings inspired by scenes from the *Iliad*, for example. Probably at some point in the mid sixth century BCE, the Homeric epics began to be written down rather than just passed down orally from bard to bard, but it was to be some time before a single, standard version of each text emerged. Evidence suggests that there were sometimes significant variations between the different versions of the *Iliad* that had been passed down until the point (somewhere in the third or second century BCE) where scholars working at the library in Alexandria compiled a definitive version of the text. It is this era from which the manuscript pictured in Figure 5.2 dates. It was at this period, too, that the *Iliad* and *Odyssey* were each divided into 24 'books': one book for each letter of the Greek alphabet. The Priam–Achilles episode you've just listened to is to be found in Book 24 and therefore belongs to the closing section of the *Iliad*, which ends with Hector's funeral at Troy. The other sections of the poem you will study in this chapter are also among the most famous sections of the *Iliad*: Book 22, Achilles' battle with the Trojan warrior Hector; and Book 6, where the main protagonists are Hector and his wife, Andromache.

Nor was it just in ancient Greece that the Homeric epic proved influential. A direct line can be traced from Homer to other epic poems, such as Virgil's *Aeneid* (written in Latin in the first century BCE), Dante's *Divine Comedy* (written in Italian in the early fourteenth century) and Milton's *Paradise Lost* (written in English in the seventeenth century). All these works hold influential places in their own literary traditions. In addition to these epic poems on new themes, there have also been influential translations of Homer into English, such as those by George Chapman (published in 1598) and Alexander Pope

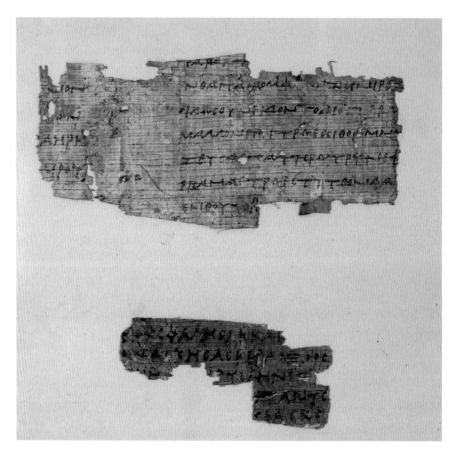

Figure 5.2 Papyrus fragment of Homer's *Iliad*, *c*.250 BCE, British Library, London, PAP 689. Photo: © British Library Board.

(published in 1715–20) which themselves inspired English poets to turn to Homeric themes. Interesting, too, is the popularity which Homer's epics have enjoyed among English-speaking readers over the last 100 years. The Penguin Classics translations of the *Odyssey* and *Iliad* (first published in 1946 and 1950, respectively) have sold well over 4 million copies between them, for example, and Homer was one of the most translated authors of the late twentieth century. Historically, Homeric epic has also inspired poems by Alfred, Lord Tennyson (1809–1892), William Butler Yeats (1865–1939) and W.H. Auden (1907–1973), and more recently has provided the impetus behind work by poets such as Michael Longley (as you have seen) and Christopher Logue (1926–2011) – as well as the St Lucian poet and playwright Derek Walcott (b.1930), whose poem *Omeros* has itself gained something of the status of a modern classic. To explain the considerable influence that Homeric poetry has enjoyed, it is evidently not enough simply to point to the fact that these epic poems are very old. So let us look at Homer's poetry in greater detail in an attempt to explain the place that the *Iliad* has traditionally occupied in the canon and why Homeric poetry has inspired – and continues to inspire – later generations.

5.4   The subject matter of the *Iliad*

Before looking at specific passages of the *Iliad*, it will be useful for you to gain an overview of the poem as a whole, so in this section I shall focus on its plot and subject matter.

The poem is set during the Trojan war – a conflict which the ancient Greeks thought had taken place several hundred years before the *Iliad* was composed (the traditional date for the destruction of Troy is 1184 BCE). According to Greek legend this war had lasted for ten years, during which an assorted army of Greeks had lain siege to the ancient city of Troy before finally claiming victory. Troy is thought to correspond to the site of Hissarlik in modern-day Turkey – a town which, as modern archaeologists have discovered, met a violent end at roughly the time in question (*c*.1220 BCE).

Modern scholars may continue to debate the extent to which the Trojan war of myth was a historical reality, but for the ancient Greeks this was an important episode in their collective past. Indeed, the original audiences of the *Iliad* would have been familiar with a whole series of myths connected with the Trojan war, knowledge of which is taken for granted in the poem. These include how the war was caused by the abduction from Greece of Helen, wife of Menelaus, by Paris, the son of the Trojan king; how the Greek fleet sailed to Troy under the leadership of Agamemnon; and how Troy was eventually captured thanks to a trick (the giant wooden horse which the Trojans took into their city unaware that it contained a number of Greek warriors). But rather than tell the story of the Trojan war from beginning to end, the action of the poem spans only 50 days and focuses on just a handful of days' fighting. As we find out in the first two lines of the *Iliad*, the story is essentially that of the 'Wrath of Achilles' and its consequences: first, Achilles' anger at the arrogant behaviour of Agamemnon (who takes away a girl given to Achilles as a battle prize); then Achilles' withdrawal from the battle, resulting in the losses suffered by the Greek forces; Patroclus' death at the hands of Hector; Achilles' return to battle; the death of Hector and the maltreatment of his corpse by Achilles; and, finally, the Priam–Achilles episode.

The focus of the action in the *Iliad* is undoubtedly the fighting, and battle scenes take up a large amount of the narrative. The devastating and disruptive effect of war is a constant theme in the poem but, importantly, war is also a way for warriors on both sides to win honour

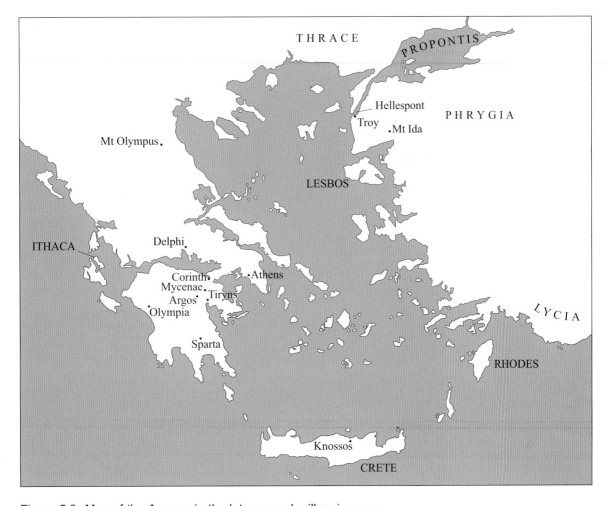

Figure 5.3 Map of the Aegean in the late second millennium BCE

and future glory (for example by killing others) and battle is presented as an engrossing spectacle in itself. Homeric society also has a clear pecking order: the central characters of the poem are not the ordinary soldiers but rather the elite Greek and Trojan leaders who, in this mythical past, are presented as stronger, braver and more beautiful than any men who have lived since. The ancient Greeks worshipped a whole series of major and minor deities: these gods, too, feature as characters in the poem and some, such as Athena and Apollo, play key roles in the fighting, weighing in on the side of either the Greeks or the Trojans. Fate also plays an important role in the poem: just as the original audience, through its familiarity with the relevant myths, would have known which of the heroes in the poem survived the war and which died at Troy, so are many heroes in the *Iliad* aware of the fate that will

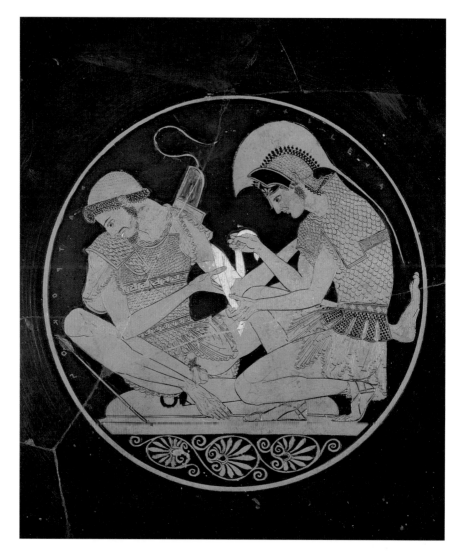

Figure 5.4 Achilles tending to Patroclus, who has been wounded by an arrow. Athenian red-figure *kylix* (drinking cup) by the Sosias Painter, *c.*500 BCE, 20cm diameter. Found at Vulci, Italy. Staatliche Museen, Berlin, inv. F2278. Photo: © The Bridgeman Art Library

befall them. And so, for example, part of the poignancy of the scene which you listened to earlier is that Achilles already knows that he is destined to die in battle and never to see his homeland and father again.

5.5 Book 22: Achilles and Hector

You are now going to listen to a short extract from Book 22 of the *Iliad* (this comes two books prior to the Priam–Achilles episode you have already heard).

Activity

Find the audio recording 'Homer's *Iliad*, Book 22: Achilles and Hector' on the module website. The recording, which lasts for just over 7 minutes, describes the encounter between Achilles and Hector outside the walls of Troy when Hector's fate is sealed.

You should listen to the extract at least twice. First, listen to the recording all the way through, aiming simply to enjoy it as a piece of poetry. Then, once you have listened to the extract for the first time, turn to Reading 5.1. This contains the words of the extract as well as accompanying notes to help you with the proper names and other details with which you may not be familiar. You may find it useful to follow this text as you listen to the extract again. As you listen for the second time, try to answer the following questions (these pick up on points made in the discussion of the *Iliad* you have just read and also look forward to further work you will do on the poem):

1 What is the setting of the scene?

2 What are the activities mentioned in this extract which have no direct connection with war and/or the ongoing battle between Achilles and Hector?

3 Which gods play an active part in the events described? Whose side are they on (if any)?

You should allow about 30 minutes for this activity.

Discussion

1 As befits a chase scene, the specific setting changes throughout the passage, though the location as a whole can neatly be summed up as 'under the walls of Troy' (l.181). The emphasis in this passage is often on movement: Hector's shaking (l.171) soon turns into a run and then we meet a flurry of verbs such as 'run', 'pursue', 'race' and 'dash', with all the time Hector's 'limbs working feverishly' (l.181). As Achilles pursues Hector, a number of sites they pass by are mentioned: the 'lookout' and 'wind-swept fig tree' (l.182); the 'wagon track' (l.183); and, in particular, the hot and cold springs (ll.184–9) and the washing tubs (ll.189–93).

245

2   The mention of the washing tubs forms the basis of a short digression about their use in peacetime. This is a place where the women of Troy used to linger to do their daily chores in a time before the Trojan plain had become a battleground: now it is a place past which men hurry in a life-and-death pursuit. This washing, then, is one arresting example of an activity which in one sense has no direct connection with the Achilles and Hector episode, but which nevertheless provides a striking contrast to the ongoing action. You probably noted others. I found myself particularly struck by the **simile**s of the falcon pursuing the pigeon (ll.175–80: 'Just as a mountain falcon …') and the hound chasing the deer (ll.234–9: 'Just as in the mountains …') – two images associated with nature (the 'natural' violence of animals perhaps contrasting with the 'unnatural' violence of war?). I also noted the simile of the horse race (ll.199–203: 'Just as some horses …') – an activity which presumably would have taken place outside the walls of Troy in times of peace, but which is now impossible for 'horse-taming Hector' to perform while the city is under siege (we shall look at these and other similes later). Zeus also comments on the sacrifices Hector used to make on Mount Ida (ll.209–11) – and so here is another activity that is distanced from the present action in both place and time (presumably these sacrifices occurred before the war, when it was safe to leave the city). An added irony here is that the Trojans will hold games and sacrifices outside the walls of Troy after Hector's death (a detail you may recall from the extract from Book 24 you listened to earlier). Another counterpoint to the pursuit of Hector by Achilles comes in the form of the discussion between the gods: this takes place on Mount Olympus (the home of the gods), far away from the scene of battle – though, of course, the outcome of their ruminations will have a direct impact on the action.

3   The gods involved in this episode are Athena, Apollo and Zeus. Most of the gods who live on Olympus are partisan in the *Iliad*. Athena is on the side of the Greeks, for example, and so as a supporter of Achilles entreats Zeus not to spare Hector (ll.220–5). Apollo, on the other hand, is on the Trojan side and so favours Hector, helping him to run faster (l.254) and only abandoning him when his fate is sealed (l.265). As the king of the gods, Zeus does not support any particular side in the *Iliad*, but rather intervenes sometimes on behalf of the Greeks, sometimes on behalf of the Trojans. Here he does pity Hector, but nevertheless allows Athena to intervene on Achilles' behalf. He later weighs the fates of the two heroes, thus condemning Hector to death (ll.260–4).

This episode from Book 22 is one of the best known in the *Iliad* – which in itself raises interesting questions about whether some sections of famous works are more 'canonical' than others. Examining key scenes such as this allows you to deepen your knowledge of the poem and to familiarise yourself with some of the characteristic features of Homeric poetry, such as the use of speeches and digressions; the intervention of the gods in human affairs; and so on. One striking technique that Homer uses in this passage is to focus on inanimate objects, in this case the washing tubs. We see another example of this in the next passage you will look at, when Hector's plumed, shining helmet plays a central role in his encounter with his wife and son.

5.6 Book 6: Hector and Andromache

The final extract of the *Iliad* I should like you to focus on is taken from Book 6 and comes from earlier in the poem than the other extracts you study in this chapter, a time when Hector is still alive and well. The setting is the city of Troy itself and, unusually for the *Iliad*, Book 6 contains a number of female characters: the short scene you will study now, for example, details an encounter between Hector and his wife, Andromache.

The context is as follows. Hector has just been home but finds Andromache gone. He is told by his housekeeper, however, that 'she went to Ilion's great tower' to watch the fighting, as she has heard that the Trojans are in difficulty. When Hector finally meets up with his wife she is accompanied by a nurse and the couple's infant son, Astyanax.

Activity

You should allow about 30 minutes for this activity.

Find the audio recording 'Homer's *Iliad*, Book 6: Hector and Andromache' on the module website. The recording lasts approximately 10 minutes. You will find this part of the poem printed in Reading 5.2. As before, there are notes to help you with the proper names and other details.

Listen to the extract all the way through and consider the following question. In order to answer, you will need to listen to the extract a second time, or, alternatively, you may choose to work with the printed text.

With which characters (if any) do your sympathies lie, and why?

As you consider this question, remember to *collect evidence* for your response. Which lines contain important information? If you were preparing a short assignment in answer to this question, which parts of the text might you choose to quote? You might also like to think about how the text shapes your opinion either in favour of or against Hector, Andromache and Astyanax.

Discussion

I hope you managed to make some headway with this question. Here is my response to compare with your own, although you may well, of course, have come up with different points from me, especially as the judgement I have asked you to make is a subjective one. Whatever conclusion you come to, the most important thing is for you to be able to back up your points with reference to the text.

I shall start by looking at the character of Hector's wife, Andromache, who is portrayed as being in a highly emotional state in this passage (for instance, she runs to Hector at l.483 and is described as weeping at ll.496 and 594). She is in this state of emotion because she is greatly concerned about her husband's fate: the reason she has left the house, for example, is to watch the battle from the vantage point of one of Troy's high towers and when she first sees Hector she wastes no time in berating him for his 'warlike spirit' (l.498). As well as being emotional, she is certainly a pitiable character, too: we learn that her whole family has been wiped out by Achilles (ll.507–26) and she is eager to avoid both the miserable fate that will befall her should Troy be captured (ll.503–7) and the prospect of her son losing his father (l.529). But she is, I think, shown to be more than just a powerless, weeping wife: she also demonstrates some practical knowledge of war when she advises Hector where to station troops (ll.530–8). As a caring mother, who has suffered greatly, and feels great loyalty to her family, there is much to warm to in Andromache's character and, for my part, I certainly found her to be a sympathetic figure.

Hector is a more problematic figure, I think. The fact that he dismisses his wife's entreaties to stay in Troy rather than fight (ll.539–47) might make him seem harsh, for example. But Hector is not without warmth, as is demonstrated when he holds his son and kisses him (ll.581–2). The wish he then utters – that his son grow up to be not just strong and brave, but also the winner of 'bloody spoils' (l.590) – may well strike a modern reader as chilling, but it is also, I think, central to understanding Hector's character. Hector is earlier described as 'Troy's only guardian' (l.494) and what characterises him, in my view, is his sense of duty towards his people (indeed, at other points in the poem it is his sense of duty, rather than a love of battle, which leads him to carry on the fight). So Hector may be uncompromising and concerned with honour, but he is also loyal, brave and an impressive warrior (his comments at ll.540–7 are revealing here).

There are, of course, other minor figures that feature in this passage: the pitiable baby, Astyanax, who is frightened by his father's plumed helmet (ll.577–8), as well as the nurse and other servants (who, typically in the *Iliad*, are cast into the background somewhat). But taken as a whole, I found the Trojans that we meet in Book 6 to be a fairly sympathetic bunch – all the more so, perhaps, because the named individuals all have their own distinct personalities (the episode of the helmet even serves to breathe life into Astyanax). And in a poem composed in Greek for consumption by Greek-speaking audiences, the extent to which the audience is invited to sympathise with the Trojans is certainly noteworthy. The outcome of this war matters not just for the warriors fighting on the plain, but also for the inhabitants of the city of Troy, for whom a Greek victory will spell complete and utter ruin.

One point that struck me about this passage is the way in which the characters talk about the future. On plenty of occasions in the *Iliad*, characters say that they do not know what the future holds: just before this passage, for instance, Hector says that he has no idea if he'll return to his family once he rejoins the battle, and Andromache's plea to him not to stay in Troy and not to 'orphan your child and make me a widow' (ll.529–30) only makes sense if his destiny is not fixed. If she were convinced that he was going to die, there would be little point in trying to resist fate. So in one sense there is everything to play for in war, but, alongside this uncertainty as regards the future, there is also more than one mention of a fixed fate. Hector, for example, says that he 'knows the day is coming when sacred Ilion will be destroyed' (ll.548–9), but that 'No man will throw me down to Hades before my destined time' (ll.597–8). He also states that 'no one escapes his fate' (l.599).

ideas of fate .

Another intriguing aspect of the poem is that characters often talk about events that will (possibly) happen in the future and which the original audience, through their knowledge of myth, know will actually come to pass. In this passage, for example, Hector talks of his 'many noble brothers, who'll fall down in the dust, slaughtered' (ll.554–5) and of Andromache being led off 'as a slave' (l.559). These reminders of the fate of Troy may well serve to increase the pathos of the scenes (and so the tender moment that Astyanax shares with his parents is all the more poignant if we recall that the eventual capture of Troy will also spell his doom – he is tossed from Troy's walls by Achilles' son, Neoptolemus). For me, then, Homer manages to achieve quite a complex effect: if the Trojans all knew with certainty what fate had in store for them, then there would not be any dramatic tension – but they do not know, and so we see the battle through their eyes, with every day bringing the prospect of defeat or victory, and life and death hanging in the balance. In other words, the outcome of every moment of battle matters. However, Homer also manages to produce pathos by reminding his audience of what fate has in store for his characters: Hector's conversations with the various members of his family are to be among his last and the lives of the women we meet in Troy will soon be changed for ever.

5.7 Homeric similes

One notable feature of Homeric poetry – and one which, I think, is important to the theme of authority – is its similes. **Simile**s are, of course, common in our everyday speech and are introduced by words such as 'like', 'as' and 'just as' ('quiet as a mouse', 'run like the wind', and so on). Homeric similes have some unusual characteristics, however. Consider the simile you met in Book 22 (lines 175–80), describing how Achilles chases Hector:

> Just as a mountain falcon, the fastest creature
> of all the ones which fly, swoops down easily
> on a trembling pigeon as it darts off in fear,
> the hawk speeding after it with piercing cries,
> heart driving it to seize the prey – in just that way
> Achilles in his fury raced ahead.

Perhaps the most noteworthy feature of Homeric similes is their sheer length. Rarely in everyday speech – or even in other forms of literature, for that matter – do we find similes as extended as these. Homeric similes have been much discussed by scholars of the *Iliad* and the purpose of this section is to allow you to think about them further.

Activity

Reading 5.3 consists of a number of examples of Homeric similes. These are all taken from Book 13 of the *Iliad*, where the Trojans are attacking the Greek ships. Read these now and, as you do so, consider the following questions:

You should allow about 30 minutes for this activity.

1   The subject of these similes is largely the warriors – but to what kind of things are they compared? What major categories emerge?

2   What, if anything, do you think these similes add to the poem? How do they alter the reader's/listener's perspective on the action?

Discussion

1   As you will no doubt have noticed, the bulk of the imagery in these similes is taken from the realm of nature. Animals feature heavily (a hawk, a boar and a bull, for example), as do natural phenomena (I counted three references to winds, plus one lightning bolt) and trees (an ash, an oak, a poplar and a pine). Aside from this, we also find a comparison to a 'pampered child', to fire, to a 'rolling boulder' caught

in a torrent and, memorably, to beans and peas bouncing off a shovel. So, while there are some odd ones out, certain themes recur. Looking at these similes, I also noted that many of the images were connected with farming: we have the tending of sheep; the farmers' binding of the bull; the beans and peas on the threshing-room floor; and oxen ploughing a field. A number of the activities mentioned are communal, too: not just the binding of the bull, but also the felling of the tree ('by working men': I.466) and the mob who chase the boar. Perhaps you noticed other patterns.

2   For me what is interesting about these similes is the way they provide a counterpoint to the main action. Many of the similes conjure up a world of peacetime activities, for example, and so, I think, serve to remind the audience of how life is lived outside wartime. Images of weather, dust clouds, torrents and boulders provide the listener with examples of natural phenomena, and these again serve to contrast with the man-made phenomenon of war. The pictures of rural life, mountains and the wilds that we are often presented with also contrast with the life to which the Trojans (and to a large extent the Greeks, too) are reduced, confined as they are to their city because of the siege. Presumably, images of rural life and natural phenomena would also have been familiar to Homer's original audience, and so these similes would have functioned as an important bridge between their world and that of the poem.

When looking at these similes, I also found myself thinking about the impression of war they give. Many of the images of rural life and farming may be seen as suggestive of a far gentler and more appealing existence as lived in peacetime and so, from one point of view, they could be said to underline the brutality of war. And other similes, too – such as those which concern the havoc wreaked by winds, water and fire – could also be said to highlight the destructive force of war. But from another point of view, Homeric similes serve to glorify war by underlining its spectacle. The Trojan war is so spectacular that, on the one hand, its effects can be compared to the most impressive forces of nature; and, on the other, the scenes of rural life to which wartime activities are likened (ploughing, threshing, tending sheep) might reasonably be thought dull and everyday when compared with the memorable events taking place on the plain of Troy. This war is unique – so unique that each of these moments in the battle is sufficiently important to be recorded in an epic poem. The events to which they are compared, however, are generic: there will be countless examples in human history of winds rousing the sea, falling boulders and oxen ploughing fields. And so war may be destructive, but I think these similes also help to suggest that it is impressive.

Figure 5.5 Achilles and Ajax, a fellow Greek warrior, playing a board game. Athenian black-figure belly amphora by Exekias from Vulci, Italy, c.550–530 BCE. Vatican Museums and Galleries 344 (ABV 145.13). Photo: © The Bridgeman Art Library

A further point to make concerns the theme of this book: namely, authority. I would be inclined to argue that these extended similes help to lend the *Iliad* an air of authority since they are instrumental in persuading the audience that the poet has a detailed and subtle understanding of the events he is describing. After all, these similes give the impression that the poet knows what the war at Troy looked *like*, what people behaved *like*. Extended similes also betray a knowledge by the poet of other realms as well, beyond the scope of war (such as farming, nature, and so on). And so this helps to reinforce the impression we gain elsewhere that the poet's knowledge is vast: he is able to recount events in great detail and recite long speeches verbatim; and he is able to speak with knowledge not only about current events in the Greek camp, on the battlefield and in Troy, but also about events that happen on Olympus among the gods. Nor is time a limiting factor: in the course of the narrative we learn about events that happened in the past (such as the way in which the washing tubs were once used outside Troy) as well as future occurrences (such as the destruction of

Troy and the fate of its various inhabitants). Events that happen the world over (not just at Troy); events which occur among men, gods and animals (many specific, some generic); events which are taken from the present, past and future: all fall within the poet's comprehension. Few authors' reach is as vast.

5.8 The authority of Homer

At this point, I should like you to take the opportunity to reflect on the work you have done on the *Iliad* in this chapter by considering the following question.

Activity

What would you say to someone who had never studied Homer before if they asked you why the *Iliad* is thought to be an important poem?

You should allow about 20 minutes for this activity.

In answering this question, you should think about the reasons that Homer occupies the position he does in the literary canon (why do people consider Homer to be important? What evidence is there that the *Iliad* has been – and continues to be – thought important?). In addition, how can Homeric poetry be said to possess 'authority' (for instance in terms of tone, subject matter, style, and so on)?

After you have collected your thoughts, you should make a short list of points in answer to this question. You may find it useful at this stage to look over some parts of this chapter again.

Discussion

I found this a tough question to answer in many ways. Certainly, I found some of the points that struck me easier to put into words than others. Here, however, is my attempt at a short list – and your points may well differ from mine:

- Age. The fact that the *Iliad* is the oldest surviving work of western literature gives it a ready-made status, I think. In a similar way, we might be interested in the oldest surviving house in a town, or the oldest surviving example of a wristwatch. And while, as you have seen, scholarly and popular conceptions of which works are considered 'canonical' are subject to variation over time, the *Iliad*'s position as 'first' does a good deal to safeguard its continued high status.

- Quality. I would argue that the quality of the poetry also makes the *Iliad* an important and canonical work, though I appreciate that this is a subjective judgement (albeit one that many critics have shared). The work that you have done on the *Iliad* in this chapter should mean that you are now in a position to make your own judgements about the quality of the poem.

- Status. The fact that so many generations have respected Homer is itself a compelling reason for us as modern readers to afford the *Iliad* a high status. For example, the *Iliad* was an important poem for the Greeks of later generations (whose civilisation is also generally held in high regard). Homeric epic can also number 'great' authors among its imitators (the epics of Virgil and Milton are regarded as 'classics', too); the *Iliad* has been much translated and is still widely studied and read; and modern poets (such as Michael Longley, but also many others) still engage with and rework Homeric poetry. The regard that previous generations, as well as our own, have had for the *Iliad* provides a compelling reason to believe that it is an important work of art.

- Characters. The people of the *Iliad* are the great heroes of yesterday, figures immortalised in myth, stronger and more beautiful than those of the present day. The characters in the poem even include the gods. In a word, the central characters in the poem are 'important' figures in their society, which makes it tempting to think, perhaps, that the poem is 'important', too (common soldiers and servants barely feature in the poem, whereas the women who feature prominently tend to be the wives, lovers and mothers of heroes).

- Authorial knowledge. As discussed above, the author of the poem is highly informed: he displays detailed knowledge of the words and actions of Greeks, Trojans and gods alike; he relates events that happen across the known world; and he is just as knowledgeable about the past and future as he is about the present. The precision of detail and his powers of description (often in the form of similes) are also convincing evidence of the author's extensive overview. (Of course, in an ancient Greek context, Homer's superior knowledge would have been put down to the fact that he was divinely inspired by the goddess(es) of poetry, the Muse(s). There is an appeal to the Muse in the very first line of the *Iliad*: 'Sing, goddess, of the wrath of Achilles, son of Peleus ...'.)

I considered other points, too. For example, how important is it that the *Iliad* comes from a culture (that of ancient Greece) which has traditionally been much admired? Or that it touches on highly charged and 'important' issues like war and death? There are no doubt a whole host of other points to make, some of which you may well have come up with in your own answer.

I think this is an interesting exercise to perform in regard to any number of works of art (of literature, art, music and so on), not least because it makes us think about the criteria we use when judging something's importance. When I was thinking about my reaction to Homeric poetry, for example, I realised at times that I was not always wholly comfortable with some of the unconscious assumptions that I was making (and that others routinely make, too), such as the idea that the *Iliad*'s authority partly stems from the fact it is populated by 'important' people (aren't common soldiers and women important, too?), or that tragic events are somehow more important than happy ones.

In the next chapter you will have the opportunity to consider from another angle the way in which classical texts possess authority, when you study *The Island* – a twentieth-century play which is based in part on a Greek tragedy: Sophocles' *Antigone*.

Conclusion

In this chapter you have made some important steps towards understanding Homeric poetry. You have also explored further the concepts of canon and authority, and have had a chance to develop your skills of close reading and close listening through your work on the poem 'Ceasefire' and extracts from the *Iliad*.

You have also gained experience of working with ancient Greek material (and its reconfiguration – or 'reception' – by a modern poet) and so have acquired further insight into what work in the discipline of Classical Studies involves. As outlined in the introduction to this chapter, Classical Studies is a broad discipline which covers the study of not only ancient Greek culture, but also the world of ancient Rome. Important aspects of Classical Studies have nevertheless been touched on, such as the incomplete nature of our sources (see Section 5.3: 'Homeric poetry and the literary canon'), the interdisciplinary nature of study (the fact that classicists often make use of different kinds of evidence – for instance, literary *and* archaeological – to build up a picture of the ancient world) and the interest that many classicists take in the way that material from the ancient world has been understood and refashioned by later thinkers and artists (such as by Longley in 'Ceasefire').

Your set work for this chapter is finished, but there are some additional optional activities for you to complete if you have time to spare.

Optional activities

Reading 5.4 consists of three further poems by Longley, all of which are based on the extracts of the *Iliad* you have listened to and read in this chapter. 'War & Peace' describes the pursuit of Hector by Achilles in *Iliad* 22, while 'The Helmet' and 'The Parting' are based on the encounter between Hector and Andromache in *Iliad* 6. You may like to read these and consider the ways in which Longley has reworked these episodes from Homer's poem.

You may also like to listen to a short audio recording, 'Lapsed classicist', by Michael Longley, which you can find on the module website. Here Longley discusses his relationship with Homer over the years. The recording includes a reading of 'Ceasefire' and some of Longley's other poems inspired by Homeric themes.

References

Johnston, I. (trans.) (2006) *Homer: The Iliad*, 2nd edn, Ar Richer Resources Publications.

Longley, M. (2006) *Collected Poems*, London, Jonathan C;

Further reading

If you would like to take your work on this chapter further, you may want to read more of the *Iliad* in the translation by Ian Johnston (2006) used here. A good, readily available translation of Homer's other epic poem, *The Odyssey*, is provided by Robert Fagles (1991). For introductions to Homer's poetry, you might find it helpful to look at William Allan (2012), a short introduction of about 70 pages, written for undergraduate students and the general reader, or Elton Barker and Joel Christensen (2013), a longer book, dealing with both the *Iliad* and *Odyssey*, but at an introductory level.

Allan, W. (2012) *Homer: The Iliad*, London, Bristol Classical Press.

Barker, E. and Christensen, J. (2013) *Homer: A Beginner's Guide*, London, Oneworld Publications.

Fagles, R. (trans.) (1991) *Homer: The Odyssey* (intro. B. Knox), Harmondsworth, Penguin.

Johnston, I. (trans.) (2006) *Homer: The Iliad*, 2nd edn, Arlington, VA, Richer Resources Publications.

Reading 5.1 Homer's *Iliad* 22, lines 166–265 (original Greek: 22.131–213)

Source: Johnston, I. (trans.) (2006) *Homer: The Iliad*, 2nd edn, Arlington, VA, Richer Resources Publications, pp. 478–80; also available online at http://records.viu.ca/~johnstoi/homer/iliad22. htm (Accessed 29 April 2014).

But Achilles was coming closer, like Enyalius,[1]
the warrior god of battle with the shining helmet.
On his right shoulder he waved his dreadful spear
made of Pelian[2] ash. The bronze around him glittered
like a blazing fire or rising sun. At that moment,   170
as he watched, Hector began to shake in fear.
His courage gone, he could no longer stand there.
Terrified, he started running, leaving the gate.
Peleus' son[3] went after him, sure of his speed on foot.
Just as a mountain falcon, the fastest creature
of all the ones which fly, swoops down easily
on a trembling pigeon as it darts off in fear,
the hawk speeding after it with piercing cries,
heart driving it to seize the prey – in just that way
Achilles in his fury raced ahead. Hector ran   180
under the walls of Troy, limbs working feverishly.
They ran on past the lookout and the wind-swept fig tree,
some distance from the wall, along the wagon track.
They reached the two fair-flowing well springs
which feed swirling Scamander's[4] stream. From one of them
hot water flows, and out of it steam rises up,
as if there were a fire burning. From the other,
cold water comes, as cold as hail or freezing snow
or melting ice, even in summer. By these springs
stood wide tubs for washing, made of beautiful stone,   190
where, in peace time, before Achaea's[5] sons arrived,
Trojan wives and lovely daughters used to wash

---

[1] **Enyalius**: another name for Ares, god of war.
[2] **Pelian**: Mount Pelion lies in mainland Greece in southern Thessaly: it takes its name from Achilles' father, Peleus.
[3] **Peleus' son**: i.e. Achilles.
[4] **Scamander**: a river flowing from Mount Ida to the Hellespont near the mouth of which the Greeks were encamped.
[5] **Achaea**: i.e. Greece: the Greeks in the *Iliad* are variously referred to as Achaeans, Argives and Danaans.

their brightly coloured clothing. The men raced past there,
one in full flight, the other one pursuing him.
The man running off in front was a brave warrior,
but the man going after him was greater. They ran fast,
for this was no contest over sacrificial beasts,
the usual prizes for a race. They were competing
for horse-taming Hector's life. Just as some horses,
sure-footed, prize-winning creatures, make the turn   200
around the post and race quickly as they strive to win
some splendid prize – a tripod[6] or a woman
honouring a man that's died – that's how these two men raced,
going three times round Priam's city[7] on their sprinting feet.
All the gods looked on. Among them the first one to speak
was Zeus,[8] father of the gods and men:

'What a sight!

My eyes can see a fine man being pursued
around the walls. How my heart pities Hector,
who's often sacrificed to me, burning
many thighs of oxen on the crests   210
of Ida[9] with its many spurs and valleys,
on the city heights, as well. And now,
godlike Achilles is pursuing him
on his quick feet round Priam's city. Come,
you gods, think hard and offer your advice –
do we wish to rescue him from death,
or kill him now, for all his bravery,
at the hands of Peleus' son, Achilles?'

Then Athena,[10]

goddess with the glittering eyes, replied to Zeus:
'Father, lord of lightning and dark clouds,   220
what are you saying? How can you want

---

[6]   **tripod**: a 'three-footed' metal support for mixing bowls, cauldrons, etc.

[7]   **Priam's city**: i.e. Troy: Priam is father of Hector and king of Troy.

[8]   **Zeus**: as befits his role as king of the gods, Zeus is neither pro-Greek (like his daughter, Athena), nor pro-Trojan, like Apollo, and so is able to provide arbitration between the warring sides. His overarching control extends even to the weather: at line 220 he is referred to as 'lord of lightning and dark clouds' and at line 226 as 'cloud-gatherer'.

[9]   **Ida**: Mount Ida is located south-east of Troy and corresponds to the present-day Kaz Dağı in northern Turkey.

[10] **Athena**: a pro-Greek goddess: in the *Iliad* she stands for organised, disciplined warfare and often acts through heroes like Odysseus and Achilles.

to snatch the man back from his wretched death.
He's mortal – his fate doomed him long ago.
Well, do as you wish, but we other gods
will not all approve your actions.'
Cloud-gatherer Zeus then answered Athena:
'Cheer up, Tritogeneia,[11] my dear child,
I'm not saying how my heart intends to act.
I want to please you. So you can do
whatever your mind tells you. Don't hold back.'   230
Athena, who was already eager, was spurred on
by Zeus' words. She rushed down from Olympus'[12] peak.
Swift Achilles was still pressing Hector hard
in that relentless chase. Just as in the mountains
a hound startles from its cover some young deer,
then goes after it through glens and valley gorges –
and even if the fawn evades it for a while,
cowering in some thicket, the dog tracks it down,
always running till he finds it – that's how Hector
could not shake off the swift-footed son of Peleus.   240
Every time he tried to dash for the Dardanian[13] gates
to get underneath the walls, so men on top
could come to his assistance by hurling spears,
Achilles would intercept him and turn him back
towards the plain, always making sure he kept
running a line between Hector and the city.
Like a dream in which a man cannot catch someone
who's running off and the other can't escape,
just as the first man can't catch up – that's how
Achilles, for all his speed, could not reach Hector,   250
while Hector was unable to evade Achilles.
But how could Hector have escaped death's fatal blow,
if Apollo[14] had not for one last time approached,
to give him strength and make his legs run faster?
Godlike Achilles, with a shake of his head,
prevented his own troops from shooting Hector
with their lethal weapons, in case some other man
hit Hector, robbed him of the glory, and left him

---

[11] **Tritogeneia**: another name for Athena.
[12] **Olympus**: a mountain in north-west Greece and, in Greek mythology, home of the gods.
[13] **Dardanian**: i.e. Trojan: Dardanus was the son of Zeus and his grandson, Tros (the great-grandfather of Priam) was the ruler of Troy.
[14] **Apollo** a pro-Trojan god: the archer-god, but also the god of disease and healing.

to come too late. But when they ran past those springs
the fourth time, Father Zeus raised his golden scales,   260
setting there two fatal lots for death's long sorrow,
one for Achilles, one for horse-taming Hector.
Seizing it in the middle, Zeus raised his balance.
Hector's fatal day sank, moving down to Hades.[15]
At once Phoebus[16] Apollo abandoned him.

[15] **Hades**: the Greek underworld (abode of the god Hades).
[16] **Phoebus**: another name for Apollo (meaning 'Shining One').

Reading 5.2 Homer's *Iliad* 6, lines 480–613 (original Greek: 6.390–502)

Source: Johnston, I. (trans.) (2006) *Homer: The Iliad*, 2nd edn, Arlington, VA, Richer Resources Publications, pp. 135–9; also available online at http://records.viu.ca/~johnstoi/homer/iliad6. htm (Accessed 29 April 2014).

Hector left the house by the same route he'd come,	480
through the well-built streets, across the mighty city,	
and reached the Scaean Gates,[17] beyond which he'd go	
out onto the plain. There his wife ran up to meet him,	
Andromache, daughter of great-hearted Eëtion,	
who'd included a large dowry with her.	
Eëtion had lived below forested Mount Placus,[18]	
in Thebe,[19] king of the Cilician[20] people. She'd become	
married wife to Hector of the shining helmet.	
Now she met him there. With her came the nurse,	
holding at her breast their happy infant child,	490
well-loved son of Hector, like a beautiful star.	
Hector had named him Scamandrius,[21] but others	
called him Astyanax, lord of the city,	
because Hector was Troy's only guardian.	
Hector looked at his son in silence, with a smile.	
Andromache stood close to him, weeping.	
Taking Hector by the hand, she spoke to him.	
'My dear husband, your warlike spirit	
will be your death. You've no compassion	
for your infant child, for me, your sad wife,	500
who before long will be your widow.	
For soon the Achaeans[22] will attack you,	
all together, and cut you down. As for me,	
it would be better, if I'm to lose you,	
to be buried in the ground. For then I'll have	
no other comfort, once you meet your death,	

---

[17] **Scaean Gates**: the main gates of Troy, built by the god Poseidon.
[18] **Placus**: a spur of Mount Ida, south-east of Troy.
[19] **Thebe**: a city in Cilicia (see next note) sacked by Achilles.
[20] **Cilician**: Cilicia was a coastal region of southern Asia Minor.
[21] **Scamandrius**: a name deriving from the River Scamander which flowed near the city of Troy.
[22] **Achaeans**: i.e. the Greeks.

except my sorrow. I have no father,
no dear mother. For lord Achilles killed
my father, when he wiped out Thebe,
city with high gates, slaying Eëtion.   510
But he didn't strip his corpse – his heart
felt too much shame for that. So he burned him
in his finely decorated armour
and raised a burial mound above the ashes.
Mountain nymphs, daughters of aegis-bearing[23] Zeus,
planted elm trees all around his body.
I had seven brothers in my home.
All went down to Hades in a single day,
for swift-footed lord Achilles killed them all,
while they were guarding their shambling oxen   520
and their white shining sheep. As for my mother,
who ruled wooded Thebe-under-Placus,
he brought her here with all his other spoils.
Then he released her for a massive ransom.
But archer goddess Artemis then killed her
in her father's house. So, Hector, you are now
my father, noble mother, brother,
and my protecting husband. So pity me.
Stay here in this tower. Don't orphan your child
and make me a widow. Place men by the fig tree,   530
for there the city is most vulnerable,
the wall most easily scaled. Three times
their best men have come there to attack,
led by the two Ajaxes,[24] the sons of Atreus,[25]
famous Idomeneus,[26] and Diomedes,[27]
Tydeus' courageous son, incited to it
by someone well versed in prophecy
or by their own hearts' inclination.'
Great Hector of the shining helmet answered her:
                                                        'Wife,
all this concerns me, too. But I'd be disgraced,   540
dreadfully shamed among Trojan men

[23] **aegis**: a divine attribute of authority, represented in art as a large all-round bib with scales.
[24] **Ajaxes**: in the *Iliad* there are two Greek warriors named Ajax: one the son of Telamos and ruler of Salamis; the other the son of Oïleus and ruler of Locris.
[25] **the sons of Atreus**: i.e. Agamemnon (leader of the Greeks) and his brother Menelaus.
[26] **Idomeneus**: leader of the Cretan forces at Troy.
[27] **Diomedes**: king of Argos and one of the foremost Greek warriors.

and Trojan women in their trailing gowns,
if I should, like a coward, slink away from war.
My heart will never prompt me to do that,
for I have learned always to be brave,
to fight alongside Trojans at the front,
striving to win fame for father and myself.
My heart and mind know well the day is coming
when sacred Ilion will be destroyed,
along with Priam of the fine ash spear   550
and Priam's people. But what pains me most
about these future sorrows is not so much
the Trojans, Hecuba,[28] or king Priam,
or even my many noble brothers,
who'll fall down in the dust, slaughtered
by their enemies. My pain focuses on you,
when one of those bronze-clad Achaeans
leads you off in tears, ends your days of freedom.
If then you come to Argos[29] as a slave,
working the loom for some other woman,   560
fetching water from Hypereia[30] or Messeis,[31]
against your will, forced by powerful Fate,
then someone seeing you as you weep
may well say:
"That woman is Hector's wife.
He was the finest warrior in battle
of all horse-taming Trojans in that war
when they fought for Troy."
                         Someone will say that,
and it will bring still more grief to you,
to be without a man like that to save you
from days of servitude. May I lie dead,   570
hidden deep under a burial mound,
before I hear about your screaming,
as you are dragged away.'
                         With these words,
glorious Hector stretched his hands out for his son.
The boy immediately shrank back against the breast
of the finely girdled nurse, crying out in terror

---

[28] **Hecuba**: wife of Priam, mother of Hector and queen of Troy.
[29] **Argos**: a city in the Peloponnese, southern Greece: but perhaps 'Argos' here simply
       indicates 'Greece'.
[30] **Hypereia**: a spring in Thessaly (northern Greece).
[31] **Messeis**: a spring in either Thessaly or Therapne, near Sparta.

to see his own dear father, scared at the sight of bronze,
the horse-hair plume nodding fearfully from his helmet top.
The child's loving father laughed, his noble mother, too.
Glorious Hector pulled the glittering helmet off   580
and set it on the ground. Then he kissed his dear son
and held him in his arms. He prayed aloud to Zeus
and the rest of the immortals.
                              'Zeus, all you other gods,
grant that this child, my son, may become,
like me, pre-eminent among the Trojans,
as strong and brave as me. Grant that he may rule
Troy with strength. May people someday say,
as he returns from war, "This man is far better
than his father." May he carry back
bloody spoils from his slaughtered enemy,   590
making his mother's heart rejoice.'
He placed his son in the hands of his dear wife.
She embraced the child on her sweet breast, smiling
through her tears. Observing her, Hector felt compassion.
He took her hand, then spoke to her.
                              'My dearest wife,
don't let your heart be sad on my account.
No man will throw me down to Hades
before my destined time. I tell you this –
no one escapes his fate, not the coward,
nor the brave man, from the moment of his birth.   600
So you should go into the house, keep busy
with your proper work, with your loom and wool,
telling your servants to set about their tasks.
War will be every man's concern, especially mine,
of all those who live in Troy.'
                              Having said these words,
glorious Hector took his plumed helmet in his hands.
His beloved wife went home, often looking back,
as she went, crying bitterly. She quickly reached
the spacious home of Hector, killer of men.
Inside she met her many servants and bid them all lament.   610
So they mourned for Hector in his own house,
though he was still alive – they thought he'd not come back,
he'd not escape the battle fury of Achaean hands.

Reading 5.3 Homer's *Iliad* 13: similes

Source: Johnston, I. (trans.) (2006) *Homer: The Iliad*, 2nd edn, Arlington, VA, Richer Resources Publications, pp. 267–94; also available online at http://records.viu.ca/~johnstoi/homer/iliad13. htm (Accessed 29 April 2014).

Lines 69–72 (13.62–5 of original Greek)

Then Poseidon left. Just as a swift-winged hawk
takes off while hovering above some high sheer rock,
swooping down over the plain to hunt another bird –
that is how Earthshaker Poseidon went off then.

Lines 160–9 (13.136–45 of original Greek)

The Trojans came on in a mass, led by Hector,
always charging forward, like a rolling boulder,
which some river in a winter flood dislodges
from a cliff beside its banks, its great flood eroding
what supports that lethal stone. In its fall, it bounces –
woods crash underneath it, as it accelerates
in a straight line, unimpeded – then it hits the plain,
where, for all its impetus, its motion stops.
That's how Hector threatened then to smash his way
with ease down to the sea, to Achaea's huts and ships.

Lines 208–13 (13.178–81 of original Greek)

Teucer[32] pulled the weapon back. Imbrius[33] collapsed.
Just as an ash tree growing on a mountain top,
visible from every side, is chopped down by bronze,
its foliage crashing to the ground – that's how he fell.
His armour, finely decorated bronze, rang out,
reverberating round him.

---

[32] **Teucer**: a Greek warrior, son of Telamon and half-brother of Ajax.
[33] **Imbrius**: a Trojan warrior, son-in-law to Priam.

Lines 280–6 (13.240–5 of original Greek)

Idomeneus[34]
went into his well-made hut, strapped fine armour
round his body, took two spears and then strode out,
looking like a lightning bolt which Cronos' son[35]
grips in his hand and hurls down from bright Olympus,
revealing in its dazzling flash a sign for mortal men,
that's how, as he moved, bronze glinted on his chest.

Lines 395–9 (13.333–7 of original Greek)

By the ships' sterns both sides met in frantic battle.
Just as keen winds sometimes whip up gusts of air,
when dirt lies heavy on the roads, and stir up
all the dust into huge clouds – that's how this fight
gathered momentum then.

Lines 462–9 (13.387–93 of original Greek)

But Idomeneus was too quick for him.
He hit Asius[36] with a spear below his chin,
forcing the bronze straight through his neck. Asius fell.
Just as a mountain oak, poplar, or tall pine falls,
cut down by working men with freshly sharpened axes,
to make timbers for some ship, that's how Asius lay,
stretched out there before his chariot and horses,
gagging, his fingers clawing at the bloody dust.

Lines 552–63 (13.468–77 of original Greek)

Deïphobus[37] finished. His words stirred the heart
in Aeneas' chest. He strode off to face Idomeneus,
fiercely eager for this fight. But no fear gripped
Idomeneus, as if he were some pampered child.
He stood his ground. Just as a wild mountain boar,
trusting its own strength, stands firm against a mob,
a crowd of men who chase it in some lonely place,
with hair bristling along its back, its eyes lit up,

---

[34] **Idomeneus**: leader of the Cretan forces at Troy.
[35] **Cronos' son**: i.e. Zeus.
[36] **Asius**: a leader of Trojan allies from the region of the Hellespont.
[37] **Deïphobus**: son of Priam and Hecuba.

like fire, gnashing its teeth ferociously, eager
to toss dogs and men aside – that's just the way
the famous spearman Idomeneus stood then,
without backing off, as swift Aeneas[38] came at him.

Lines 579–87 (13.489–95 of original Greek)

Aeneas
called out to those companions he'd caught sight of –
Deïphobus, Paris,[39] and Agenor[40] – leaders,
just as he was, of those Trojan warriors.
Men came up behind them. Just as a flock of sheep
follows the ram from pasture to their water,
filling the shepherd's heart with joy, so Aeneas
was happy in his chest to see that band of soldiers
standing there around him.

Lines 671–6 (13.570–3 of original Greek)

When that spear struck Adamas,[41] he doubled up,
bent down over the spear, writhing like a bull
which farmers in the mountains bind with willow shoots
and drag along by force, against the creature's will.
That's how Adamas, once hit, twitched there for a while,
but not for long.

Lines 689–95 (13.586–92 of original Greek)

Priam's son[42] hit Menelaus[43] with his arrow –
on the front plate of his armour, in the chest.
The keen arrow bounded off. Just as black beans or peas
fly off a broad shovel on large threshing floors,
driven by the sharp wind or winnower's strength –
that's how the arrow point glanced off the breast plate,
then flew aside, away from glorious Menelaus.

---

[38] **Aeneas**: a Trojan warrior, son of Prince Anchises and the goddess Aphrodite.
[39] **Paris**: aka Alexander, son of Priam and Hecuba, and the Trojan husband of Helen.
[40] **Agenor**: a Trojan warrior.
[41] **Adamas**: a Trojan warrior.
[42] **Priam's son**: Helenus, twin brother of the prophetess Cassandra.
[43] **Menelaus**: Greek warrior: brother of Agamemnon; king of Sparta; and the Greek husband of Helen.

Lines 827–35 (13.701–8 of original Greek)

Ajax, son of Oïleus,[44] would not move away
from Ajax, son of Telamon[45] – he fought beside him.
Just as in a meadow a pair of wine-dark oxen
strain with the same heart to pull a jointed plough,
beads of sweat running from the bottom of their horns,
with nothing but a well-polished yoke between them,
as they labour down the furrows, till the plough
slices through the edges of the field – that's the way
the two Ajaxes stood together then, side by side.

Lines 932–9 (13.795–801 of original Greek)

Just like blasts of storming winds
striking the earth under Father Zeus' thunder,
then with a roar slicing into the sea, whipping up
a crowd of surging waves across a booming ocean,
with lines of arching foam, one following another –
that's how Trojans marched behind their leaders,
in a tight formation, one behind the other,
glittering in bronze.

---

[44] **Ajax, son of Oïleus**: Greek warrior, the ruler of Salamis.
[45] **Ajax, son of Telamon**: Greek warrior, the ruler of Locris.

Reading 5.4 Three poems by Michael Longley

Source: Longley, M. (2006) *Collected Poems*, **London, Jonathan Cape, pp. 225 and 226.**

War & Peace

Achilles hunts down Hector like a sparrowhawk
Screeching after a horror-struck collared-dove
That flails just in front of her executioner, so
Hector strains under the walls of Troy to stay alive.
Past the windbent wild fig tree and the lookout
Post they both accelerate away from the town
Along a cart-track as far as double well-heads
That gush into the eddying Scamander, in one
Warm water steaming like smoke from a bonfire,
The other running cold as hailstones, snow water,
Handy for the laundry-cisterns carved out of stone
Where Trojan housewives and their pretty daughters
Used to rinse glistening clothes in the good old days,
On washdays before the Greek soldiers came to Troy.

similes

The Helmet

When Shiny Hector reached out for his son, the wean[46]
Squirmed and buried his head between his nurse's breasts
And howled, terrorised by his father, by flashing bronze
And the nightmarish nodding of the horse-hair crest.

His daddy laughed, his mammy laughed, and his daddy
Took off the helmet and laid it on the ground to gleam,
Then kissed the babbie and dandled him in his arms and
Prayed that his son might grow up bloodier than him.

The Parting

He: 'Leave it to the big boys, Andromache.'
'Hector, my darling husband, och, och,'[47] she.

---

[46] **wean**: a Northern Irish word that refers to a young child ('wee one').
[47] **och**: a Northern Irish word, used to express exasperation or disapproval.

Chapter 6

The Island

Lynda Prescott with Fiona Richards

Contents

Aims

This chapter will:

- offer a further perspective on the theme of 'remaking authority' through study of an overtly political play that draws on a classical, canonical text

- help you to develop your skills in reading modern drama, paying attention to different voices, silences, non-verbal sounds and physical elements

- develop your awareness of the performance history dimension of drama.

Materials you will need

In this chapter, you will need to listen to the following audio recordings, which can be found on the module website:

- Soweto Blues
- Bring Him Back Home
- Sizothabatha Umthwalo
- What a System, What a Crime.

You will also be directed to the 'Moving on to A105 website' for some optional readings.

Introduction

At the start of the previous chapter you looked at a modern poem by Michael Longley that reworks a famous moment from Homer's *Iliad*. James Robson's discussion showed how the 1990s' Irish political and social context of Longley's poem combines with the mythical past of Homer's epic, illuminating the 'themes of death, grief, empathy and the painful realities of coming to terms with one's (former) enemies' (Chapter 5, Section 5.1). In this chapter you will continue to investigate the reworking of ancient Greek texts in the modern world, but this time the focus shifts to South Africa during the period of apartheid, and to a different form of literature: drama. Through studying the play *The Island*, you will again see how an ancient, canonical text (in this case Sophocles' play *Antigone*) has been reworked in a modern context to combine powerful new meanings with the essential elements of the original text.

Apartheid

Originally coined in the 1930s, the term 'apartheid' literally means 'apartness'. The word belongs to the language known as Afrikaans, a modified form of Dutch, and one of two European languages (the other being English) used by European settlers in South Africa. Over the course of several centuries, the Afrikaans-speakers, or Afrikaners, established themselves as a powerful minority, exercising control of South Africa's government. The predominantly Afrikaner National Party began using the term 'apartheid' in the early 1940s to describe a social system of racial segregation, and from 1948, when the National Party narrowly defeated more moderate interests in the country's elections, apartheid became enshrined in South Africa's laws. The Population Registration Act 1949 assigned every South African to a racial group: white, black, Asian or coloured (that is, of mixed race), and restrictions were established as to where different races could live and work. From 1952 onwards new, tighter **pass laws** meant that all non-whites were required to carry identity documents (passbooks) showing their racial group and the areas they were allowed to go to, for both residence and employment. Enforcing these laws entailed heavy policing and repression of the non-white majority.

Resistance to apartheid took many political forms, but the African National Congress (ANC), founded in 1912, was an especially prominent force. One of its leaders, a young black lawyer called Nelson Mandela (1918–2013), was sentenced to life imprisonment in 1964, but continued to inspire black Africans from his prison cell on the notorious Robben Island until his release in 1990. Apartheid was gradually dismantled under the leadership of the National Party's F.W. de Klerk (b.1936), and in 1994 Mandela was elected as South Africa's first black president, heading a government of national unity. Mandela and de Klerk shared the Nobel Peace Prize in 1993 'for their work for the peaceful termination of the apartheid regime, and for laying the foundations for a new, democratic South Africa' (The Nobel Foundation, 1993).

6.1   Introducing *The Island*

An overview of Sophocles' *Antigone*

Sophocles was one of the most famous dramatists of ancient Greece and was born near Athens at the start of the fifth century BCE. His three plays derived from the myth of Oedipus and his family (*King Oedipus*, *Oedipus at Colonus* and *Antigone*) occupy an important place in the canon of western drama. *Antigone* in particular has been a potent text for actors and theatre directors all around the world, the tragic figure of Antigone, daughter of Oedipus, standing as an example of heroic resistance against the forces of oppression. Eileen Battersby, in her article 'A Greek tragedy for our times', describes *Antigone* as 'a foundation text of European theatre' (2004, p. 55), but there have been many productions in various languages and cultures outside of Europe, too. (You can read part of Battersby's article on the 'Moving on to A105' website.)

Africa has generated its fair share of *Antigone*s, although the South African play we have chosen for you to study here is not a direct adaptation of Sophocles' play. Instead, *The Island* contains parts of Sophocles' drama as a play-within-a-play, and although you will come across some explanations of the plot of *Antigone* as you read *The Island*, you will probably find it easier to follow the play if you know the outlines of the *Antigone* story.

Activity

If you have studied AA100 *The arts past and present*, you will already be familiar with a modern adaptation of *Antigone*: *The Burial at Thebes* by Seamus Heaney (1939–2013). However, since *The Island* presents only sections from Sophocles' play, you may want to refresh your memory of the plot of *Antigone*. You will find a short outline of the play on the 'Moving on to A105' website. If you have not studied AA100, nor read the play in any other form, you should access and read this synopsis now.

Performing *Antigone*: the Serpent Players

There is a rather dramatic backstory behind the play you are about to study. It begins in June 1965, when some amateur actors from New Brighton, a black township near Port Elizabeth on South Africa's

Eastern Cape coast, were rehearsing a production of Sophocles' *Antigone*. Three days before the first performance, the actor playing Haemon, King Creon's son, was arrested. At this period of South Africa's history there was nothing unusual about such an arrest: the actors in the New Brighton group, the Serpent Players, were all black, and so subject to the draconian restrictions of racial segregation or apartheid described above. Police surveillance and arrest were commonplace, with offenders who broke the pass laws being cursorily tried in 'Native Commissioner's Courts' and then, more often than not, jailed. The prisoners considered to pose most political risk were sent to an offshore jail in Table Bay, near Cape Town, called Robben Island (Figure 6.1). This was the destination of Norman Ntshinga, who would have been the Serpent Players' Haemon; other prisoners on Robben Island at the time included members of the banned ANC, including Mandela.

Figure 6.1 Robben Island Prison, Cape Town, South Africa. Photographed by Fraser Hall. Photo: © Robert Harding World Imagery/Fraser Hall/Getty Images

The Serpent Players' production of *Antigone* went ahead, with John Kani taking over the role of Haemon. As it happened, Kani's brother was also a prisoner on Robben Island, and in his letters he reported that Sophocles' play had found a new audience in the island prison. Ntshinga and another imprisoned Player, Sipho 'Sharkey' Mguqulwa, arranged a two-man version of *Antigone* as part of a prison entertainment, 'on the basis of their memory of the play they were to have done when they were arrested' (Fugard, 1993, p. xxviii). This was not a unique event: in 1970, at a Christmas concert in the prison, there would be a fuller version of *Antigone* with Mandela playing the part of Creon (Mandela, 1994, p. 540). (You can read a short account of Mandela's experience of playing Creon on the 'Moving on to A105' website.)

Meanwhile, the depleted Serpent Players were beginning to branch out from their repertoire of western classical drama. One thing that certainly *was* unusual about this theatre group was its connection with a white playwright and director, Athol Fugard, who lived in Port Elizabeth and, despite the laws insisting on segregation in the theatre, had worked with the Serpent Players since 1963. After directing adaptations of modern as well as ancient drama with the Players, Fugard began workshop improvisations with members of the group that took them in quite new directions. He was influenced by his reading of *Towards a Poor Theatre*, by the Polish theatre director and innovator Jerzy Grotowski (1968), which steered away from theatre as 'spectacle' and emphasised the importance of the actor as a creator as much as an interpreter. And in two of the Serpent Players, John Kani and Winston Ntshona, Fugard found actors who were utterly committed not only to acting but also to the kind of creative, improvisatory approaches that he was keen to develop. The most significant products of this collaboration were two plays that now, when published, bear on their title page not the name of a single author but the words 'Devised by Athol Fugard, John Kani and Winston Ntshona'.

Staging *The Island*: finding a performance space and an audience

The first of these collaborative plays devised by Fugard, Kani and Ntshona, *Sizwe Bansi is Dead*, is based on the idea of a rural migrant worker taking the passbook of a dead man in order to continue working in Port Elizabeth. The play was first performed in Cape Town, at a theatre called The Space, in October 1972. The Space, which was actually a converted warehouse, had been established earlier that year by Brian Astbury, a theatre photographer, and his wife Yvonne Bryceland, an actress who worked closely with Fugard. Having been set up as a 'club', the theatre managed to evade the censorship that might otherwise have prevented a politically provocative play like *Sizwe Bansi* seeing the light of day. It also managed to attract audiences that were diverse in terms of both race and class. Although anti-apartheid theatre was emerging as a powerful force across the country – the South African Black Theatre Union was set up in July 1972 in Durban – plays performed at The Space reached a public that was, according to one American academic, 'more diverse than the audience for Black Consciousness Movement drama, and more vocally dissident than the audience for "western" theatrical experiments' (Kruger, 1999, p. 165). It is worth briefly thinking about South African theatres in relation to our theme of authority, and the role of cultural institutions as gatekeepers.

During the apartheid regime, and especially in the late 1950s and early 1960s, a number of new theatres were built in South Africa with financial support from municipal or civic authorities. But these subsidised theatres, like other established mainstream venues, barred black actors and audience members, and their repertoires, which were influenced by the policies of South Africa's Performing Arts Councils, looked towards European and North American drama rather than plays reflecting contemporary South African society. Nevertheless, 'alternative' theatre venues also emerged, often associated with the work of particular theatre practitioners. The Space Theatre was one of these, followed by the Market Theatre in Johannesburg, which opened in 1976 and became known as South Africa's 'Theatre of the Struggle'. Post-apartheid, the Market Theatre is still flourishing and since 1995 it has received state subsidy: in the space of two decades, the 'alternative' became 'mainstream'.

Back in the 1970s, and under the restrictions of apartheid, The Space was also the venue at which the second Fugard/Kani/Ntshona play, now known as *The Island*, was performed. The germ of the play was that two-man version of *Antigone* enacted by the real-life imprisoned Serpent Players on Robben Island, mentioned above. However, this subject was even more politically sensitive than that of *Sizwe Bansi*, since it dealt with prison conditions, a topic surrounded by legal prohibitions. So for its first performance in July 1973, the play was disguised under the title *Die Hodoshe Span* ('Hodoshe' being the name given to one of the prison warders in the play, and 'span' referring to his 'work team'). At the time of this first performance the play still did not exist in written form. It was directed by Fugard, and the actors, Kani and Ntshona playing the parts of 'John' and 'Winston', relied on the improvisations they had developed in two weeks of intensive workshops with Fugard in order to present this play with another play enclosed inside it. So, strikingly for our purposes, this is a 'text' that at its first public appearance was not written down, although it relied in places on a translation of Sophocles' written text. And, as you will now see, it is also a play that begins without voices.

6.2 Reading *The Island*

Although the ideal way to approach a play is to see it in performance, the academic study of drama often involves simply reading the text on the page. *The Island* is quite a short play, and the full text, along with some explanatory notes, has been reproduced for you as Reading 6.1. (Note that the page references given for the play in this chapter refer to this reading.) You may choose to read the play now from beginning to end, or to read it in sections as you work through the activities and discussions below. If you opt to read the whole play now, I recommend that you read the relevant scenes again while carrying out the activities in this section.

If you have studied AA100 and read *Doctor Faustus* by Christopher Marlowe (1564–1593), you will quickly notice that the experience of reading a modern play is very different. A play like *Dr Faustus*, besides being written mostly in **blank verse**, includes very few direct indications as to what is actually happening on the stage. In a modern play, as well as the differences in language, there are often copious stage directions. Often these italicised directions are as important as the words spoken by the play's characters, and our first activity focuses closely on the opening stage directions that lead us into the play.

Activity

You should allow about 20 minutes for this activity.

Read (or re-read) the opening stage directions of the play at the beginning of Reading 6.1. They are exceptionally long and on stage the mime described in the second paragraph (beginning 'The long drawn-out wail …') can last for several minutes. As you read, try to visualise John's and Winston's movements. Then select one or two words and phrases from the text of the stage directions to answer the following questions:

1　What does the opening sand-digging mime say about the life of prisoners on Robben Island?

2　How does the mood change once the men are back inside their cell?

3　Although there are no spoken words in this opening, a number of sounds are indicated: what are they?

Discussion

1　The stage directions are fairly explicit about what the opening mime is meant to convey: 'an image of back-breaking and grotesquely futile labour'. Although the audience cannot, of course, see the piles of sand that 'never diminish', if the mime is skilfully done the self-defeating nature of the two-handed digging-and-emptying becomes apparent. You might also have noted that this labour is described as 'interminable'; on stage, even a few minutes spent on repetitive movements like these can seem to stretch out for a long time, so the audience soon feels the tedium of the prisoners' existence. However, the pace changes with the next phase of the mime, the degrading three-legged run back to the cell, with beatings thrown in.

2   Once back in the cell (the central raised area described at the beginning of the stage directions), the prisoners can give in to 'total exhaustion'. However, Winston soon begins to express his sense of 'anger and outrage', so in answer to this question you might have selected stage directions relating to both elements of this mood change.

3   Exhaustion can easily be expressed through silence, but we can imagine this silence broken by Winston's soft moaning, building up gradually to the out-and-out 'noise' of rage. Besides these inarticulate sounds, and the men's earlier 'grunts' during the digging mime, you probably noted the external sounds of the opening siren and the whistle that marks the end of the digging – sharp, intrusive noises representing the invisible powers of those who control the prisoners' existence. Less strident but still unpleasant sounds mentioned at the end of the second paragraph are 'the squeal of the wheelbarrows' and 'the hum of Hodoshe, the green carrion fly': the full significance of 'Hodoshe' will become apparent only as the play goes on.

Scene 1: memory and imagination

During the opening mime we form our first impressions of the characters, John and Winston, and begin to appreciate the importance of the relationship between them. We know from the cast list that these two black prisoners are the only characters to appear in the play. The white warder, whom they call 'Hodoshe', remains offstage and invisible. In fact, the whole superstructure of state authority, as represented in the prison setting, is revealed to the audience only by indirect means. We have already noted the siren and whistle in the opening mime, but as the play continues we shall also begin to understand more about how the prison regime operates, not just through physical brutality but also through raising and then destroying prisoners' hopes; we learn all this through the dialogue between John and Winston. As the opening scene moves from mime into speech we quickly develop a sense of the

Figure 6.2 'Breaking Rock', 1966. Photographed by Cloete Breytenbach. Photo: © Cloete Breytenbach/UWC-Robben Island Museum Mayibuye Archives. This photograph was taken during a press visit organised by the South African government. The photo shoot was staged

characters' individuality as well as a sense of the ever-shifting relationship between them.

Activity

You should allow about an hour for this activity.

Read (or re-read) the whole of Scene 1 (the longest in the play) in Reading 6.1, referring to the notes when you come across non-English words. (Two non-English languages feature prominently in the play: the European Afrikaans, mentioned in the text box on apartheid, and the African Xhosa. The use of these two languages in the play is discussed in more detail in Book 3, Chapter 1.) As you read, make brief notes on the characters John and Winston, identifying points of difference between them as well as shared characteristics.

Discussion

At the end of the opening mime we saw that Winston was filled with uncontrollable rage and John was trying to placate him. This continues when the dialogue begins, with Winston calling angrily for Hodoshe and John persuading him to be quiet. But there is a quick 'reversal of earlier roles' (p. 308) as Winston tends to John's injured ear, so here, right at the start of the play, the idea of brotherhood and mutual support is established. This is reinforced by Winston's utterance of the Xhosa rallying cry, '*Nyana we Sizwe!*' ('Son of the Land!' or 'Brother!'), and by their sharing of memories about St George's Strand. You might also have noted John's attempt to amuse Winston with his invented 'News bulletin and weather forecast' (p. 309), an example of his readiness to break into mimicry and improvisation. As the scene progresses, you may have become more aware of John's enthusiasm for the play-acting plan he has committed himself and Winston to, and his determination to make Winston learn his part. So even in this first part of the dialogue our understanding of the two characters is becoming richer and fuller. You may well have noted other points, especially as the scene progresses. As you built up your picture of the two characters, you may also have found yourself reflecting on the relationship between them and the way they use this relationship to survive.

In looking at the first part of the play's dialogue we have already touched on the two concepts mentioned in the heading to this section: memory (here, of the seaside) and imagination (John's 'news bulletin'). These two concepts are especially important at this point in the play since both these qualities enable the men to move beyond the present moment: the sharing of memories and imaginative projections is an important part of their survival strategies

Activity

Look back through Scene 1 again, noting when John and Winston 'take themselves out' of their prison cell through the exercise of imagination.

You should allow about 20 minutes for this activity.

Discussion

There are several possibilities you may have noted here, including John's and Winston's nightly ritual of entertaining each other with re-creations of favourite movies (p. 317), and John's one-sided telephone conversation with 'Scott' and 'Sky' in a **shebeen** back home in New Brighton, using just an empty mug as a prop (pp. 317–18). These examples involve a dramatic element, and we see how much John, in particular, relishes acting. So it seems almost natural that while other prisoners are rehearsing songs or practising the Zulu war dance for the prison concert (p. 311), John should be persuading Winston to join him in a piece of drama. We may be initially surprised at their material, *The Trial of Antigone*, but, as you have seen, this is actually a historically authentic choice; even had we not known this, John validates the Sophocles connection by recalling for Winston the 1965 New Brighton production of the play (pp. 314–15). As he imitates 'Georgie', 'Mulligan' and 'Nomhle' in their various roles, John's re-enactment grounds Sophocles' play firmly in the everyday life that he and Winston knew before their incarceration. And his efforts clearly galvanise Winston, who, after much reluctance, declares that he has memorised the plot of the play (p. 315). Already, then, there are suggestions that imagination, exercised here through both formal and informal acting, can have a transformative power.

Figure 6.3 John Kani and Winston Ntshona 'phoning home' in a 1995 revival of *The Island* at the Market Theatre, Johannesburg, South Africa. Photographed by Ruphin Coudyzer. Photo: © Ruphin Coudyzer FPPSA – www.ruphin.com

Looking back over this first scene as a whole, we can hardly fail to notice the ever-changing mood of the play, inviting a corresponding range of responses from the audience. In the theatre, with the constant visible reminder of the constraints of the prison cell (a tiny floor-space), the audience would be conscious of the men's ingenuity in surmounting the horror of the prison's inhuman conditions. But John's closing words, 'Tell her also … it's starting to get cold now, but the worst is still coming' (p. 318), remind us that the dominant mode of the play is tragedy.

Scenes 2 and 3: imprisonment and the meaning of freedom

The next two scenes of the play are set a few days later, both on the same night, so we shall consider them together.

Activity

Read (or re-read) Scenes 2 and 3 in Reading 6.1. Then jot down some responses to the following questions:

1 What major ideas, or themes, are being brought to the audience's attention?

2 What actually happens in the course of these two scenes?

You should allow about an hour and a half for this activity.

Discussion

1 It would be difficult to consider these scenes without reflecting on the ideas presented in the heading to this section. To be imprisoned for political reasons under desperately inhumane conditions, as John and Winston are, is to be condemned to a kind of living death. In Winston's case, serving a life sentence, the contradictions implied in the idea of a living death are sharpened to the point of absurdity (I'm thinking here of the most serious senses of 'absurd' – illogical, meaningless, or, in the words of the *Oxford English Dictionary*, 'out of harmony with reason or propriety'). But for John, receiving news that his sentence has been commuted, the idea of freedom suddenly comes tantalisingly close; being a free man again will mean not only the restoration of identity, dignity and choice, but also escaping the fate of someone like 'Old Harry' who has been turned 'into stone' by the prison regime (p. 331).

Another major theme you may have homed in on concerns the nature and purpose of drama. This theme surfaces in comic mode at the beginning of Scene 2, when we see Winston in his ludicrous *Antigone* 'costume', but John soon urges him to 'try to understand, man, ... this is Theatre' (p. 320): the laughter they anticipate from the prison audience will be followed by the moment 'when our Antigone hits them with her words' (p. 321). Winston is not yet convinced, and in a central speech in Scene 2 (p. 322) he questions the uses of what is, in effect, dramatic fiction in a situation like his, so horribly hemmed in by reality: 'Only last night you tell me that this Antigone is a bloody ... what you call it ... legend! A Greek one at that. Bloody thing never even happened. Not even history! Look, brother, I got no time for bullshit. Fuck legends.'

Winston is really the character to watch, as he tests out his own limitations, particularly in having to dress and think like a woman, and we do, I think, see him change during the course of the play. At this point he is simply goaded by John's response, which asserts the importance of playing *Antigone* as a way of expressing their convictions, their ideals, in the face of oppression. In fact, John's position has a great weight of theatre history behind it. As I pointed out at the beginning of this chapter, the character of Antigone stands as a symbol of heroic resistance; thus, Sophocles' play has often been used to give voice to resistance at moments of political crisis. A canonical work of European culture, *Antigone* shares in the kind of authoritative status that, as you saw in the last chapter, ancient Greek texts often embody. Even a fragmentary amateur version of *Antigone*, such as John and Winston's, borrows and builds on the authority of Sophocles' play, reworking it for an entirely different context from that of the original. Of course, an academic explanation like this is one thing, but the experience of watching a character like Winston grow into the role of Antigone is another thing altogether. This growth is closer to the surface than in many plays, since Winston and John to some extent play themselves, notably through using their own names, and although neither Kani nor Ntshona experienced imprisonment on Robben Island, they were certainly close to people who did, and, as actors, they 'stand in' for those people.

2   Your answer to the question of what actually happens may have been quite brief. We see Winston dressing up, and the ensuing quarrel is arguably an 'event', but probably, if we were to summarise the action of the play, we would consider John's news of his sentence being reduced to be the most significant thing that happens in these two scenes. You probably noticed, though, that this news is delivered offstage: the audience does not witness the dramatic moment of the prison governor's announcement. And later, as John reflects on the tactics of the prison authorities – 'the whole bloody thing is most probably a trick anyway' (p. 327) – we, too, may begin to ask whether this has been the life-transforming event that it seems at first to be, or whether it is a cruel kind of pretence.

In thinking more generally about the balance between the two elements we've been considering – themes and events – you've probably come to realise that, at the level of plot, the whole action of the play so far could be summed up fairly briefly. The chain of events the audience needs to understand in order to make sense of *The Island* has mostly been completed before the play opens: the story of how John and Winston came to be incarcerated in a notorious jail is treated only retrospectively. No great discoveries or revelations occur during the course of the play, but, as you will see in the next section, there is a dramatic climax in Scene 4. Even the events in the story of Antigone – the second level of narrative within the play – are pared down to the formal trial (see pp. 332–7), focusing attention on the conflict between the individual and the state. Like many modern plays, *The Island* is not overly concerned with telling a story, but neither is it an abstract debate about political or aesthetic issues. Rather, the major questions that arise during the play surface directly through the exploration of characters and their situations. And despite the absence of scenery, props and other devices geared towards theatrical illusion, the play is firmly grounded in the physical realities of life in the island prison.

Scene 4: performing Antigone

Activity

Now read (or re-read) the final scene, paying attention to the opening stage directions and the use of language.

You should allow about 40 minutes for this activity.

1   How might an actual theatre audience be positioned in relation to the imaginary prison audience?

2   How does the characters' speech differ in this scene from the way they speak in earlier scenes?

Discussion

1   It is in this final scene that we see how closely the classical drama of *Antigone*, in all its power and solemnity, is woven together with the fate of black South Africans suffering under apartheid. The congruence is achieved very simply, by converting the central cell area into a stage, complete with blanket backdrop, on which John appears first as a kind of Master of Ceremonies, introducing the play, and then as Creon confronting Winston's Antigone. This means that when, on pp. 332–4, John addresses 'Captain Prinsloo, Hodoshe, Warders, … and Gentlemen' (you may have noted the significant pause before the prisoners are addressed as 'gentlemen'), he is actually speaking straight to the theatre audience. As the real-life audience takes on the role of prison audience, then, it finds itself involved very directly in the merging of the classical and contemporary stories.

2   This change in the relationship between audience and stage is accompanied by a marked change in the play's language, nothing less than a complete shift in **register**. The dialogue so far has been naturalistic, with short, sometimes disjointed, utterances peppered with slang and the odd Afrikaans' phrase. However, you may have noted that in this scene the characters still speak forcefully, but much more formally, using words like 'defiance', 'transgression', 'impunity'. The length of John's opening speeches – the first a kind of prologue, and the second spoken in the role of Creon – also imposes an entirely different pace on the scene. However, the opening phrase of Winston's final speech as Antigone, before he tears off his wig (p. 337), may have reminded you of Winston's own 'voice'. At this point, his words 'Brothers and Sisters of the Land!' (the inclusive 'sisters' here makes it clear that he is addressing not just the all-male prison audience) echo the Xhosa rallying cry '*Nyana we Sizwe!*' that we heard first at the start of the play (p. 308) and then twice, emphatically, at the end of Scene 3 (p. 332).

The whole of Winston-as-Antigone's farewell speech is poetic in its simplicity, and although he refers to 'the Island' as the place of incarceration, rather than the tomb to which Sophocles' Antigone is consigned, his words stay close to those of the character in Sophocles' play (in a modern English translation, of course). However, it is when he speaks to the audience in his own character that the most profound effects are achieved, for here Sophocles' words pierce through the play text directly, unchanged. At the climax of the play, then, Antigone's words, with all the weight and authority of classical tradition behind them, are bestowed on Winston in his own person, rather than as an actor playing Antigone, in a vivid and moving demonstration of their common fate and common humanity.

The play ends, as it began, with an extended mime. We gradually move from the world of theatre, as John and Winston come out of their roles and take down their makeshift 'set', to the world of the prison. Their shackled three-legged run recapitulates the second phase of the long mime in Scene 1, and the wail of the siren takes the audience back to the moment before the stage lights first came up at the very beginning of the play. You might want to pause here and consider briefly the effects of the play's circular structure, and the possible meanings implied. But any extended discussion about *The Island*'s meaning must also take into account the context within which it is performed, and this is why I should like us to now turn to the play's performance history.

Figure 6.4 John and Winston playing Antigone and Creon in a 1995 revival of *The Island* at the Market Theatre, Johannesburg, South Africa. Photographed by Ruphin Coudyzer. Photo: © Ruphin Coudyzer FPPSA – www.ruphin.com

6.3 *The Island*'s performance history

After its obscure and precarious premiere in Cape Town under the title *Die Hodoshe Span*, the play quickly acquired an international reputation, appearing in London, newly retitled, just a few months later. This was partly because of lucky timing: in 1971 Fugard had travelled to Britain to direct one of his plays, *Boesman and Lena*, at London's Royal Court Theatre Upstairs, and when plans were made for a season of South African drama at the Royal Court in the winter of 1973, he was invited back. So after an anxious wait for passports, Kani, Ntshona and Fugard brought their production of *Sizwe Bansi is Dead* to London and, alongside it, their new play *The Island*, for the opening of the Royal Court's South African season in December 1973.

There was much acclaim for the plays, and particularly for the inspired performances by Kani and Ntshona. But there were also objections: one South African newspaper, for example, reported that the South African Embassy in London had received complaints about the play's 'propaganda' element *(Eastern Province Herald*, quoted in The Open University, 1991, p. 92).

The following year both plays transferred to the Edison Theatre, New York, and the texts, along with that of Fugard's single-authored play, *Statements after an Arrest under the Immorality Act*, were published by Oxford University Press. *The Island* was thus well on the way to international recognition, and it was this that secured the play protection from censorship in South Africa, where the first 'open' production took place at a new arts centre in Johannesburg in 1977.

The play was also performed elsewhere, especially in Africa (there were notable productions in Zimbabwe in 1985 and 1999, for example), and by other actors, but Kani and Ntshona continued to be involved with *The Island* for three decades. In one of their revivals, in Cape Town in 1985, the following statement was made in the programme and subsequently quoted in a Cape Town newspaper:

> We, John Kani and Winston Ntshona, declare every single performance of this play, *The Island*, as an endorsement of the local and international call for the immediate release of Mr Nelson Mandela and all political prisoners and detainees. We earnestly

hope that this call will receive the support of all well-meaning South Africans.

(*Weekend Argus*, quoted in The Open University, 1991, p. 92)

Ten years later Kani and Ntshona were actually able to perform the play in Johannesburg again, to an audience that included Nelson Mandela, by then president of South Africa, and 300 former political prisoners. At the end of the performance the audience and cast joined in singing the national (ANC) anthem: *The Island* had become an act of celebration.

Activity

Think about your own response to the play: how useful would the terms 'propaganda' or 'protest' be in articulating this response?

You should allow about 10 minutes for this activity.

Discussion

This is another of those questions for which there will be as many different answers as there are people answering it. You might have reflected that *The Island* makes no direct reference to the South African government, or to Mandela. It would be difficult, then, to argue that the play is simply propaganda or 'protest theatre', although it may include some of those elements. For some of us, studying the play in the twenty-first century long after the dismantling of apartheid in South Africa, the political dimension might appear to be mainly a matter of historical interest. But the play continues to be performed in new contexts. For example, when Kani and Ntshona performed the play during their 2002 tour of the United Kingdom, the programme notes (along with large theatre posters) drew attention to the work of the human rights organisation Amnesty International. Audiences were thus prompted to think about the current plight of political prisoners around the world rather than back to the specifics of South Africa under apartheid.

One of the ideas running through 'Voices, texts and material culture', which you will explore in more detail in Book 4, is that context always affects meaning. Contexts are particularly important in the case of drama, since performance, by definition, is linked to a particular place at a particular time and happens in the presence of particular people. So performances of *The Island* in South Africa, both during and after apartheid, inevitably sound a different note from performances in the west. In his book on Fugard's work, Dennis Walder draws on the idea of theatre as a form of bearing witness – a function associated strongly with twentieth-century European drama – to account for *The Island's* continuing relevance:

> [I]f, as I would argue, *The Island* did bear witness, rather than articulate a call to arms, then I would also argue that it continues to do so – not because things have stayed the same, but because they have changed. Nobody gets detained on Robben Island any more; and the draconian laws that led to imprisonment for dissent have been repealed. But the extreme experience to which the play testifies, and the way in which the prisoners resist and survive if only temporarily by play acting, has not dated, in a world in which the experience of being detained and tortured for one's racial identity remains depressingly familiar.
>
> (2003, pp. 58–9)

6.4 Anti-apartheid protest music

Fiona Richards

Parallels to the dramatic impact of *The Island* can be found in South African music, some of which played an important part in the protests against apartheid (see the reference to Defiance Campaign songs in Reading 6.1, p. 326). There are numerous examples of songs expressing anger at forced evictions and working conditions, while during hunger strikes freedom songs served as a type of spiritual nourishment. Often these songs were short and simple, in order to enable participation and so that their sentiments could be clearly heard and understood. Figure 6.5 shows an example of one of these compact songs, with repeating phrases and uncomplicated rhythms.

Figure 6.5 'Siph'Amandla' from Nyberg, A. (ed.) (1990) *Freedom is Coming: Songs of Protest and Praise from South Africa*, Glasgow, Wild Goose Publications, p. 19

Activity

Find the recordings of the openings of two protest songs, 'Soweto Blues' (1976) and 'Bring Him Back Home' (1987), on the module website. They were composed by the eminent South African jazz musician Hugh Masekela (b.1939). 'Soweto Blues' is sung by Masekela's former wife, Miriam Makeba (1932–2008), nicknamed 'Mama Africa' after her work as a civil rights activist.

Listen to the songs now. How do they differ in musical style?

You should allow about 15 minutes for this activity.

Discussion

The first is a blues song, languid and reflective, focusing on the tragedy of the Soweto riots of 1976, in which hundreds of young people were shot dead by the police. You can hear references such as 'bullets dying' and then the somewhat sardonic interjection, 'Just a little atrocity deep in the city'. The mixing of English with black African language is in itself a type of protest, enhanced by the earthy tones of Makeba's voice. The second song, 'Bring Him Back Home', was part of the campaign to free Mandela, and you might have commented on its upbeat and forceful nature, with punchy rhythms and prominent trumpet melody (played by Masekela). You might also have noted the change in sentiment during the intervening years – from grieving to a determination to see change.

The Robben Island Singers are former freedom fighters who were once imprisoned with Nelson Mandela. The three men, Grant Shezi, Muntu Nxumalo and Thembinkosi Sithole, were in prison for ten, thirteen and nine years respectively, and now use the songs and stories from this time to inspire others. You can find an example of their harmonised singing on the module website. The motivational song 'Sizothabatha Umthwalo' ('We Will Take Our Belongings') concerns packing up and leaving the country to join Umkhonto Wessizwe (the armed wing of the ANC) for military training.

While in prison, singing could be a means of both survival and protest, with songs used to build community and for expressive purposes. It was common for prisoners to challenge prison authorities by improvising new lyrics to a familiar melody, and traditional folk songs could take on new meanings.

Activity

Finish your work in this section by listening to 'What a System, What a Crime', sung by the Robben Island Singers. You can find this on the module website. Here the Singers take a well-known tune, 'Oh My Darling, Clementine', giving it original and satirical words of protest against the regime.

6.5 Authority and identity

Returning to *The Island*, and at a distance now of several decades from its first 'open' production, we can attempt to sum up the play's significance in relation to questions of authority. *The Island* has been seen by audiences throughout the world, and has accumulated prestige – and consequent authority – by association with influential figures such as the director Peter Brook, who arranged a restaging of the play with Kani and Ntshona at the Bouffes du Nord, Paris, in 1999. Kani and Ntshona's long involvement with the play has also lent considerable authority to their performances; it must be impossible for other actors to take on the roles of John and Winston without a keen awareness of their originators. But the play's emphasis on the theme of identity goes beyond association with these actors: as Walder notes, '"John" and "Winston" … perform their resistance to imprisonment by taking on apparently innocuous, "classical" identities' (2003, p. 59). The play not only appropriates the cultural authority of Sophocles' tragedy by reworking the conflict between Antigone and Creon, but also uses this vehicle to assert the importance of identity on behalf of those who are oppressed or marginalised. As in Michael Longley's reworking of a part of the *Iliad* in his poem 'Ceasefire', a political point is being made. If *The Island* has become a canonical modern play – as arguably it has – it is because it fuses its basis in Greek tragedy with a wider concern for individual identity in the conflict between private and public morality.

Conclusion

This chapter and the previous one have both shown how texts from ancient Greece have provided a foundation for quite different works produced many centuries later. This suggests that artistic canons are dynamic not simply because they change over time, as you saw in the first part of this book, but also because canonical works may embody the potential to generate new texts that draw on some of the authority of the originals.

Reading *The Island* also forms part of your study of the academic subject Literature, which you have explored here through one of its oldest genres: drama. You will encounter further examples of dramatic writing in Book 3, but there the perspective will be different, as you will be approaching this material from the angle of Creative Writing, another branch of the larger subject we generally call 'English'. However, your study of *The Island*, a play that grew out of improvisation and collaboration, serves as a reminder that creativity is a quality that pervades the arts, and manifests itself not just in the written productions of individual authors but across a very wide spectrum of activities that incorporate making and performing.

References

Battersby, E. (2004) 'A Greek tragedy for our times', *The Irish Times*, 3 April (City edition; Weekend), p. 55.

Fugard, A. (1993) *The Township Plays* (ed. D. Walder), Oxford, Oxford University Press.

Grotowski, J. (1968) *Towards a Poor Theatre*, Holstebro, Odin Teatret.

Kruger, L. (1999) *The Drama of South Africa*, London, Routledge.

Mandela, N. (1994) *Long Walk to Freedom: The Autobiography of Nelson Mandela*, London, Abacus.

The Nobel Foundation (1993) 'Presentation speech for the Nobel Peace Prize 1993' [Online]. Available at http://nobelprize.org/nobel_prizes/peace/laureates/1993/presentation-speech.html (Accessed 30 April 2014).

The Open University (1991) *A319, Block 4: Literature and Ideology*, Milton Keynes, The Open University.

Walder, D. (2003) *Athol Fugard*, Tavistock, Northcote House.

Further reading

Dennis Walder's edition of Fugard's *Township Plays* includes a number of other play-scripts. One already referred to in this chapter and well worth reading is *Sizwe Bansi is Dead*, another collaboration between Athol Fugard, John Kani and Winston Ntshona. See:

Fugard, A. (1993) *The Township Plays* (ed. D. Walder), Oxford, Oxford University Press.

If your interests lie mainly in the way that late twentieth-century and twenty-first-century literature reuses and transforms texts from ancient Greece (and Rome), you might want to explore The Open University website devoted to *Classical Receptions in Drama and Poetry in English from c.1970 to the Present*: http://www2.open.ac.uk/ClassicalStudies/GreekPlays/index.html

Reading 6.1 *The Island*

Source: Fugard, A. (1993) *The Township Plays* **(ed. D. Walder), Oxford, Oxford University Press, pp. 194–227 and 231.**

The Island was devised by Athol Fugard, John Kani and Winston Ntshona. It was first performed on 2 July 1973, and was directed by Athol Fugard, with John Kani as John and Winston Ntshona as Winston. The version of the text included in this reading was edited with notes by Dennis Walder.

Characters:

JOHN

WINSTON

Scene 1

Centre stage: a raised area representing a cell on Robben Island[1]. Blankets and sleeping-mats – the prisoners sleep on the floor – are neatly folded. In one corner are a bucket of water and two tin mugs.

The long drawn-out wail of a siren. Stage-lights come up to reveal a moat of harsh, white light around the cell. In it the two prisoners – John stage-right and Winston stage-left – mime the digging of sand. They wear the prison uniform of khaki shirt and short trousers. Their heads are shaven. It is an image of back-breaking and grotesquely futile labour. Each in turn fills a wheelbarrow and then with great effort pushes it to where the other man is digging, and empties it. As a result, the piles of sand never diminish. Their labour is interminable. The only sounds are their grunts as they dig, the squeal of the wheelbarrows as they circle the cell, and the hum of Hodoshe[2], the green carrion fly.

A whistle is blown. They stop digging and come together, standing side by side as they are handcuffed together and shackled at the ankles. Another whistle. They start to run … John mumbling a prayer, Winston muttering a rhythm for their three-legged run.

They do not run fast enough. They get beaten … Winston receiving a bad blow to the eye and John spraining an ankle. In this condition they arrive finally at the cell

---

[1] **a cell on Robben Island**: small island about seven miles off the Atlantic coast at Cape Town, a place of banishment or imprisonment since the beginning of white settlement. A leper colony for much of the nineteenth century, it was also used to imprison African chiefs who resisted the whites, and as a mental asylum. In 1959 a maximum security prison was built, at first housing convicted criminal offenders as well as 'politicals'. The prisoners were black, the warders white. The prison had a capacity of 650 prisoners.

[2] **Hodoshe**: the Afrikaans word for a carrion fly, but also the name of the chief warder.

door. Handcuffs and shackles are taken off. After being searched, they lurch into their cell. The door closes behind them. Both men sink to the floor.

A moment of total exhaustion until slowly, painfully, they start to explore their respective injuries ... Winston his eye, and John his ankle. Winston is moaning softly and this eventually draws John's attention away from his ankle. He crawls to Winston and examines the injured eye. It needs attention. Winston's moaning is slowly turning into a sound of inarticulate outrage, growing in volume and violence. John urinates into one hand and tries to clean the other man's eye with it, but Winston's anger and outrage are now uncontrollable. He breaks away from John and crawls around the cell, blind with rage and pain. John tries to placate him ... the noise could bring back the warders and still more trouble. Winston eventually finds the cell door but before he can start banging on it John pulls him away.

WINSTON   [*calling*]. Hodoshe!

JOHN   Leave him, Winston. Listen to me, man! If he comes now we'll be in bigger shit.

WINSTON   I want Hodoshe. I want him now! I want to take him to the office. He must read my warrant. I was sentenced to Life, brother, not bloody Death!

JOHN   Please, Winston! He made us run. ...

WINSTON   I want Hodoshe!

JOHN   He made us run. He's happy now. Leave him. Maybe he'll let us go back to the quarry tomorrow. ...

[*Winston is suddenly silent. For a moment John thinks his words are having an effect, but then he realizes that the other man is looking at his ear. Winston touches it. It is bleeding. A sudden spasm of fear from John, who puts a hand to his ear. His fingers come away with blood on them. The two men look at each other.*]

WINSTON   *Nyana we Sizwe!* [3]

[*In a reversal of earlier roles Winston now gets John down on the floor of the cell so as to examine the injured ear. He has to wipe blood and sweat out of his eyes in order to see clearly. John winces with pain. Winston keeps restraining him.*]

WINSTON   [*eventually*]. It's not too bad. [*Using his shirt-tail he cleans the injured ear.*]

---

[3]   *Nyana we Sizwe*: an ancient Xhosa rallying cry, used again at the end of Scene 3, meaning 'Son of the Land!' or 'Brother!'

JOHN   [*through clenched teeth as Winston tends his ear*]. Hell, *ons was gemoer vandag!*[4] [*A weak smile.*] News bulletin and weather forecast! Black Domination was chased by White Domination. Black Domination lost its shoes and collected a few bruises. Black Domination will run barefoot to the quarry tomorrow. Conditions locally remain unchanged – thunderstorms with the possibility of cold showers and rain. Elsewhere, fine and warm!

[*Winston has now finished tending John's ear and settles down on the floor beside him. He clears his nose, ears, and eyes of sand.*]

WINSTON   Sand! Same old sea and sand I used to play with when I was young. St George's Strand[5]. New Year's Day. Sand dunes. Sand castles ....

JOHN   *Ja,*[6] we used to go there too. Last .... [*Pause and then a small laugh. He shakes his head.*] The Christmas before they arrested me, we were down there. All of us. Honeybush. My little Monde played in the sand. We'd given her one of those little buckets and spades for Christmas.

WINSTON   *Ja.*

JOHN   Anyway, it was Daddy's turn today. [*Shaking his head ruefully.*] *Haai,*[7] Winston, this one goes on the record. 'Struesgod! I'm a man, brother. A man! But if Hodoshe had kept us at those wheelbarrows five minutes longer ...! There would have been a baby on the Island tonight. I nearly cried.

WINSTON   *Ja.*

JOHN   There was no end to it, except one of us!

WINSTON   That's right.

JOHN   This morning, when he said: 'You two! The beach!' ... I thought, Okay, so it's my turn to empty the sea into a hole. He likes that one. But when he pointed to the wheelbarrows, and I saw his idea ...! [*Shaking his head.*] I laughed at first. Then I wasn't laughing. Then I hated you. You looked so stupid, *broer!*[8]

WINSTON   That's what he wanted.

---

4 **Hell, ons was gemoer vandag!**: (Afrikaans) Hell, we were really beaten up today!
5 **St George's Strand**: a beach near Port Elizabeth.
6 **Ja**: (Afrikaans) Yes
7 **Haai**: exclamation of surprise or alarm (from Xhosa 'hayi' = no).
8 **broer**: brother.

JOHN   It was going to last forever, man! Because of *you*. And for *you*, because of *me*. *Moer!* [9] He's cleverer than I thought.

WINSTON   If he was God, he would have done it.

JOHN   What?

WINSTON   Broken us. Men get tired. Hey! There's a thought. We're still alive because Hodoshe got tired.

JOHN   Tomorrow?

WINSTON   We'll see.

JOHN   If he takes us back there … If I hear that wheelbarrow … of yours again, coming with another bloody load of … eternity!

WINSTON   [*with calm resignation*]. We'll see.

[*Pause. John looks at Winston.*]

JOHN   [*with quiet emphasis, as if the other man did not fully understand the significance of what he had said*]. I *hated* you, Winston.

WINSTON   [*meeting John's eyes*]. I hated *you.*

[*John puts a hand on Winston's shoulder. Their brotherhood is intact. He gets slowly to his feet.*]

JOHN   Where's the *lap*?

WINSTON   Somewhere. Look for it.

JOHN   Hey! You had it last.

[*Limping around the cell looking for their wash-rag.*]

WINSTON   *Haai*, man! You got no wife here. Look for the rag yourself.

JOHN   [*finding the rag beside the water bucket*]. Look where it is. Look! Hodoshe comes in here and sees it. 'Whose *lappie* is that?' Then what do you say?

WINSTON   'It's his rag, sir.'

JOHN   Yes? Okay. 'It's my rag, sir.' When you wash, use your shirt.

WINSTON   Okay, okay! 'It's our rag, sir!'

JOHN   That'll be the bloody day!

[*John, getting ready to wash, starts to take off his shirt. Winston produces a cigarette butt, matches, and flint from their hiding-place under the water bucket. He settles down for a smoke.*]

[9]   ***Moer!***: (Afrikaans) a term of abuse, equivalent to 'Fuck!'

Shit, today was long. Hey, Winston, suppose the watch of the chap behind the siren is slow! We could still be there, man! [*He pulls out three or four rusty nails from a secret pocket in his trousers. He holds them out to Winston.*] Hey, there.

WINSTON   What?

JOHN   With the others.

WINSTON   [*taking the nails*]. What's this?

JOHN   Necklace, man. With the others.

WINSTON   Necklace?

JOHN   Antigone's necklace.

WINSTON   *Ag,*[10] shit, man!

[*Slams the nails down on the cell floor and goes on smoking.*]

Antigone! Go to hell, man, John.

JOHN   Hey, don't start any nonsense now. You promised. [*Limps over to Winston's bed-roll and produces a half-completed necklace made of nails and string.*] It's nearly finished. Look. Three fingers, one nail. … three fingers, one nail … [*Places the necklace beside Winston who is shaking his head, smoking aggressively, and muttering away.*] Don't start any nonsense now, Winston. There's six days to go to the concert. We're committed. We promised the chaps we'd do something. This *Antigone* is just right for us. Six more days and we'll make it.

[*He continues washing.*]

WINSTON   Jesus, John! We were down on the beach today. Hodoshe made us run. Can't you just leave a man …?

JOHN   To hell with you! Who do you think ran with you? I'm also tired, but we can't back out now. Come on! Three fingers ….

WINSTON   … one nail! [*Shaking his head.*] *Haai* … *haai* … *haai!*

JOHN   Stop moaning and get on with it. Shit, Winston! What sort of progress is this? [*Abandoning his wash.*] Listen. Listen! Number 42 is practising the Zulu War Dance. Down there they're rehearsing their songs. It's just in this *moer* cell that there's always an argument. Today you want to do it, tomorrow you don't want to do it. How the hell must I know what to report to the chaps tomorrow if we go back to the quarry?

---

[10]   *Ag*: (Afrikaans exclamation) Oh (pronounced like German 'ach').

[*Winston is unyielding. His obstinacy gets the better of John, who eventually throws the wash-rag at him.*]

There! Wash!

[*John applies himself to the necklace while Winston still muttering away in an undertone, starts to clean himself.*]

How can I be sure of anything when you carry on like this? We've still got to learn the words, the moves. Shit! It could be so bloody good, man.

[*Winston mutters protests all the way through this speech of John's. The latter holds up the necklace.*]

Nearly finished! Look at it! Three fingers ....

WINSTON   ... one nail.

JOHN   *Ja!* Simple. Do you still remember all I told you yesterday? Bet you've bloody forgotten. How can I carry on like this? I can't move on, man. Over the whole bloody lot again! Who Antigone is ... who Creon is ....

WINSTON   Antigone is mother to Polynices ....

JOHN   *Haai, haai, haai* ... shit, Winston! [*Now really exasperated.*] How many times must I tell you that Antigone is the sister to the two brothers? Not the mother. That's another play.[11]

WINSTON   Oh.

JOHN   That's all you know! 'Oh.' [*He abandons the necklace and fishes out a piece of chalk from a crack in the floor.*] Come here. This is the last time. 'Struesgod. The last time.

WINSTON   *Ag,* no, John.

JOHN   Come! I'm putting this plot down for the last time! If you don't learn it tonight I'm going to report you to the old men tomorrow. And remember, *broer*, those old men will make Hodoshe and his tricks look like a little boy.

WINSTON   Jesus Christ! Learn to dig for Hodoshe, learn to run for Hodoshe, and what happens when I get back to the cell? Learn to read *Antigone*!

JOHN   Come! And shut up! [*He pulls the reluctant Winston down beside him on the floor. Winston continues to clean himself with the rag while John lays out the 'plot' of* Antigone.] If you would just stop moaning, you would learn faster. Now listen!

[11]   **That's another play**: Sophocles' *Oedipus Rex*, in which the mother of Polynices (Jocasta, not Antigone) has a major role.

WINSTON	Okay, do it.
JOHN	Listen! It is the Trial of Antigone. Right?
WINSTON	So you say.
JOHN	First, the accused. Who is the accused?
WINSTON	Antigone.
JOHN	Coming from you that's bloody progress. [*Writing away on the cell floor with his chalk.*] Next the State. Who is the State?
WINSTON	Creon.
JOHN	King Creon. Creon is the State. Now … what did Antigone do?
WINSTON	Antigone buried her brother Eteocles.
JOHN	No, no, no! Shit, Winston, when are you going to remember this thing? I told you, man, Antigone buried Polynices. The traitor! The one who I said was on *our* side. Right?
WINSTON	Right.
JOHN	Stage one of the Trial. [*Writing on the floor.*] The State lays its charges against the Accused … and lists counts … you know the way they do it. Stage two is Pleading. What does Antigone plead? Guilty or Not Guilty?
WINSTON	Not Guilty.
JOHN	[*trying to be tactful*]. Now look, Winston, we're not going to argue. Between me and you, in this cell, we know that she's Not Guilty. But in the play she pleads Guilty.
WINSTON	No, man, John! Antigone is Not Guilty. …
JOHN	In the play ….
WINSTON	[*losing his temper*]. To hell with the play! Antigone had every right to bury her brother.
JOHN	Don't say 'To hell with the play'. We've got to do the bloody thing. And in the play she pleads Guilty. Get that straight. Antigone pleads ….
WINSTON	[*giving up in disgust*]. Okay, do it your way.
JOHN	It's not my way! In the play ….
WINSTON	Guilty!
JOHN	Yes, Guilty! [*Writes furiously on the floor.*]
WINSTON	Guilty.

JOHN Stage three, Pleading in Mitigation of Sentence. Stage four, Sentence, State Summary, and something from you ... Farewell Words. Now learn that.

WINSTON Hey?

JOHN [*getting up*]. Learn that!

WINSTON But we've just done it!

JOHN I've just done it. Now you learn it.

WINSTON [*throwing aside the wash-rag with disgust before applying himself to learning the 'plot'*]. Learn to run, learn to read. ...

JOHN And don't throw the rag there! [*Retrieving the rag and placing it in its correct place.*] Don't be so bloody difficult, man. We're nearly there. You'll be proud of this thing when we've done it.

[*Limps to his bed-roll and produces a pendant made from a jam-tin lid and twine.*]

Look. Winston, look! Creon's medallion. Good, hey! [*Hangs it around his neck.*] I'll finish the necklace while you learn that. [*He strings on the remaining nails.*] Jesus, Winston! June 1965.[12]

WINSTON What?

JOHN This, man. *Antigone*. In New Brighton. St Stephen's Hall. The place was packed, man! All the big people. Front row ... dignitaries. Shit, those were the days. Georgie was Creon. You know Georgie?

WINSTON The teacher?

JOHN That's him. He played Creon. Should have seen him, Winston. Short and fat, with big eyes, but by the time the play was finished he was as tall as the roof.

[*Onto his legs in an imitation of Georgie's Creon.*]

'My Councillors, now that the Gods have brought our City safe through a storm of troubles to tranquillity. ...' And old Mulligan! Another short-arsed teacher. With a beard! He used to go up to the Queen. ... [*Another imitation.*] 'Your Majesty, prepare for grief, but do not weep.'

[*The necklace in his hands.*]

---

[12] **June 1965**: recalling the Serpent Players' production of *Antigone*, with Nomhle Nkonyeni and George Mnci, which took place in St Stephen's Hall, New Brighton, as a police round-up in the area was in full force. 'Mulligan' Mbikwane was another Player in the production, as were 'Sipho' and 'Simon'.

Nearly finished!

Nomhle played Antigone. A bastard of a lady that one, but a beautiful bitch. Can't get her out of my mind tonight.

WINSTON   [*indicating the 'plot'*]. I know this.

JOHN   You sure?

WINSTON   This? ... it's here. [*Tapping his head.*]

JOHN   You're not bullshitting, hey? [*He rubs out the 'plot' and then paces the cell.*] Right. The Trial of Antigone. Who is the Accused?

WINSTON   Antigone.

JOHN   Who is the State?

WINSTON   King Creon.

JOHN   Stage one.

WINSTON   [*supremely self-confident*]. Antigone lays charges ....

JOHN   NO, SHIT, MAN, WINSTON!!!

[*Winston pulls John down and stifles his protests with a hand over his mouth.*]

WINSTON   Okay ... okay ... listen, John ... listen. ... The State lays charges against Antigone.

[*Pause.*]

JOHN   Be careful!

WINSTON   The State lays charges against Antigone.

JOHN   Stage two.

WINSTON   Pleading.

JOHN   What does she plead? Guilty or Not Guilty?

WINSTON   Guilty.

JOHN   Stage three.

WINSTON   Pleading in Mitigation of Sentence.

JOHN   Stage four.

WINSTON   State Summary, Sentence, and Farewell Words.

JOHN   [*very excited*]. He's got it! That's my man. See how easy it is, Winston? Tomorrow, just the words.

[*Winston gets onto his legs, John puts away the props. Mats and blankets are unrolled. The two men prepare for sleep.*]

JOHN   Hell, I hope we go back to the quarry tomorrow. There's still a lot of things we need for props and costumes. Your wig! The boys in Number Fourteen said they'd try and smuggle me a piece of rope from the jetty.

WINSTON   *Ja*, I hope we're back there. I want to try and get some tobacco through to Sipho.

JOHN   Sipho?

WINSTON   Back in solitary.

JOHN   Again!

WINSTON   *Ja.*

JOHN   Oh hell!

WINSTON   Simon passed the word.

JOHN   What was it this time?

WINSTON   Complained about the food I think. Demanded to see the book of Prison Regulations.

JOHN   Why don't they leave him alone for a bit?

WINSTON   Because he doesn't leave them alone.

JOHN   You're right. I'm glad I'm not in Number Twenty-two with him. One man starts getting hard-arsed like that and the whole lot of you end up in the shit.

            [*Winston's bed is ready. He lies down.*]

            You know what I'm saying?

WINSTON   *Ja.*

JOHN   What?

WINSTON   What 'What'?

JOHN   What am I saying?

WINSTON   *Haai,* Johnny, man! I'm tired now! Let a man ....

JOHN   I'm saying Don't Be hard-Arsed! You! When Hodoshe opens that door tomorrow say '*Ja, Baas*' the right way. I don't want to be back on that bloody beach tomorrow just because you feel like being difficult.

WINSTON   [*wearily*]. Okay, man, Johnny.

JOHN   You're not alone in this cell. I'm here too.

WINSTON   Jesus, you think I don't know that!

JOHN   People must remember their responsibilities to others.

WINSTON   I'm glad to hear you say that, because I was just going to remind you that it is your turn tonight.

JOHN   What do you mean? Wasn't it my turn last night?

WINSTON   [*shaking his head emphatically*]. *Haai, haai.* Don't you remember? Last night I took you to bioscope.

JOHN   Hey, by the way! So you did. Bloody good film too. 'Fastest Gun in the West'. Glenn Ford.

[*Whips out a six-shooter and guns down a few bad men.*]

You were bullshitting me a bit, though. How the hell can Glenn Ford shoot backwards through his legs? I tried to work that one out on the beach. [*He is now seated on his bed-roll. After a moment's thought he holds up an empty mug as a telephone-receiver and starts to dial. Winston watches him with puzzlement.*]

Operator, put me through to New Brighton, please … yes, New Brighton, Port Elizabeth. The number is 414624. … Yes, mine is local … local. …

WINSTON   [*recognizing the telephone number*]. The Shop!

[*He sits upright with excitement as John launches into the telephone conversation.*]

JOHN   That you, Scott? Hello, man! Guess who! … You got it! You bastard! Hell, shit, Scott, man … how things with you? No, still inside. Give the news, man … you don't say! No, we don't hear anything here … not a word. … What's that? Business is bad? … You bloody undertaker! People aren't dying fast enough! No, things are fine here. …

[*Winston, squirming with excitement, has been trying unsuccessfully to interrupt John's torrent of words and laughter. He finally succeeds in drawing John's attention.*]

WINSTON   Who else is there? Who's with Scott?

JOHN   Hey, Scott, who's there with you? … Oh no! … call him to the phone, man. …

WINSTON   Who's it?

JOHN   [*ignoring Winston*]. Just for a minute, man, please, Scott. … [*Ecstatic response from John as another voice comes over the phone.*] Hello there, you beautiful bastard … how's it, man? …

WINSTON   Who the hell is it, man?

JOHN   [*hand over the receiver*]. Sky!

[*Winston can no longer contain his excitement. He scrambles out of his bed to join John, and joins in the fun with questions and remarks whispered into John's ear. Both men enjoy it enormously.*]

How's it with Mangi? Where's Vusi? How are the chaps keeping, Sky? Winston? … All right, man. He's here next to me. No, fine, man, fine, man … small accident today when he collided with Hodoshe, but nothing to moan about. His right eye bruised, that's all. Hey, Winston's asking how are the punkies[13] doing? [*Big laugh.*] You bloody lover boy! Leave something for us, man!

[*John becomes aware of Winston trying to interrupt again: to Winston.*] Okay … okay….

[*Back to the telephone.*] Listen, Sky, Winston says if you get a chance go down to Dora Street, to his wife. Tell V., Winston says he's okay, things are fine. Winston says she must carry on … nothing has happened … tell her to take care of everything and everybody. … *Ja.* … .

[*The mention of his wife guillotines Winston's excitement and fun. After a few seconds of silence, he crawls back heavily to his bed and lies down. A similar shift in mood takes place in John.*]

And look, Sky, you're not far from Gratten Street. Cross over to it, man, drop in on number thirty-eight, talk to Princess, my wife. How is she keeping? Ask her for me. I haven't received a letter for three months now. Why aren't they writing? Tell her to write, man. I want to know how the children are keeping. Is Monde still at school? How's my twin baby, my Father and Mother? Is the old girl sick? They mustn't be afraid to tell me. I want to know. I know it's an effort to write, but it means a lot to us here. Tell her … this was another day. They're not very different here. We were down on the beach. The wind was blowing. The sand got in our eyes. The sea was rough. I couldn't see the mainland properly. Tell them that maybe tomorrow we'll go to the quarry. It's not so bad there. We'll be with the others. Tell her also … it's starting to get cold now, but the worst is still coming.

[*Slow fade to blackout.*]

---

[13] **punkies**: 'good-time' girls at the shebeen.

Scene 2

The cell, a few days later.

John is hidden under a blanket. Winston is in the process of putting on Antigone's wig and false breasts.

JOHN   Okay?

WINSTON   [*still busy*]. No.

JOHN   Okay?

WINSTON   No.

JOHN   Okay?

WINSTON   No.

      [*Pause*]

JOHN   Okay?

      [*Winston is ready. He stands waiting. John slowly lifts the blanket and looks. He can't believe his eyes. Winston is a very funny sight. John's amazement turns into laughter, which builds steadily. He bangs on the cell wall.*]

      Hey, Norman. Norman! Come this side, man. I got it here. *Poes!*[14]

      [*John launches into an extravagant send-up of Winston's Antigone. He circles 'her' admiringly, he fondles her breasts, he walks arm in arm with her down Main Street, collapsing with laughter between each 'turn'. He climaxes everything by dropping his trousers.*]

      Speedy Gonzales! Here I come!

      [*This last joke is too much for Winston who has endured the whole performance with mounting but suppressed anger. He tears off the wig and breasts, throws them down on the cell floor, and storms over to the water bucket where he starts to clean himself.*]

WINSTON   It's finished! I'm not doing it. Take your Antigone and shove it up your arse!

JOHN   [*trying to control himself*]. Wait, man. Wait ….

      [*He starts laughing again.*]

WINSTON   There is nothing to wait for, my friend, I'm not doing it.

JOHN   Please, Winston!

---

[14] *Poes!*: (Afrikaans) obscene slang: 'Cunt!'

WINSTON   You can laugh as much as you like, my friend, but just let's get one thing straight, I'm *not* doing Antigone. And in case you want to know why ... I'm a man, not a bloody woman.

JOHN   When did I say otherwise?

WINSTON   What were you laughing at?

JOHN   I'm not laughing now.

WINSTON   What are you doing, crying?

[*Another burst of laughter from John.*]

There you go again, more laughing! Shit, man, you want me to go out there tomorrow night and make a bloody fool of myself? You think I don't know what will happen after that? Every time I run to the quarry ... 'Nyah ... nyah. ... Here comes Antigone! ... Help the poor lady! ...' Well, you can go to hell with your Antigone.

JOHN   I wasn't laughing at you.

WINSTON   Then who were you laughing at? Who else was here that dressed himself as a lady and made a bloody fool of himself?

JOHN   [*now trying very hard to placate the other man*]. Okay Winston, Okay! I'm not laughing any more.

WINSTON   You can go to hell with what you're saying.

JOHN   Look, Winston, try to understand, man, ... this is Theatre.

WINSTON   You call laughing at me, Theatre? Then go to hell with your Theatre!

JOHN   Please, Winston, just stop talking and listen to me.

WINSTON   No! You get this brother, ... I am not doing your Antigone! I would rather run the whole day for Hodoshe. At least I know where I stand with him. All *he* wants is to make me a 'boy' ... not a bloody woman.

JOHN   Okay, okay ....

WINSTON   Nothing you can say ...

JOHN   [*shouting the other man down*]. Will you bloody listen!

WINSTON   [*throwing the wash-rag down violently*]. Okay. I'm listening.

JOHN   Sure I laughed. *Ja ... I laughed.* But can I tell you why I laughed? I was preparing you for ... stage fright! You think I don't know what I'm doing in this cell? This is preparation for stage fright! I know those bastards out there. When you get in front of them, sure they'll laugh ... 'Nyah, nyah!' ...

they'll laugh. But just remember this, brother, nobody laughs forever! There'll come a time when they'll stop laughing, and that will be the time when our Antigone hits them with her words.

WINSTON   You're day-dreaming, John. Just get it into your head that I'm not doing Antigone. It's as simple as that.

JOHN   [*realizing for the first time that Winston needs to be handled very carefully*]. Hey, Winston! Hold on there, man. We've only got one more day to go! They've given us the best spot in the programme. We end the show! You can't back out now.

WINSTON   You think I can't? Just wait and see.

JOHN   Winston! You want to get me into trouble? Is that what you want?

WINSTON   Okay, I won't back out.

JOHN   [*delighted with his easy victory*]. That's my man!

WINSTON   [*retrieving the wig and false breasts off the floor and slamming them into John's hands*]. Here's Antigone … take these titties and hair and play Antigone. I'm going to play Creon. Do you understand what I'm saying? Take your two titties …. I'll have my balls and play Creon. [*Turns his back on a flabbergasted John, fishes out a cigarette-butt and matches from under the water bucket, and settles down for a smoke.*]

JOHN   [*after a stunned silence*]. You won't make it! I thought about that one, days ago. It's too late now to learn Creon's words.

WINSTON   [*smoking*]. I hate to say it, but that is just too bad. I am not doing Antigone.

[*John is now furious. After a moment's hesitation he stuffs on the wig and false breasts and confronts Winston.*]

JOHN   Look at me. Now laugh.

[*Winston tries, but the laugh is forced and soon dies away.*]

Go on.

[*Pause.*]

Go on laughing! Why did you stop? Must I tell you why? Because behind all this rubbish is me, and you know it's me. You think those bastards out there won't know it's you? Yes, they'll laugh. But who cares about that as long as they laugh in the beginning and listen at the end. That's all we want them to do … listen at the end!

WINSTON	I don't care what you say, John. I'm not doing Antigone.
JOHN	Winston … you're being difficult. You promised ….
WINSTON	Go to hell, man. Only last night you tell me that this Antigone is a bloody … what you call it … legend! A Greek one at that. Bloody thing never even happened. Not even history! Look, brother, I got no time for bullshit. Fuck legends. Me? … I live my life here! I know why I'm here, and it's history, not legends. I had my chat with a magistrate in Cradock[15] and now I'm here. Your Antigone is a child's play, man.
JOHN	Winston! That's Hodoshe's talk.
WINSTON	You can go to hell with that one too.
JOHN	Hodoshe's talk, Winston! That's what he says all the time. What he wants us to say all our lives. Our convictions, our ideals … that's what he calls them … child's play. Everything we fucking do is 'child's play' … when we ran that whole day in the sun and pushed those wheelbarrows, when we cry, when we shit … child's play! Look, brother, … I've had enough! No one is going to stop me doing Antigone ….

[*The two men break apart suddenly, drop their trousers, and stand facing the wall with arms outstretched. Hodoshe calls John.*]

Yes, sir!

[*He then pulls up his trousers and leaves the cell. When he has left, Winston pulls up his trousers and starts muttering with savage satisfaction at the thought of John in Hodoshe's hands.*]

WINSTON	There he goes. Serves him right. I just hope Hodoshe teaches him a lesson. Antigone is important! Antigone this! Antigone that! Shit, man. Nobody can sleep in this bloody cell because of all that bullshit. Polynices! Eteocles! The other prisoners too. Nobody gets any peace and quiet because of that bloody Antigone! I hope Hodoshe gives it to him.

[*He is now at the cell door. He listens, then moves over to the wig on the floor and circles it. He finally picks it up. Moves back to the cell door to make sure no one is coming. The water bucket gives him an idea. He puts on the wig and, after some difficulty, manages to see his reflection in the*

---

[15]   **Cradock**: Eastern Cape Town, to which those rounded up in the Port Elizabeth area were taken.

water. A good laugh, which he cuts off abruptly. He moves around the cell trying out a few of Antigone's poses. None of them work. He feels a fool. He finally tears off the wig and throws it down on the floor with disgust.]

Ag, voetsek![16]

[*Hands in pockets, he paces the cell with grim determination.*]

I'm not going to do it. And I'm going to tell him. When he comes back. For once he must just shut that big bloody mouth of his and listen. To me! I'm not going to argue, but 'struesgod that …!

[*The wig on the floor. He stamps on it.*]

Shit, man! If he wants a woman in the cell he must send for his wife, and I don't give a damn how he does it. I didn't walk with those men and burn my bloody passbook in front of that police station, and have a magistrate send me here for life so that he can dress me up like a woman and make a bloody fool of me. I'm going to tell him. When he walks through that door.

[*John returns. Winston is so involved in the problem of Antigone that at first he does not register John's strangely vacant manner.*]

Listen, *broer*, I'm not trying to be difficult, but this Antigone! No! Please listen to me, John. 'Struesgod I can't do it. I mean, let's try something else, like singing or something. You always got ideas. You know I can sing or dance. But not Antigone. Please, John.

JOHN   [*quietly*]. Winston ….

WINSTON   [*still blind to the other man's manner*]. Don't let's argue, man. We're been together in this cell too long now to quarrel about rubbish. But you know me. If there's one thing I can't stand it's people laughing at me. If I go out there tomorrow night and those bastards start laughing I'll fuck up the first one I lay my hands on. You saw yourself what happened in here when you started laughing. I wanted to *moer* you,[17] John. I'm not joking. I really wanted to …. Hey, are you listening to me? [*Looking squarely at John.*]

---

[16] *Ag voetsek!*: (Afrikaans) offensive command, originally to a dog, as in 'Oh, fuck off!'
[17] **I wanted to *moer* you**: (Afrikaans) I wanted to fuck (beat) you up.

JOHN	Winston … I've got something to tell you.
WINSTON	[*registering John's manner for the first time*]. What's the matter? Hodoshe? What happened? Are we in shit? Solitary?
JOHN	My appeal was heard last Wednesday. Sentence reduced. I've got three months to go.
	[*Long silence. Winston is stunned. Eventually ….*]
WINSTON	Three ….
JOHN	… months to go.
WINSTON	Three ….
JOHN	*Ja*. That's what Prinsloo said.
WINSTON	John!
	[*Winston explodes with joy. The men embrace. They dance a jig in the cell. Winston finally tears himself away and starts to hammer on the cell walls so as to pass on the news to other prisoners.*]
	Norman! Norman!! John. Three months to go. *Ja* …. Just been told ….
	[*Winston's excitement makes John nervous. He pulls Winston away from the wall.*]
JOHN	Winston! Not yet, man. We'll tell them at the quarry tomorrow. Let me just live with it for a little while.
WINSTON	Okay, okay …. How did it happen?
	[*He pulls John down to the floor. They sit close together.*]
JOHN	Jesus, I'm so mixed up, man! *Ja* … the door opened and I saw Hodoshe. Ooo God, I said to myself. Trouble! Here we go again! All because of you and the noise you were making. Went down the corridor straight to Number Four … Solitary and Spare Diet!! But at the end, instead of turning right, we turned left into the main block, all the way through it to Prinsloo's office.
WINSTON	Prinsloo!
JOHN	I'm telling you. Prinsloo himself, man. We waited outside for a little bit, then Hodoshe pushed me in. Prinsloo was behind his desk, busy with some papers. He pulled out one and said to me: 'You are very lucky. Your lawyers have been working on your case. The sentence has been reduced from ten years, to three.'
WINSTON	What did Hodoshe say?

JOHN	Nothing. But he looked unhappy.
	[*They laugh.*]
	Hey, something else. Hodoshe let me walk back here by myself! He didn't follow me.
WINSTON	Of course. You are free.
JOHN	*Haai*, Winston, not yet. Those three months … ! Or suppose it's a trick.
WINSTON	What do you mean?
JOHN	Those bastards will do anything to break you. If the wheelbarrows and the quarry don't do it, they'll try something else. Remember that last visit of wives, when they lined up all the men on the other side …. 'Take a good look and say goodbye! Back to the cells!'
WINSTON	You say you saw Prinsloo?
JOHN	Prinsloo himself. Bastard didn't even stand up when I walked in. And by the way … I had to sign. *Ja*! I had to sign a form to say that I had been officially told of the result of my appeal … that I had three months to go. *Ja*. I signed!
WINSTON	[*without the slightest doubt*]. It's three months, John.
JOHN	[*relaxing and living with the reality for the first time*]. Hell, Winston, at the end of those three months, it will be three years together in this cell. Three years ago I stood in front of that magistrate at Kirkwood – bastard didn't even look at me: 'Ten years!' I watched ten years of my life drift away like smoke from a cigarette while he fidgeted and scratched his arse. That same night back in the prison van to the cells at Rooihel. First time we met!
WINSTON	*Ja*. We had just got back from our trial in Cradock.
JOHN	You, Temba, …
WINSTON	Sipho ….
JOHN	Hell, man!
WINSTON	First time we got close to each other was the next morning in the yard, when they lined us up for the vans ….
JOHN	And married us!
	[*They lock left and right hands together to suggest handcuffs.*]
WINSTON	Who was that old man … remember him? … in the corner handcuffed to Sipho?

JOHN   Sipho?

WINSTON   *Ja,* the one who started the singing.

JOHN   [*remembering*]. Peter. Tatu[18] Peter.

WINSTON   That's him!

JOHN   Hell, it comes back now, man! Pulling through the big gates, wives and mothers running next to the vans, trying to say goodbye … all of us inside fighting for a last look through the window.

WINSTON   [*shaking his head*]. Shit!

JOHN   Bet you've forgotten the song the old man started?

            [*Winston tries to remember. John starts singing softly. It is one of the Defiance Campaign songs.*[19] *Winston joins in.*]

WINSTON   [*shaking his head ruefully*]. By the time we reach Humansdorp though, nobody was singing.

JOHN   Fuck singing. I wanted to piss. Hey! I had my one free hand on my balls, holding on. I'd made a mistake when we left the Rooihel. Drank a gallon of water thinking of those five hundred miles ahead. Jesus! There was the bucket in the corner! But we were packed in so tight, remember, we couldn't move. I tried to pull you but it was no bloody good. So I held on – Humansdorp, Storms River, Blaaukrantz … held on. But at Knysna, to hell with it, I let go!

            [*Gesture to indicate the release of his bladder. Winston finds this enormously funny. John joins in.*]

            You were also wet by then!

WINSTON   Never!

JOHN   Okay, let's say that by George nobody was dry. Remember the stop there?

WINSTON   *Ja.* I thought they were going to let us walk around a bit.

JOHN   Not a damn! Fill up with petrol and then on. Hey, but what about those locals, the Coloured prisoners, when we pulled away. Remember? Coming to their cell windows and shouting … 'Courage, Brothers! Courage!' After that … ! Jesus I was tired. Didn't we fall asleep? Standing like that?

WINSTON   What do you mean standing? It was impossible to fall.

[18] **Tatu:** (Xhosa) father, a respectful term/mode of address to an older man.
[19] **Defiance Campaign songs**: a reference to the 1952 mass Campaign of passive resistance and defiance against apartheid, when more than 8000 people were arrested.

JOHN   Then the docks, the boat …. It was my first time on one. I had nothing to vomit up, but my God I tried.

WINSTON   What about me?

JOHN   Then we saw this place for the first time. It almost looked pretty, hey, with all the mist around it.

WINSTON   I was too sick to see anything, *broer.*

JOHN   Remember your words when we jumped off onto the jetty?

[*Pause. The two men look at each other.*]

Heavy words, Winston. You looked back at the mountains … 'Farewell Africa!' I've never forgotten them. That was three years ago.

WINSTON   And now, for you, it's three months to go.

[*Pause. The mood of innocent celebration has passed. John realizes what his good news means to the other man.*]

JOHN   To hell with everything. Let's go to bed.

[*Winston doesn't move. John finds Antigone's wig.*]

We'll talk about Antigone tomorrow.

[*John prepares for bed.*]

Hey, Winston! I just realized. My family! Princess and the children. Do you think they've been told? Jesus, man, maybe they're also saying … three months! Those three months are going to feel as long as the three years. Time passes slowly when you've got something … to wait for ….

[*Pause. Winston still hasn't moved. John changes his tone.*]

Look, in this cell we're going to forget those three months. The whole bloody thing is most probably a trick anyway. So let's just forget about it. We run to the quarry tomorrow. Together. So let's sleep.

Scene 3

The cell, later the same night. Both men are in bed. Winston is apparently asleep. John, however, is awake, rolling restlessly from side to side. He eventually gets up and goes quietly to the bucket for a drink of water, then back to his bed. He doesn't lie down, however. Pulling the blanket around his shoulders, he starts to think about the three months. He starts counting the days on the fingers of one hand. Behind him Winston sits up and watches him in silence for a few moments.

WINSTON   [*with a strange smile*]. You're counting!

JOHN	[*with a start*]. What! Hey, Winston, you gave me a fright, man. I thought you were asleep. What's the matter? Can't you sleep?
WINSTON	[*ignoring the question, still smiling*]. You've started counting the days now.
JOHN	[*unable to resist the temptation to talk, moving over to Winston's bed*]. *Ja.*
WINSTON	How many?
JOHN	Ninety-two.
WINSTON	You see!
JOHN	[*excited*]. Simple, man. Look … twenty days left in this month, thirty days in June, thirty one in July, eleven days in August … ninety-two.
WINSTON	[*still smiling, but watching John carefully*]. Tomorrow?
JOHN	Ninety-one.
WINSTON	And the next day?
JOHN	Ninety.
WINSTON	Then one day it will be eighty!
JOHN	*Ja!*
WINSTON	Then seventy.
JOHN	Hey, Winston, time doesn't pass so fast.
WINSTON	Then only sixty more days.
JOHN	That's just two months here on the Island.
WINSTON	Fifty … forty days in the quarry.
JOHN	Jesus, Winston!
WINSTON	Thirty.
JOHN	One month. Only one month to go.
WINSTON	Twenty … [*holding up his hands*] then ten … five, four, three, two … tomorrow!
	[*The anticipation of that moment is too much for John.*]
JOHN	NO! Please, man, Winston. It hurts. Leave those three months alone. I'm going to sleep!
	[*Back to his bed, where he curls up in a tight ball and tries determinedly to sleep. Winston lies down again and stares up at the ceiling. After a pause he speaks quietly.*]

WINSTON   They won't keep you here for the full three months. Only two months. Then down to the jetty into a ferry-boat … you'll say goodbye to this place … and straight to Victor Verster[20] Prison on the mainland.

[*Against his will, John starts to listen. He eventually sits upright and completely surrenders himself to Winston's description of the last few days of his confinement.*]

Life will change for you there. It will be much easier. Because you won't take Hodoshe with you. He'll stay here with me, on the Island. They'll put you to work in the vineyards at Victor Verster, John. There are no quarries there. Eating grapes, oranges … they'll change your diet … Diet C,[21] and exercises so that you'll look good when they let you out finally. At night you'll play games … Ludo, draughts, snakes and ladders! Then one day they'll call you into the office, with a van waiting outside to take you back. The same five hundred miles. But this time they'll let you sit. You won't have to stand the whole way like you did coming here. And there won't be handcuffs. Maybe they'll even stop on the way so that you can have a pee. Yes, I'm sure they will. You might even sleep over somewhere. Then finally Port Elizabeth. Rooihol Prison again, John! That's very near home, man. New Brighton is next door! Through your cell window you'll see people moving up and down in the street, hear the buses roaring. Then one night you won't sleep again, because you'll be counting. Not days, as you are doing now, but hours. And the next morning, that beautiful morning, John, they'll take you straight out of your cell to the Discharge Office where they'll give you a new khaki shirt, long khaki trousers, brown shoes. And your belongings! I almost forgot about your belongings.

JOHN   Hey, by the way! I was wearing a white shirt, black tie, grey flannel trousers … brown Crockett shoes … socks? [*A little laugh.*] I can't remember my socks! A check jacket … and my watch! I was wearing my watch!

WINSTON   They'll wrap them up in a parcel. You'll have it under your arm when they lead you to the gate. And outside, John, outside that gate, New Brighton will be waiting for you. Your mother, your father, Princess and the children … and when they open it ….

[20] **Victor Verster**: prison for 'politicals' en route to release, in Paarl, near Cape Town.
[21] **Diet C**: most prisoners were kept on the worst diet, Diet D.

[*Once again, but more violently this time, John breaks the mood as the anticipation of the moment of freedom becomes too much for him.*]

JOHN   Stop it, Winston! Leave those three months alone for Christ's sake. I want to sleep.

[*He tries to get away from Winston, but the latter goes after him. Winston has now also abandoned his false smile.*]

WINSTON   [*stopping John as he tries to crawl away*]. But it's not finished, John!

JOHN   Leave me alone!

WINSTON   It doesn't end there. Your people will take you home. Thirty-eight, Gratten Street, John! Remember it? Everybody will be waiting for you … aunts, uncles, friends, neighbours. They'll put you in a chair, John, like a king, give you anything you want … cakes, sweets, cool drinks … and then you'll start to talk. You'll tell them about this place, John, about Hodoshe, about the quarry, and about your good friend Winston who you left behind. But you still won't be happy, hey. Because you'll need a fuck. A really wild one!

JOHN   Stop it, Winston!

WINSTON   [*relentless*]. And that is why at ten o'clock that night you'll slip out through the back door and make your way to Sky's place. Imagine it, man! All the boys waiting for you … Georgie, Mangi, Vusumzi. They'll fill you up with booze. They'll look after you. They know what it's like inside. They'll fix you up with a woman ….

JOHN   NO!

WINSTON   Set you up with her in a comfortable joint, and then leave you alone. You'll watch her, watch her take her clothes off, you'll take your pants off, get near her, feel her, feel it …. *Ja,* you'll feel it. It will be wet ….

JOHN   WINSTON!

WINSTON   Wet *poes,* John! And you'll fuck it wild!

[*John turns finally to face Winston. A long silence as the two men confront each other. John is appalled at what he sees.*]

JOHN   Winston? What's happening? Why are you punishing me?

WINSTON   [*quietly*]. You stink, John. You stink of beer, of company, of *poes,* of freedom …. Your freedom stinks, John, and it's driving me mad.

JOHN   No, Winston!

WINSTON   Yes! Don't deny it. Three months time, at this hour, you'll be
           wiping beer off your face, your hands on your balls, and *poes*
           waiting for you. You will laugh, you will drink, you will fuck
           and forget.

           [*John's denials have no effect on Winston.*]

           Stop bullshitting me! We've got no time left for that. There's
           only two months left between us. [*Pause.*] You know where I
           ended up this morning, John? In the quarry. Next to old
           Harry. Do you know old Harry, John?

JOHN   Yes.

WINSTON   Yes what? Speak, man!

JOHN   Old Harry, Cell Twenty-three, seventy years, serving Life!

WINSTON   That's not what I'm talking about. When you go to the
           quarry tomorrow, take a good look at old Harry. Look into
           his eyes, John. Look at his hands. They've changed him.
           They've turned him into stone. Watch him work with that
           chisel and hammer. Twenty perfect blocks of stone every day.
           Nobody else can do it like him. He loves stone. That's why
           they're nice to him. He's forgotten himself. He's forgotten
           everything   why he's here, where he comes from.

           That's happening to me, John. I've forgotten why I'm here.

JOHN   No.

WINSTON   Why am I here?

JOHN   You put your head on the block for others.

WINSTON   Fuck the others.

JOHN   Don't say that! Remember our ideals ….

WINSTON   Fuck our ideals ….

JOHN   No, Winston … our slogans, our children's freedom ….

WINSTON   Fuck slogans, fuck politics … fuck everything, John. Why am
           I here? I'm jealous of your freedom, John. I also want to
           count. God also gave me ten fingers, but what do I count?
           My life? How do I count it, John? One … one … another
           day comes … one …. Help me, John! … Another day …
           one … one …. Help me, brother! … one ….

[*John has sunk to the floor, helpless in the face of the other man's torment and pain. Winston almost seems to bend under the weight of the life stretching ahead of him on the Island. For a few seconds he lives in silence with his reality, then slowly straightens up. He turns and looks at John. When he speaks again, it is the voice of a man who has come to terms with his fate, massively compassionate.*]

Nyana we Sizwe!

[*John looks up at him.*]

Nyana we Sizwe … it's all over now. All over. [*He moves over to John.*] Forget me ….

[*John attempts a last, limp denial.*]

No, John! Forget me … because I'm going to forget you. Yes, I will forget you. Others will come in here, John, count, go, and I'll forget them. Still more will come, count like you, go like you, and I will forget them. And then one day, it will all be over.

[*A lighting change suggests the passage of time. Winston collects their props together for Antigone.*]

Come. They're waiting.

JOHN   Do you know your words?

WINSTON   Yes. Come, we'll be late for the concert.

Scene 4

The two men convert their cell-area into a stage for the prison concert. Their blankets are hung to provide a makeshift backdrop behind which Winston appears with their props. John comes forward and addresses the audience. He is not yet in his Creon costume.

JOHN   Captain Prinsloo, Hodoshe, Warders, … and Gentlemen! Two brothers of the House of Labdacus found themselves on opposite sides in battle, the one defending the State, the other attacking it. They both died on the battlefield. King Creon, Head of the State, decided that the one who had defended the State would be buried with all religious rites due to the noble dead. But the other one, the traitor Polynices, who had come back from exile intending to burn and destroy his fatherland, to drink the blood of his masters, was to have no grave, no mourning. He was to lie on the open fields to rot, or at most be food for the jackals. It was a law. But Antigone, their sister, defied the law and buried the body of her brother Polynices. She was caught and arrested. That is why tonight the Hodoshe Span,[22] Cell Forty-two, presents for your entertainment: 'The Trial and Punishment of Antigone'.

[*He disappears behind the blankets. They simulate a fanfare of trumpets. At its height the blankets open and he steps out as Creon. In addition to his pendant, there is some sort of crown, and a blanket draped over his shoulders as a robe.*]

My People! Creon stands before his palace and greets you! Stop! Stop! What's that I hear? You, good man, speak up. Did I hear 'Hail the King'? My good people, I am your *servant* ... a happy one, but still your servant. How many times must I ask you, implore you to see in these symbols of office nothing more, or less, than you would in the uniform of the humblest menial in your house. Creon's crown is as simple, and I hope as clean, as the apron Nanny wears.[23] And even as Nanny smiles and is your happy servant because she sees her charge ... your child! ... waxing fat in that little cradle, so too does Creon – your obedient servant! – stand here and smile. For what does he see? Fatness and happiness! How else does one measure the success of a state? By the sumptuousness of the palaces built for its king and princes? The magnificence of the temples erected to its gods? The achievements of its scientists and technicians which can now send rockets to the moon? No! These count for nothing beside the fatness and happiness of its people.

But have you ever paused to ask yourself whose responsibility it is to maintain that fatness and happiness? The answer is simple, is it not? ... your servant the king! But have you then gone on to ask yourself what does the king need to maintain his happy state of affairs? What, other than his silly crown, are the tools with which a king fashions the happiness of his people? The answer is equally simple, my

---

[22] ***Hodoshe Span***: (Afrikaans) the Hodoshe team of prisoners.

[23] **Creon's crown is ... as clean as the apron Nanny wears**: John, as Creon, uses a domestic comparison, referring to the common role of black women in white homes, looking after the children.

good people. The law! Yes. The law. A three-lettered word, and how many times haven't you glibly used it, never bothering to ask yourselves, 'What, then, is the law?' Or if you have, then making recourse to such clichés as 'the law states this' … or 'the law states that'. The law states or maintains nothing, good people. The law defends! The law is no more or less than a shield in your faithful servant's hand to protect YOU! But even as a shield would be useless in one hand, to defend, without a sword in the other, to strike … so too the law has its edge. The penalty! We have come through difficult times. I am sure it is needless for me to remind you of the constant troubles on our borders … those despicable rats who would gnaw away at our fatness and happiness. We have been diligent in dealing with them. But unfortunately there are still at large subversive elements … there are still amongst us a few rats that are not satisfied, and to them I must show this face of Creon … so different to the one that hails my happy people! It is with a heavy heart, and you shall see why soon enough, that I must tell you that we have caught another one. That is why I have assembled you here. Let what follows be a living lesson for those among you misguided enough still to harbour sympathy for rats! The shield has defended. Now the sword must strike! Bring in the accused.

[*Winston, dressed as Antigone, enters. He wears the wig, the necklace of nails, and a blanket around his waist as a skirt.*]

Your name!

WINSTON	Antigone, daughter of Oedipus, sister of Eteocles and Polynices.
JOHN	You are accused that, in defiance of the law, you buried the body of the traitor Polynices.
WINSTON	I buried the body of my brother Polynices.
JOHN	Did you know there was a law forbidding that?
WINSTON	Yes.
JOHN	Yet you defied it.
WINSTON	Yes.
JOHN	Did you know the consequences of such defiance?
WINSTON	Yes.

JOHN	What did you plead to the charges laid against you? Guilty or Not Guilty?
WINSTON	Guilty.
JOHN	Antigone, you have pleaded guilty. Is there anything you wish to say in mitigation? This is your last chance. Speak.
WINSTON	Who made the law forbidding the burial of my brother?
JOHN	The State.
WINSTON	Who is the State?
JOHN	As King I am its manifest symbol.
WINSTON	So you made the law.
JOHN	Yes, for the State.
WINSTON	Are you God?
JOHN	Watch your words, little girl!
WINSTON	You said it was my chance to speak.
JOHN	But not to ridicule.
WINSTON	I've got no time to waste on that. Your sentence on my life hangs waiting on your lips.
JOHN	Then speak on.
WINSTON	When Polynices died in battle, all that remained was the empty husk of his body. He could neither harm nor help any man again. What lay on the battlefield waiting for Hodoshe to turn rotten, belonged to God. You are only a man, Creon. Even as there are laws made by men, so too there are others that come from God. He watches my soul for a transgression even as your spies hide in the bush at night to see who is transgressing your laws. Guilty against God I will not be for any man on this earth. Even without your law, Creon, and the threat of death to whoever defied it, I know I must die. Because of your law and my defiance, that fate is now very near. So much the better. Your threat is nothing to me, Creon. But if I had let my mother's son, a Son of the Land, lie there as food for the carrion fly, Hodoshe, my soul would never have known peace. Do you understand anything of what I am saying, Creon?
JOHN	Your words reveal only that obstinacy of spirit which has brought nothing but tragedy to your people. First you break the law. Now you insult the State.

WINSTON	Just because I ask you to remember that you are only a man?
JOHN	And to add insult to injury you gloat over your deeds! No, Antigone, you will not escape with impunity. Were you my own child, you would not escape full punishment.
WINSTON	Full punishment? Would you like to do more than just kill me?
JOHN	That is all I wish.
WINSTON	Then let us not waste any time. Stop talking. I buried my brother. That is an honourable thing, Creon. All these people in your state would say so too, if fear of you and another law did not force them into silence.
JOHN	You are wrong. None of my people think the way you do.
WINSTON	Yes they do, but no one dares tell you so. You will not sleep peacefully, Creon.
JOHN	You add shamelessness to your crimes, Antigone.
WINSTON	I do not feel any shame at having honoured my brother.
JOHN	Was he that died with him not also your brother?
WINSTON	He was.
JOHN	And so you honour the one and insult the other.
WINSTON	I shared my love, not my hate.
JOHN	Go then and share your love among the dead. I will have no rats' law here while yet I live.
WINSTON	We are wasting time, Creon. Stop talking. Your words defeat your purpose. They are prolonging my life.
JOHN	[*again addressing the audience*]. You have heard all the relevant facts. Needless now to call the state witnesses who would testify beyond reasonable doubt that the accused is guilty. Nor, for that matter, is it in the best interests of the State to disclose their identity. There was a law. The law was broken. The law stipulated its penalty. My hands are tied.

Take her from where she stands, straight to the Island! There wall her up in a cell for life, with enough food to acquit ourselves of the taint of her blood. |

WINSTON [*to the audience*]. Brothers and Sisters of the Land! I go now on my last journey. I must leave the light of day forever, for the Island, strange and cold, to be lost between life and death. So, to my grave, my everlasting prison, condemned alive to solitary death.

[*Tearing off his wig and confronting the audience as Winston, not Antigone.*]

Gods of our Fathers! My Land! My Home!

Time waits no longer. I go now to my living death, because I honoured those things to which honour belongs.

[*The two men take off their costumes and then strike their 'set'. They then come together and, as in the beginning, their hands come together to suggest handcuffs, and their right and left legs to suggest ankle-chains. They start running ... John mumbling a prayer, and Winston a rhythm for their three-legged run.*
The siren wails.
Fade to blackout.]

Afterword

How significant is the idea of authority in the Arts and Humanities? Having now explored this issue from the perspective of several different academic disciplines, you have quite a lot of material on which to base an answer to this question. But as with most big questions, there is no easy or right answer. We'd certainly want to acknowledge the power and influence of traditions, institutions and the reputations that build up around particular people and particular works. But, as we have seen, traditions and reputations are seldom static, and perhaps of equal importance in the field of Arts and Humanities are the challenges to authority that bring about change. In the second part of this book we have seen challenges to authority that were both direct, in the case of the Protestant Reformation of the sixteenth century, and indirect, in the case of *The Island*, which offered a challenge to the political authority that sustained apartheid by appealing to the authority of a classical text. When you move on to Book 4 of this module you will have further opportunities to focus on processes of change, first within a concentrated case study rooted in a particular place and time, and second by considering the 'afterlives' of objects that have found their way into *different* places, periods and contexts.

But for now, what have we learned about voices, texts, images and objects in relation to this idea of change? It is clear that the value or worth of particular cultural products is always susceptible to change – the reputation of Caravaggio, discussed in Chapter 3, might be a case in point. Thinking back to the final chapter of Book 1, in which the early modern book is presented as 'solid but unstable', it is also clear that 'texts', especially written texts, are not always as settled as we at first assume. Chapter 1 of this book discussed the way that scriptural writings come together in combination, enabling us to take a brief look behind the concept of fixed canons of religious writing and glimpse something of the process of canon-formation. And in Chapter 2 we saw that even one of the most canonical works of classical music, Handel's *Messiah*, has no single, 'authoritative', score.

Staying with written texts for the moment, another factor that sometimes makes it difficult to identify a definitive version of a text is that it may have begun its life not in the semi-permanent form of writing, but in oral form. In Chapter 5 we saw how Homer's *Iliad* was gradually transformed from an epic sung piecemeal by bards at festivals and banquets to a written text standardised by Alexandrian scholars – a process that took several centuries. The same long transition from oral transmission to writing is also true, of course, of the Buddhist *sutta* we read in Chapter 1. In Chapter 6 we saw a much swifter move from spoken word to written text in the case of *The Island*, but it is still significant that the play was not actually written down at the time of its first performance, and it went on being adapted in performance by the actors John Kani and Winston Ntshona.

Orality thus turns out to be another important strand in relation to textual study. As well as the situations where voices sometimes carry the whole weight of texts before they are written down, we've also encountered voices performing a range of functions: preaching (think back to Chapter 4 and Luther's Lenten sermons, spoken to a church congregation before being published), singing, acting, and so on. These are literal voices, though while we are thinking about voices we might also note some of the metaphorical voices we have encountered, such as the collective voices of the authorities that select and shape various kinds of canon.

Authority will continue to be a major theme throughout this module, so do try to hold on to some of the insights you've developed in the course of Book 2 and bring them back into the frame when you sense they are relevant to the work you will be doing in Books 3 and 4. For now, you will probably want to take a little time to review and reflect briefly on the very varied approaches to voices, texts, images and objects that have opened up in this book. In particular, you might want to think about how the academic disciplines represented here differ from each other, not just in terms of the subject matter they deal with, but also in terms of the kinds of questions they ask and the kinds of skills they require of you. At the same time, try to keep aware of the overlaps and connections between different disciplines: sometimes you will find these links in an explicit way, for example in an opera's libretto, but sometimes you will discern them for yourself as you consciously try to adopt an open and interdisciplinary approach to a topic.

When you move on to Book 3 you will encounter two new disciplines, English Language Studies and Creative Writing, deliberately placed alongside each other so that you can examine the basic ingredients from which any verbal composition is constructed. Book 3, 'Doing things with words', should provide you with new perspectives to look back on some of the work you have done here in this book, as well as breaking new ground.

Glossary

allegory

In art and literature, a method of representing an abstract quality or idea, usually of a moral or political nature, through a series of symbols and personifications (that is, objects and figures representing abstract qualities and ideas).

alliteration

(Sometimes known as 'head rhyme'.) The repetition of a speech sound, usually a consonant, in a sequence of words. The recurrent sound is generally at the beginning of a word or a stressed syllable.

aria

The Italian word for 'air'. Although it carries a number of meanings in relation to music, it is most commonly used to describe an expressive piece written for solo voice. Arias are featured in large-scale vocal works, including operas, oratorios and cantatas.

baritone

A type of male voice between tenor and bass.

Baroque

A term that originally designated a complex and ornate style in art and architecture. Now used to embrace all of the arts (including music and literature) in the period between c.1600 and c.1750.

blank verse

A flexible, unrhymed English verse form, based on a pattern of five stressed syllables per line. Not to be confused with the even more flexible 'free verse' (which can be quite irregular), blank verse was the dominant verse form in early modern drama, favoured by Marlowe, Shakespeare and their contemporaries.

Carnival

A period immediately before Lent in the Christian calendar, when traditionally early modern Europeans were allowed to indulge in excessive eating, drinking and other riotous behaviour that was largely forbidden for the rest of the year.

chiaroscuro

From the Italian chiaro (light) and oscuro (dark). Used to refer to the effects of light and shadow within a painting, especially when they are strongly contrasting.

chord

A musical chord is formed when two or more pitches are played simultaneously as one unit. The adjective used to describe a texture using a succession of chords is 'chordal'.

Classical

The Classical period in western music is used as a description of music of the late eighteenth and early nineteenth centuries. The leading exponents of this style are Wolfgang Amadeus Mozart (1756–1791), Joseph Haydn (1732–1809), Ludwig van Beethoven (1770–1827) and Franz Schubert (1797–1828). Classical music follows the same principles of order and balance as described under classicism.

classicism

A term used within Art History primarily with reference to works inspired by the models provided by ancient Greece and Rome, in the form of poems, plays, temples, statues, vases, and so forth. The underlying aim of classicism as it was practised in western Europe from the Renaissance onwards was to present an idealised vision of the world. The term is also associated with a set of abstract design principles, such as order, harmony, proportion and balance, so that a work of art can be described as classical even if it does not reveal a direct debt to Graeco-Roman models.

Communion

A Christian service and sacrament commemorating Christ's Last Supper with his disciples.

composition

In art, analysing the composition of a painting involves looking at the way in which all of its elements – figures, figure groups, objects, colours, light and shade, background, middle ground and foreground, scale and perspective – are arranged.

counterpoint

The textural interweaving of different melodic and rhythmic patterns. The adjective is 'contrapuntal'.

curator

A curator (also sometimes termed a 'keeper') is responsible for the care of objects in the collection of a museum, art gallery or similar institution. His or her activities may include making acquisitions for the collection and staging temporary exhibitions.

dhamma

The Pali term for the truth of how things are, and practices that lead to knowledge and understanding of that truth. The Sanskrit term is *dharma*.

Diet

A national assembly of representatives from the member states of the Holy Roman empire.

epic poem

'Epic' is the name given to long, narrative poems which take as their starting point the deeds of gods and heroes, the oldest surviving example of which is Homer's *Iliad*. The term derives from the Greek for 'word' (epos). Epic poetry characteristically adheres to set conventions, such as the inclusion of lengthy speeches and repeated phrases. Characteristic of Greek and Latin epic is the fact that it is composed in a poetic metre known as dactylic hexameter.

Eucharist

Another word for Communion.

excommunication

Officially exclusion from the Church, both as a community and as an institution.

the Fall

The loss of humankind's pristine innocence and tranquillity, associated in Jewish and Christian tradition with the temptation and disobedience of Adam and Eve in the Garden of Eden, as described in the first book of the Bible, Genesis.

form

This term is used across a number of Arts disciplines, sometimes with subtly different meanings. In the visual arts it refers to the sum of the characteristics which determine the physical appearance of a work of art. So for an art historian 'form' may include the following: treatment of pictorial space; perspectival devices and features; composition or arrangement of pictorial components; choice and arrangement of colour; tonal values; scale; and choice, use and method of application of materials. In Music, the term is used to refer to the overall structure or plan of the work. The same generally holds true in Literary Studies, and might include references to specific poetic forms, such as blank verse. However, the terms 'form' and 'genre' are sometimes used interchangeably in Literary Studies.

genre painting

Figurative works that purport to represent ordinary everyday life, and which were much influenced by the work of the seventeenth-century Dutch school.

genres

This French term for type or species is used in several Arts disciplines. Art historians use it to distinguish between different types of picture, such as portrait, landscape and still life. In Music, a genre is a type of musical work, for example symphony, opera, oratorio. In Literary Studies the commonest use of genre is, similarly, to categorise different varieties of written work, such as fiction, poetry or drama, with numerous sub-divisions (for example: novel, gothic novel).

Habsburgs

One of the most powerful ruling families in Europe in the early modern period. They held the prestigious title of Holy Roman emperor, whose territories covered much of central Europe, throughout this time.

harmony

In music, harmony is created when different pitches are played together at the same time. Some harmonies are consonant, which means the pitches are blended together to make pleasing sounds that are easy to listen to. Others are dissonant, where sounds created by certain pitch combinations are relatively harsh and grating. Two or more pitches played simultaneously as one unit are called a chord.

Huguenots

A name for French Protestants in the sixteenth and seventeenth centuries, first used as a term of abuse by their opponents.

iconography

Within Art History, this is the study of visual themes, symbols and motifs, understood to be derived from literary sources and whose meanings have culturally specific significance.

iconophobia

A strong aversion to all religious images.

idolatry

The worship of an image that is believed to have a superhuman or divine power.

Impressionist

The term refers to a late nineteenth-century art movement characterised by formal experimentation and a sketchy application of paint, resulting from the artist's desire to capture a fleeting impression on the canvas. The term 'Impressionism' was coined in 1874 by the French art critic Louis Leroy in his review of the first of a series of exhibitions of paintings by a group of artists who included Claude Monet (1840–1926), Camille Pissarro (1830–1903), Auguste Renoir (1841–1919), Berthe Morisot (1841–1895), Edgar Degas (1834–1917) and Alfred Sisley (1839–1899). Édouard Manet (1832–1883) is often associated with the Impressionists, but never showed his work in any of their exhibitions.

indulgence

A remission of the punishment for sins after death. Medieval popes granted and sold indulgences, based on their claim to control the keys to the kingdom of heaven granted to Peter, the first pope.

installation

An installation is usually a three-dimensional work of art that is placed within or outside a museum or gallery, but is no longer sufficiently object-like or self-contained in its form to be considered a sculpture, or can no longer be called sculpture on account of the different materials of which it is made. Installation has been one of the dominant media for contemporary art, from the 1960s through to the present.

karma

The Sanskrit word for 'action'. The word implies the idea that whatever is done in this life is influenced by the circumstances of previous lives, and that actions in this life will in turn influence lives to come.

libretto

The text for an extended vocal work, particularly an opera. The writer of such a text is called a librettist.

lyre

An ancient Greek instrument rather like a small harp.

mantra

Any formula of words or syllables whose sound is said to have great potency. The words or syllables spoken by the practitioner are understood on various levels, from their literal meaning to elaborate symbolic interpretations.

Marianum

A representation of Mary (the mother of Jesus) holding the Christ child, with golden rays of the sun behind her, while she stamps on a serpent representing Satan.

meditation

A practice used for religious and therapeutic purposes. In Buddhism there are two types of meditation: meditation to calm the mind and meditation to develop understanding of *dhamma*.

melody

A melody, or tune, is created by combining rhythm and pitch. The way in which these two elements are manipulated to create melody can produce a range of effects. A melody can be constructed from several phrases.

minuet

A stately dance in a moderate or slow triple time.

nibbana

The Pali term (in Sanskrit the term is nirvana) used in Buddhism to refer to the highest possible happiness. It means literally 'blowing out'.

The things that are blown out are the 'fires' of greed, hatred and ignorance, which prevent ordinary people from being happy.

opera buffa

A type of light-hearted or comic opera popular in the Classical period.

Pali

An ancient language developed in the Indian subcontinent and used to record early Buddhist texts.

pass laws

Legislation introduced by the South African government in 1923 and again in 1952 to restrict the movements of non-whites. The 1952 Act made it compulsory for all black Africans over the age of 16 to carry 'passbooks' at all times. The passbook provided proof of permission (or proof that permission had not been granted) to live and/or work in a specific area. Failure to produce a passbook on demand meant arrest and automatic penalties, including imprisonment.

pediment

The crowning, triangular part of an architectural façade.

phrase

A musical phrase is a short, self-contained group of notes, rather like a phrase in writing or speaking.

pitch

The way in which notes sound high or low in relation to one another.

polyptych

A picture or carving, used as an altarpiece, consisting of a central section with an even number of folding shutters to each side.

portico

A colonnaded porch attached to a building. If topped by a pediment, it is known as a temple front.

Post-Impressionist

A term coined by the British critic Roger Fry to distinguish the work of several French painters working towards the end of the nineteenth century – most notably Paul Cézanne (1839–1906), Paul Gauguin

(1848–1903), Vincent Van Gogh (1853–1890) and Georges Seurat (1859–1891). Not much unites these painters other than the fact they followed on the heels of the Impressionists and painted in a more artificial palette, with expressive brush strokes and a thicker application of paint – all of which draws attention to the flatness of the canvas support.

quatrain

A four-line stanza-form, very common in English poetry, with a range of possible rhyme schemes.

Reformation

A period of major religious upheaval and division among European Christians, initiated in 1517 by the Protestant reformer Martin Luther (1483–1546) and others, who objected to various aspects of the beliefs and practices of the medieval Roman Catholic Church.

register

A distinctive use of language, written or spoken, for a particular situation.

relic

A relic is literally 'that which is left behind' and in medieval and early modern history it refers specifically to an object that was associated with a saint, martyr or other holy person, or, in some cases, part of their body.

Renaissance

A term, meaning 'rebirth', used to describe both a historical period (approximately 1400 to 1600), and a process of cultural transformation. It relates in particular to the resurgence of interest in, and attempts to emulate, the artistic and intellectual heritage of ancient Greece and Rome.

rhyme scheme

The order and arrangement of rhymes, either throughout a whole poem or in a typical stanza.

rhythm

In music, the way in which sounds are distributed over time. These sounds can last for varied lengths of time. Some notes are short and will seem to move fast, while others will last longer and could seem to move more slowly. Some rhythms are even and smooth, while others are uneven.

Sanskrit

An ancient Indian language used primarily for religious texts.

scherzo

Literally, 'joke'. Since Beethoven's time, it has been applied to movements that replace the more stately minuet.

shebeen

An unlicensed establishment selling alcohol to black Africans, who, under apartheid, could not enter bars reserved for white people.

simile

A figure of speech in which two different things are explicitly compared, using the words 'like' or 'as'.

still life

Inanimate objects, such as fruits, flowers, drinking vessels and other containers, as represented in painting.

sutta

The Pali term for a thread. It is used to mean a text from the Buddhist tradition that is said to have been composed by the Buddha.

tempo (plural tempi)

The term used to describe the speed of a piece of music. To create contrast and interest, composers often vary the tempo within a musical work.

texture

In music, the term is used to refer to the ways in which different lines of music interweave. The simplest musical texture is a single unaccompanied melodic line, while combinations of voices and instruments playing different parts simultaneously create more complex musical textures.

tipitaka

Literally meaning the 'three baskets', this term denotes the collection of Buddhist texts.

triptych

A picture or carving, used as an altarpiece, consisting of three parts: a central section with folding shutters to each side. If there are more than three panels to the altarpiece it is called a polyptych.

unison

In music, this means all instruments or voices playing the same notes.

Acknowledgements

Chapter 1

'Karaniya Metta Sutta: The Buddha's Words on Loving-kindness' (Khp 9), translated from the Pali by The Amaravati Sangha. Access to Insight, 17 June 2010, http://www.accesstoinsight.org/tipitaka/kn/khp/khp.9.amar.html.

Chapter 2

Adams, J. (2008) *Hallelujah Junction*. Faber and Faber Limited.

Porter, C. (1934) 'Anything goes'; Warner/Chappell Music Limited.

Chapter 3

Tate (2010) 'The Unilever Series: Ai Weiwei: Sunflower Seeds' [Online]. © Tate 2014.

Chapter 4

Beveridge, H. (trans.) (1994) *Institutes of the Christian Religion* by John Calvin, W M B. Eerdmans Publishing Company. Reproduced with permission from the Copyright Clearance Centre.

Chapter 5

Longley, M. (2006) *Collected Poems*. Random House.

Homer, *The Illiad*. Translation by Ian Johnston, Malaspina University-College, Nanaimo, BC, Canada.

Chapter 6

Nyberg, A. (1990) 'Siph' Amandla', *Freedom is Coming: Songs of Protest and Praise from South Africa*. © The Iona Community, published by Wild Goose Publications, through the Pearce Institute, Glasgow, Scotland.

Fugard, A. et al. (1993) *The Township Plays*. By Permission of Oxford University Press and the author.

Index

Page numbers in **bold** refer to figures.